CYBER MELTDOWN

RON RHODES

HARVEST HOUSE PUBLISHERS

EUGENE, OREGON

Cover by Dugan Design Group, Bloomington, Minnesota

Cover photos © Argus, Alx / Fotolia

CYBER MELTDOWN
Copyright © 2011 by Ron Rhodes
Published by Harvest House Publishers
Eugene, Oregon 97402
www.harvesthousepublishers.com

Library of Congress Cataloging-in-Publication Data
Rhodes, Ron.
    Cyber meltdown / Ron Rhodes.
        p. cm.
    Includes bibliographical references.
    ISBN 978-0-7369-4417-5 (pbk.)
    ISBN 987-0-7369-4423-6 (eBook)
    1. Bible—Prophecies—Cyberterrorism. 2. Cyberterrorism—Biblical teaching. 3. Bible—
Prophecies—End of the world. 4. End of the world—Biblical teaching. I. Title.
    BS649.C83R46 2011
    236'.9—dc22
                                                                      2010052597

Printed in the United States of America

11 12 13 14 15 16 17 18 19 / LB-SK / 10 9 8 7 6 5 4 3 2 1

While I was writing this book, my mother entered her heavenly home, face-to-face with the Lord Jesus Christ, reunited with her husband, one of her sons, a grandson, her mother and father, and all of her Christian loved ones who are with the Lord. It is fitting—indeed, a joy—to publicly acknowledge her powerful Christian example to me through the years and her much-appreciated ongoing role as prayer warrior, cheering squad, comforter, nurturer, and friend, not only for me but also for my whole family and many others. She was truly one of a kind. I look forward to our glorious reunion (1 Thessalonians 4:13-17).

This book is lovingly dedicated to Alpha Rhodes.

Acknowledgments

As has been our habit for a number of years, Bob Hawkins Jr., LaRae Weikert, and I met for breakfast one morning in early 2010. Bob is the president of Harvest House Publishers; LaRae is the vice president of the editorial department. We like to meet periodically, toss around ideas for future book projects, and enjoy a nice meal.

On this particular morning, I shared with them my desire to write *Cyber Meltdown*—a book that deals with such things as computer viruses, cyber attacks, cyber war, cyberterrorism, and the way these things may relate to biblical prophecy. It is definitely a different kind of book, and I so appreciate the way Bob and LaRae both immediately got behind it. A special thanks go not only to them but also to the entire team at Harvest House—too many folks to mention but all greatly appreciated.

Of course, as always, I want to also publicly thank my wife, Kerri, and my two grown children, David and Kylie—both college students. They continue to be marvelous gifts to me from the Lord, vessels of God's love, grace, and encouragement. I am blessed.

Your nation, the United States, is under attack from foreign enemies. You are already aware of the international threat posed by terrorist organizations like al-Qaida, and you know only too well what the acts of real-world, real-life violence wrought by such groups can do to America's citizens...

Another shadow conflict is taking place behind the veil of modern technology. Every minute of the day, external foes are mounting assaults on American infrastructure, civilian American assets, and American military targets. Those enemies do this through the virtual world. Their foot soldiers are an army of disparate computer hackers,* ranging from state-sponsored operatives to ordinary people in almost every nation on the planet.

PHIL ELMORE,
"Why We Need Cyber-Warriors Now,"
WorldNetDaily

---

* Here, *hackers* refers to skilled computer programmers who are adept at writing computer code and gaining unauthorized access to computers and networks. In popular usage In the media, the term often refers to cyber criminals.

CONTENTS

TECHNOLOGIES THAT AMAZE

When I was a doctoral student at Dallas Theological Seminary in the early 1980s, all of my fellow doctoral students were Trekkies—every last one was a fan of the original *Star Trek* television series and also the movies.

We enjoyed talking about some of the amazing technologies these futuristic characters used. On one occasion, a security system performed a retina scan before permitting Captain Kirk to access a data file. "That'll never happen in real life," some of my fellow doctoral students said. But they were wrong—retina scans are now part of a recent field known as biometrics. Everyone has a unique retina, so a retina scan is ideal for security purposes.

The Internet also became popular when I was a seminary student. Of course, back then I used a dial-up modem that by today's standards was glacially slow. At the time, my friends and I thought the technology was amazing.

And new technologies continue to emerge. They are neither good nor bad in themselves, but they can be *used* for good or bad. This is important to understand. As I relate some of these technologies to the fulfillment of important biblical prophecies, we must remember that these technologies themselves are not inherently evil. Thomas Ice and Timothy Demy put it well:

[Evil] is a theological issue, not a technological one! Those who lack a proper theological framework erroneously assign evil (or virtue) to inanimate objects or tools, rather than to the human heart. Like any other tools of daily existence, technology is merely one means through which human desire is displayed.[1]

The same computers on which these pages were typed could just as easily have been used for unscrupulous hacking into corporate records or for espionage. It is characteristic of a fallen world that those things that God created for good, men and women will use for evil. The ramifications of original sin are as real in technology as they are in theology.[2]

This is a point that certainly applies to cyberspace. Indeed, cyberspace is wonderful in many ways. Many Christian ministries are accessible on the Internet, including mine. But cyberspace can also be used for evil purposes, such as pornography, identity theft, and terrorism.

WHAT IS CYBERSPACE?

In this book, we will explore various kinds of cyber attacks. In fact, by the time you finish reading, you will have a new appreciation for some of the hidden dangers of cyberspace. But what is cyberspace? This definition is from the recent textbook *Cyberpower and National Security*:

[Cyberspace is] a global domain within the information environment whose distinctive and unique character is framed by the use of electronics and the electromagnetic spectrum to create, store, modify, exchange, and exploit information via interdependent and interconnected networks using information-communication technologies.[3]

Phew—that's a pretty technical description. We can simplify things by saying that cyberspace includes the Internet, where you "surf the Web" and retrieve your e-mail. But cyberspace also includes other (often private) networks and associated infrastructures where information is stored, retrieved, and modified.

Richard Clarke, in his recent book *Cyber War: The Next Threat to National Security and What to Do About It*, makes things a bit more understandable when he says that cyberspace refers to "all of the computer networks in the world and everything they connect and control."[4] He clarifies that cyberspace is more than just the Internet. The Internet is an open system of freely connectable networks intended for general access. One computer can potentially connect with any other computer if they are both connected to the Internet. (Of course, security software is designed to limit who has access to what.)

Cyberspace, however, goes beyond that. Cyberspace includes not only the Internet but also networks of computers that outsiders are not supposed to be able to freely access. For example, corporations have private networks that contain sensitive product data or marketing strategies. Military networks store data on the latest weapon technologies. Such private networks feel very much like the Internet, but they are intended to be separate from the Internet.

Cyberspace also includes control systems that enable machines to communicate with other machines. For example, electronic control panels can communicate with water pumps, elevators, electrical generators, traffic lights, and so on—nearby or far away.

Even further, Cyberspace includes a flow of data, such as stock market trades and the credit card transaction at the local Target store where you just shopped. These things and much more are all parts of cyberspace. Clearly, the Internet is only a part of cyberspace.

"HEY, HOW'D YOU GET INTO MY NETWORK?"

The private networks I mentioned above are intended to be closed from Internet traffic so that the average Joe, like you and me, cannot gain access. Sometimes these closed-off networks are referred to as *intranets*. *Net* obviously means network. *Intra* means "inside" or "within." So an intranet is a network that is to be used *within* a limited group of users (such as a corporation or government agency). Only those inside the group are supposed to be able to access it, whether from a computer that is physically connected to it or remotely through the Internet, logging on with a secure username and password. Those outside the group—people who are just surfing the Internet and are not affiliated with the group—are blocked from accessing this intranet.

But here's the problem: These intranets are not always secure. Sometimes the digital equivalent of an open door is left open, and anybody who finds the door can walk in through the Internet. Some people, while surfing the Web, innocently and inadvertently stumble into such intranets with no intention to do anything wrong. Others purposefully force their way through the door to engage in cyber espionage.

The harsh reality to remember is that the cyber world is not as secure as it seems. In fact, every layer of the cyber world—including hardware (such as electrical grids or nuclear reactors), software (like Microsoft Word), networks (even at the Department of Defense), and the people who run it—is susceptible to a variety of security breakdowns. I will illustrate this throughout the rest of this book. You will probably be shocked by what you learn!

RELENTLESS CYBER ATTACKS

Today, cyber attacks are increasing so fast that keeping track of them is nearly impossible.[5] Consider our government, for example. *Politico*, a reliable news website, reports that computer attacks have relentlessly assaulted Congress, the Senate, and other government entities in recent times: "Senate Sergeant-at-Arms Terrance Gainer tells *Politico* that the number of 'security events' per month has shot up to 1.8 billion (yes, billion)."[6] Moreover, 13.9 million computer attacks are launched each day against the Senate Security Operations Center. That is staggering. Not a moment passes that is free of attack.

Computer security personnel inform us that many of these attacks take place through flaws in such applications as those in Microsoft Office (Microsoft Word is a popular culprit) and Adobe Acrobat. Such applications have security flaws that allow hackers to access things they are not supposed to see. (You may use Microsoft Word and Adobe Acrobat, just as I do. Remember that your best defense is to always run updates of these software programs as soon as they become available. These updates increase your system's security.)

Politico also reveals that in less than half a year, "87 Senate offices,

13 Senate committees, and 7 other offices were attacked by spear-phishing attacks, which appeared as e-mail messages to staffers, urging them to open infected attachments or click on bad links."[7] *Spear-phishing* messages look legitimate because they appear to be from someone you actually know (for example, the senator you work for). Once you open the infected attachment or click on a bad link, your computer and the network it is connected to become infected with a virus that will spy on all your keystrokes and secretly e-mail that data back to the cyber criminal who sent the e-mail.

Is it any wonder that computer security has become a hot new field brimming with high-paying jobs that are often filled by computer techies right out of college? The work can be lucrative because the government and corporations will pay big to remain cyber secure.

CIVILIAN CASUALTIES

It is one thing for our government to suffer such cyber problems. It is another thing altogether for you and me—right where we live, in our cozy little neighborhoods, at our jobs, and as we travel—to get slammed and injured by cyber attacks. Without meaning to sound alarmist, cyber attacks can be launched from anywhere in the world and can...

> reach out from cyberspace into the physical dimension and cause giant electrical generators to shred themselves, trains to derail, high-tension power transmission lines to burn, gas pipelines to explode, aircraft to crash, weapons to malfunction, funds to disappear, and enemy units to walk into ambushes.[8]

One digital-agenda commissioner offered this lament:

> When your money is quietly stolen from your bank account or your country is shut down, as happened to Estonia in 2007, the threat suddenly becomes very real...To anyone thinking that cyber attacks are an abstract concept, I would say that for millions of people each year there are already direct practical consequences.[9]

To illustrate the damage cyber attacks can do, this commissioner pointed to the Conficker Botnet—that is, the Conficker Robot Network, comprised of thousands of computers over a large geographical area that have been infected by a virus that allows a devious hacker to steal money and classified information. The Conficker Botnet also stopped a mission by French jet fighters in 2009 and shut down British and German army websites. Conficker is a nasty cyber bug!

The Stuxnet cyber attack was launched more than a year ago but is still active at the time of this writing. Stuxnet has affected nuclear reactors in Iran and China, prompting widespread speculation that secret Israeli and U.S. intelligence services are involved. Stuxnet has been so catastrophically effective that I devote an entire chapter to it in this book.

We must acknowledge that the whole world is vulnerable to cyber attacks. Computer security researcher and former U.S. National Security Agency officer Charlie Miller has publicly stated that "a hostile power could devastate" the European Union "for slightly more than $100 million and a team of 750 spies and hackers."[10] A high-finance cyber attack could bring any country to its knees.

If you think America is safe, read on. You will soon discover that this country is more vulnerable to cyber attacks than most others.

THE PLAN FOR THIS BOOK

In this book, I first discuss cyberspace and the staggering number of things that can go very, very wrong in it. Some of the material will alarm you, some will stun you, some will make you mad, some may make you paranoid…but all of it is utterly relevant to each of our lives. I then relate certain cyber technologies to end-time biblical prophecy. I think you will find this part of the book especially eye-opening.

By the time you finish the book, you will be much more cyber wise and will increase your understanding of Bible prophecy. You will also appreciate in a new way that regardless of man's technological inventions, God is in control, Christ is coming again, and the last book in the Bible (Revelation) demonstrates that we win in the end!

PART 1

A SOBERING CYBER WAKE-UP CALL

PROBING U.S. VULNERABILITIES

You might be surprised to learn that the United States is highly vulnerable to severe injury from cyber weapons. In fact, Richard Clarke, former antiterrorism czar to Bill Clinton and George W. Bush, warns that great damage could be inflicted on America in a mere 15 minutes. In his book *Cyber War: The Next National Security Threat and What to Do About It*, he warns of a possible "electronic Pearl Harbor," the likes of which we have never seen before. Here is the apocalyptic scenario he paints, all based on a single massive cyber attack.*

- The unclassified Department of Defense network known as the NIPRNET collapses, with heavy-duty routers throughout the network failing and constantly rebooting.

- The Department of Defense classified networks grind to a halt.

- Computer networks at the Pentagon collapse.

- Internet service providers go into meltdown.

- Meltdowns also take place at major financial computer

---

* Specific aspects of this scenario are confirmed many times over in the books and articles on cyber attacks I consulted for this book.

centers in New York. Terabytes* of financial data are wiped
clean, so no one knows who owns what.

- The computer systems at the Federal Aviation Administration's National Air Traffic Control Center in Herndon,
Virginia, collapse.

- Computer systems at alternate air traffic control centers go
down, so they cannot see what aircraft are aloft.

- Multiple airline midair collisions ensue.

- Infrastructure attacks cause large refinery fires and explosions in various cities.

- Chemical plants malfunction with lethal clouds of chlo-
rine gas spewing into the air.

- Major gas pipelines explode in various suburbs.

- Subway trains crash in multiple cities.

- Traffic lights go out all over the country, resulting in thousands of casualties due to collisions.

- Freight trains derail across the country.

- Blackouts occur in major cities due to power grid failures.

- Communication, weather, and navigation satellites deviate
from their orbits, completely disrupting service.

- Food and medical supplies are depleted at local stores due
to the disruption in transportation.

- Communication breaks down on many different levels—
including between the different sectors of our government
and military.[1]

Clarke soberly warns that in all the wars America has participated in,
no one nation has ever done this kind of damage to cities in the United
States. "A sophisticated cyber war attack by one of several nation-states

---

* A terabyte is equivalent to 1 trillion bytes (1 million megabytes, or 1000 gigabytes).

could do that today, in fifteen minutes, without a single terrorist or soldier ever appearing in this country."[2]

You might think all this sounds rather alarmist. But keep in mind that Richard Clarke is a credible source who has had continued access to reliable intelligence data, and he has a long track record of being right.[3]

Even worse, we may never know with certainty who is responsible for cyber attacks. Was it Russia? Was it China? Was it North Korea? Was it Iran? Such ambiguity makes retaliation much more difficult. This anonymity could encourage many anti-America countries to engage in such attacks.

ASSESSING OUR LEVEL OF READINESS

During the NFL preseason, professional football teams compete in order to see how adept their players are individually and how well the team functions as a whole. These preseason games demonstrate to the coaches what their team is doing right and what changes need to be made. Some preseason games are like a rude awakening—a sudden and unanticipated heads-up that they may be in for a losing season unless they make some changes.

This is similar to some cyber-readiness tests that the United States has participated in recently. Such tests are engineered to reveal what would happen if our country experienced a full-fledged cyber attack.

- How much damage would the United States sustain from a cyber attack?

- How would a cyber attack affect the civilian population, corporate America, and the military?

- How would the government itself react to a cyber attack, and how quickly?

- Would life go on as normal?

- Would we survive?

Let me tell you about a few of these cyber tests and what they reveal about U.S. preparedness.

CYBER SHOCKWAVE

In the interests of national survival, our government gathered a group of highly informed people—people with important jobs, people who know a lot about governing, national security, and planning—and challenged them to produce a realistic simulation of what might really happen in this country during a bona fide cyber attack.

The event was hosted by the Bipartisan Policy Center (hereafter BPC) and was appropriately called Cyber ShockWave. It was held at the Mandarin Oriental Hotel in Washington DC on February 16, 2010, and it simulated an attack that was to unfold over a single day in July 2011. The simulation provided an unprecedented firsthand look at how our government would react during such a crisis.

Knowing how important it was for the simulation to be realistic, the people and organizations chosen to oversee its design were known for their acumen in technology and national security. The simulation was designed by former CIA director general Michael Hayden and the BPC National Security Preparedness Group, and it was led by the cochairs of the 9/11 Commission: Governor Thomas Kean and Congressman Lee Hamilton. To further ensure a realistic simulation, Cyber ShockWave was developed in partnership with General Dynamics Advanced Information Systems, Georgetown University, PayPal, and SMobile Systems. The collective goal was to "highlight the immediate, real dangers of cyberterrorism by bringing together a bipartisan group of former senior administration and national security officials playing the roles of Cabinet members."[4] These were the pivotal role players in the simulation:

- Michael Chertoff, former secretary of homeland security, acted as national security advisor.

- John Negropontas, director of national intelligence, played secretary of state.

- Fran Townsend, White House homeland security advisor, played secretary of homeland security.

- John McLaughlin, director of central intelligence, played director of national intelligence.

- Senator Bennett Johnston played the secretary of energy.
- Stephen Friedman, director of the National Economic Council, played secretary of treasury.
- Deputy Attorney General Jamie Gorelick played attorney general.
- White House Press Secretary Joe Lockhart played counselor to the president.
- Stewart Baker, general counsel of the National Security Agency, played cyber coordinator.
- Charles F. Wald, deputy commander U.S. European Command, played secretary of defense.

This impressive Cabinet, whose mission was to advise the president and formulate an appropriate response to a cyber attack as it was in progress, did not know the scenario in advance. The simulation was driven by mock incoming intelligence reports and news reports, and all reactions of Cabinet members were in real time with no breaks given. The benefit of such an approach was that the simulation shed much-needed light on the way difficult split-second decisions must be made as a cyber attack unfolds and causes a cacophony of problems.

In this scenario, Cabinet members arise one morning, assuming they are beginning a status-quo day. Suddenly their smartphones ring, and a controlled but charged voice instructs them to drop whatever they are doing and come in for an emergency meeting. Everyone rushes to the meeting, where they hear these alarming words:

> We've encountered a crisis—some form of cyber attack—and we suspect involvement from another country. Already, some 20 million smart phones of our citizens have stopped working. And that figure is escalating by the minute. Our tech team tells us that all this is due to malware [a destructive software program] that was apparently preplanted in the smart phones months before through a March Madness basketball application that many people innocently downloaded.

Less than half an hour later, the team is updated.

> The attack has continued to escalate. An electronic energy
> trading platform has been shut down, and the power grid
> on the eastern seaboard has been crippled.[5]

As things continue to deteriorate during the day, Cabinet members advise the president on suggested courses of action. In many cases, decisions must be rendered almost instantly. Each Cabinet member realizes that if the president waits too long to act, things can get exponentially worse.

Once the Cyber ShockWave simulation was completed, and after a collective sigh of relief, a discussion ensued among participants and partners. The discussion was moderated by Wolf Blitzer of CNN. The purpose was to ascertain what course of action the U.S. government should take to avoid a real-world, large-scale cyber attack.

The various officials in attendance offered some sobering comments. Michael Chertoff, former secretary of homeland security, chaired the simulated National Security Council. He gave this warning:

> [Cyberterrorism] ought to be treated as a threat of suffi-
> cient seriousness that we give it the priority attention we've
> given weapons of mass destruction. [Cyberterrorism is]
> more complicated by the fact that it involves every indi-
> vidual. Anybody who has a smart phone, who downloads
> an app or gets on his or her PC, is engaged in this process.

He stressed that we should not wait, but quickly "come together in a nonpartisan way and figure out the answer to questions as opposed to kicking the can down the road until we're in an emergency."[6]

John McLaughlin, director of central intelligence, played the role of director of national intelligence. He likewise urged that the United States must act now in order to prepare for such an event, which will surely one day come upon us.

> A useful aspect of something like this simulation is it helps
> people visualize what is realistic and possible in some

circumstances. The smart thing is to prepare now, to do the legislation now, to do the bipartisan work now, to do the intelligence work now, the foreign policy work. These are all very complicated things and we need to get started on them.[7]

Stephen Friedman, director of the National Economic Council, played the role of secretary of the treasury. He agreed that immediate action was necessary. "There is no question in my mind that this is a predictable surprise and we need to get our act together."[8] The obvious implication is that we currently do *not* have our act together, as we will see in this book.

As might be expected, controversial legal questions about personal privacy versus national security surfaced during the panel discussion. Deputy Attorney General Jamie Gorelick, who played the role of attorney general, noted with obvious concern, "We have to come to grips with the implications for our personal privacy and the relationship between the federal government and the private sector."[9] (We will see that as cyber technologies continue to develop, our personal privacy continues to wane.)

Jason Grumet, founder and president of the Bipartisan Policy Center, concluded by affirming what everyone else already knew. "Cyber ShockWave demonstrated the tremendous challenges the government has in dealing with potential cyber attacks."[10]

CYBER STORM

Cyber ShockWave is not the only official U.S. exercise of its kind. The Central Intelligence Agency has held an annual cyber war exercise called Silent Horizon since 2007. The Department of Homeland Security (DHS) runs an annual exercise titled Cyber Storm, which simulates a large-scale cyber attack on critical infrastructure.

Cyber Storm III was held in September 2010. It was a three-day cooperative effort that simulated more than 1500 increasingly sophisticated cyber threats against critical government systems. Janet Napolitano, secretary of the Department of Homeland Security, summarized the purpose of the exercise. "Securing America's cyber infrastructure requires close coordination with our federal, state, international, and private-sector partners. Exercises like Cyber Storm III allow us to build upon the significant progress we've made in responding to evolving cyber threats."[11]

Cyber Storm III was something akin to a fire drill for online government systems. It was a huge effort, involving a collaboration of seven cabinet-level departments (the Departments of Justice, Energy, Defense, State, and Transportation, as well as the White House and the U.S. National Security Agency), eleven states (including California, New York, and Pennsylvania), twelve countries (Australia, Britain, Canada, France, Germany, Hungary, Japan, Italy, the Netherlands, New Zealand, Sweden, and Switzerland), and sixty private companies (including banking, chemical, communications, nuclear energy, and IT companies). Thousands of representatives of government and industry are included.[12]

The test is sponsored by the National Cybersecurity and Communications Integration Center (NCCIC)—the U.S. national Internet security coordination center that opened in October 2009. This organization serves as the coordinating center for U.S. cyber security operations and houses U.S. government computer experts and their private-sector counterparts under one roof. The Pentagon and National Security Agency were both involved in the planning process for the exercise.

The Cyber Storm exercise seeks to determine whether participants "can prepare for and respond to cyber attacks, exercise strategic decision making under pressure in accordance with DHS guidelines, and effectively share information across agencies in a secure manner."[13] The guidelines relate to the National Cyber Incident Response Plan, released by the Department of Homeland Security in late 2009.

Why are so many government departments, companies, states, and countries involved? Phil Reitinger, deputy undersecretary of the DHS National Protection and Programs Directorate, answers: "One of the things that I think is critical to recognize about cyberspace is [that] it's beyond the capability of any one government agency to respond, or even one government or one private-sector entity. This really requires a joint response." So, to get a realistic picture of what a major cyber attack would look like requires the involvement of many people, organizations, and governments.[14]

Cyber Storm leaders emphasized that we are no longer facing small incidents where someone says, "Hey, someone hacked my website and changed my home page." Instead, we regularly face "advanced, targeted attacks that use the Internet's fundamental elements against itself—with the goal of compromising trusted transactions and relationships."[15] In other words, hostile hackers now have the ability to invade our military and corporate networks to engage in espionage and network disruption, to severely damage our civilian infrastructure (such as electrical power grids), to engage in financial crimes relating to banks and credit card companies, and much more.

The exercise does not entail actually attacking an operating network, but rather simulates such an attack, with participants receiving a series of bulletins about new cyber attack events. During Cyber Storm III, participants from the U.S. government, state governments, foreign governments, and private companies responded to an unfolding cyber attack at an exercise control center at U.S. Secret Service headquarters in Washington DC.

As was true with Cyber ShockWave, Cyber Storm III confirmed the great vulnerabilities in the United States that must be rectified to keep our country safe. As well, the exercise pointed to the need for our government officials to act quickly in building cyber defenses.

THE TERRORIST CYBER THREAT TO THE UNITED STATES

Jim Setde, retired director of the FBI's computer crime squad, once commented, "You bring me a select group of hackers and within 90 days I'll bring this country to its knees."[16] And today's Middle Eastern terrorist organizations have the financial backing of oil-rich countries (such as Saudi Arabia, Iran, Syria, and others), so they can afford not just a "select group of hackers" but a whole army of them.[17]

The Department of Defense defines terrorism as "the calculated use of unlawful violence or threat of unlawful violence to inculcate fear, intended to coerce or to intimidate governments or societies in the pursuit of goals that are generally political, religious, or ideological." Based on this definition, the following definition is suggested for cyberterrorism:

> A computer based attack or threat of attack intended to intimidate or coerce governments or societies in pursuit of goals that are political, religious, or ideological. The attack should be sufficiently destructive or disruptive to generate fear comparable to that from physical acts of terrorism. Attacks that lead to death or bodily injury, extended power outages, plane crashes, water contamination, or major economic losses would be examples.[18]

Today, terrorists can engage in cyber attacks while sitting in the comfort of their own living rooms. Cyberspace undoubtedly gives a sense of empowerment to terrorists that they have never enjoyed before because they can accomplish their tasks throughout the world without ever leaving their own country.[19]

Another factor that makes cyberspace especially appealing to terrorists is that it is economical. For just a few thousand dollars or even less, one can obtain current cyber technology suitable for engaging in a variety of terrorist acts against the United States. The potential return on investment is therefore very appealing to terrorists.

CYBER JIHAD

Some Islamic terrorists consider cyberspace a means of fulfilling jihad. *Jihad* comes from the Arabic word *jihadi*, which principally means "to struggle" or "to strive in the path of Allah." The term has made headlines many times in recent years as terrorist activity has escalated around the world. Seemingly, whenever the United States takes a stand against terrorist Muslims, a jihad or "holy war" is declared against the United States. The term is more generally taken among militant Muslims to refer to armed fighting and warfare in defending Islam and standing against evil.

Islamic scholar Jamal Elias claims that for most Muslims today, "any war that is viewed as a defense of one's own country, home, or community is called a jihad. This understanding is very similar to what is called 'just war' in Western society."[20]

Radical Islamic fundamentalists are well known for their use of arms and explosives in defending their version of Islam. The goal of jihad, in their thinking, is to terrorize perceived enemies of Islam into submission and retreat. These Muslims seek to emulate the behavior of Muhammad (Sura 33:21), for he often led Islamic forces into battle to make Islam dominant during his time. He shed other people's blood to bolster Islam throughout the Arabian Peninsula.[21] "Muhammad's mission was to conquer the world for Allah. The goal of jihad, or holy war, is to establish Islamic authority over the whole world. Islam teaches that Allah is the only authority, and all political systems must be based on Allah's teaching."[22] Islamic history clearly reveals that jihad has been a primary tool of religious expansionism for militant practitioners of Muhammad's religion.

This radical form of jihad is taken much more seriously today than it used to be, if only because of the sheer number of radical Muslims threatening it against various countries, and because of the growing availability of weapons of mass destruction. Most Muslims are by no means radical fundamentalists, but even a minority can be a substantial threat. Islam has 1.3 billion adherents, so even a very small minority can involve tens of millions of people who can cause a great deal of trouble in the world, not only for the West but also for moderate Muslim governments.[23]

Islamic fundamentalists often cite verses from the Quran to support their view that armed conflict is permissible or even compulsory in the defense of Islam.

- "Fighting is prescribed for you, and ye dislike it. But it is possible that ye dislike a thing which is good for you" (Sura 2:216).

- "Therefore, when ye meet the unbelievers (in fight), smite at their necks; At length, when ye have thoroughly subdued them, bind a bond firmly (on them)" (Sura 47:4).

- "But when the forbidden months are past, then fight and slay the pagans wherever ye find them, and seize them, beleaguer them, and lie in wait for them in every stratagem (of war)" (Sura 9:5).

In 1998, five Muslim caliphates (governments)—representing five radical Muslim factions—signed a *fatwa* (a written decision) declaring a holy war against the United States. The document they signed includes these words:

> For over seven years the United States has been occupying the lands of Islam and the holiest of places, the Arabian Peninsula, plundering its riches, dictating to its rulers, humiliating its people, terrorizing its neighbors, and turning its bases in the Peninsula into a spearhead through which to fight the neighboring Muslim peoples…[There has been] aggression against the Iraqi people…[Their aim has been to] serve the Jews' petty state…[They express] eagerness to destroy Iraq…All these crimes and sins committed by the Americans are a clear declaration of war on Allah, his messenger, and Muslims…The ruling to kill the Americans and their allies—civilians and military—is an individual duty for every Muslim who can do it in any country in which it is possible to do it…This is in accordance with the words of Almighty Allah, "and fight the pagans altogether as they fight you altogether," and "fight them until there is no more tumult or oppression, and there prevail justice and faith in Allah."[24]

Who can doubt that the September 11, 2001 attack against the World Trade Center and Pentagon was a manifestation of this *fatwa*, written just three years earlier? Americans have taken jihad very seriously since that day.

Many extremist Muslims certainly have a religious motivation to participate in jihad, for Muslims who lose their lives in service to Allah are guaranteed entrance into Paradise (Hadith 9:459). According to Muslim tradition, Muhammad said, "The person who participates in (holy battles) in Allah's cause and nothing compels him to do so except belief in Allah and His Apostles, will be recompensed by Allah either with a reward, or booty (if he survives) or will be admitted to Paradise (if he is killed in the battle as a martyr)" (Hadith 1:35).

All of this is foundational to my main point: Cyberspace is an ideal terrain for extremist Muslims to carry out jihad against countries they consider to be enemies, including the "Greater Satan" (the United States) and the "Lesser Satan" (Israel). Jeffrey Carr talks about this form of jihad in his book *Inside Cyber Warfare*. He notes that some Islamic hackers speak about cyber attacks in religious terms, affirming that their attacks are tantamount to fighting jihad against Islam's enemies. One such Muslim hacker urged his comrades to engage in cyber attacks against Israel: "Use [the hacking skills] God has given you as bullets in the face of the Jewish Zionists. We cannot fight them with our bodies, but we can fight them with our minds and hands...By God, this is Jihad."[25]

In view of all this, we can understand why so many in our current government are fighting feverishly to beef up the cyber security in this country—especially Senator John McCain. Let us be clear that the terrorists' motivation is not only political (to thwart supposed U.S. imperialism) but also religious (to destroy the enemies of Islam and force the entire world into submission to the Islamic faith).

With that kind of motivation, terrorists are likely to use a cyber attack to cripple the U.S. infrastructure (such as our electrical grid), economy, and military. They will undoubtedly use cyberspace to inflict whatever damage they can in the United States.

AN ELECTRONIC PEARL HARBOR

I very much enjoyed my visit to Honolulu, where I had the opportunity to visit Pearl Harbor. In fact, I had the opportunity to speak at Calvary Chapel Pearl Harbor.

While I was there, I discovered that prior to Japan's attack against the naval fleet at Pearl Harbor, some in our own intelligence community were concerned about the possibility of such an attack. But such a scenario seemed too infeasible and far-fetched to take seriously. In hindsight, we know better.

Today some may be tempted to think that the "electronic Pearl Harbor" discussed in this chapter may seem too infeasible and far-fetched to take seriously. The rest of this book could change their minds.

CYBER WARFARE: A GROWING GLOBAL MENACE

cAfee, the leading computer security company, published a hard-hitting report titled *In the Crossfire: Critical Infrastructure in the Age of Cyber War.* The report suggests that the use of cyber attacks as strategic weapons by governments and political organizations is escalating at a breathless pace. The survey follows closely on the heels of the cyber attacks on Google and several other companies. The McAfee report includes this frank note:

> We believe that governments around the world are building up their offensive security capabilities. Leaders in this area, as identified in our *2009 Virtual Criminology Report,* are the U.S., Russia, France, Israel, and China, in no particular order. *Cyber* is part of the arsenal governmental, political, and terrorist organizations want to have at their disposal.[1]

Multiple news programs have reported that the world has now embarked on a new arms race. "The weapons this time are malicious data-packets of the kind hitherto employed mainly by spammers... Nations will use their cyber tools to wreak economic havoc and social disruption."[2] Who would have thought that cyber warfare would one day become a national security problem for the United States? Today it is an immeasurably intense concern.

One reason for the concern is that cyber warfare can cause a variety of injuries, including disabling our country's infrastructure (such as our electrical grid), penetrating and stealing data from our military computer networks, stealing data from major corporations (including defense contractors), manipulating and stealing money from banks and credit card companies, and any number of other crippling activities.[3] Our country has already suffered attack in these and other ways.

The United States faces a clear and present danger from the cyber war capabilities of countries around the world. Defense Secretary Robert Gates tells us that the United States is "under cyber attack virtually all the time, every day."[4] These attacks come from many different countries.

Admiral Mike McConnell, former director of national intelligence, tells us that "the vast majority of the industrialized countries in the world today have cyber-attack capabilities."[5] In fact, more than 140 countries currently do. These countries can plant a variety of electronic viruses and bugs into key utility, military, and financial network systems that can wreak all kinds of havoc.[6] To make matters more complicated, our sophisticated adversaries can route their technological attacks through proxies and obfuscate their identities. Figuring out the source of an attack can be difficult, though sometimes not impossible.

We have already had some scary moments in this country. For example, U.S. cyber experts have discovered that computer hackers from Russia and/or China (we are not absolutely sure which) have successfully planted software in the U.S. electricity grid infrastructure. These *logic bombs* could be activated from a remote location to sabotage the electrical system at a later date. The originators can send a signal from their country through the Internet, and *zap*, there goes our electricity grid. Further, North Korean hackers have disrupted the servers of the Department of Homeland Security, the U.S. Treasury, and several other government departments, along with a number of regular Internet providers, by flooding them with requests for data. A

Pentagon server used for logistical communications in armed conflict was also impeded by a cyber attack.[7]

The big concern to U.S. government officials is that major cyber attacks—much more potent than the ones mentioned above—have already been inflicted against other countries, and the results have been positively frightening. One naturally wonders whether the United States could be next. This is the reason for the Cyber ShockWave and Cyber Storm exercises mentioned in chapter 1.

In the pages that follow, we will consider several real-world examples of cyber attacks launched against key countries in the past few years. I think you will agree with me that all of this has profound implications for our lives. We have entered a new era of perpetual cyber threats. ⨯

RUSSIA'S TACTICAL CYBER WARFARE CAPABILITIES

The Second Russian–Chechen War (1997–2001)

Before the turn of the new millennium, the Russian military invaded Chechnya in an attempt to reinstall a Moscow-friendly regime. During the conflict, Russia and Chechnya engaged in cyber warfare against each other. These relatively mild cyber attacks were attempts to control and shape public perception of the conflict. However, Russian Federal Security Service hackers outmaneuvered the Chechen hackers and knocked out several strategic Chechen websites.[8]

The Russia–Estonia Conflict (2007)

More recently, the Russians launched a substantive three-week cyber attack against Estonia in 2007. The conflict emerged because the Estonians intended to remove a Soviet war memorial from Tallinn. The Russian cyber attack was primarily aimed at the Estonian presidency and parliament, government ministries, political parties, three of Estonia's six news organizations, two major banks, and several communications firms.[9]

In computerese, the Russians slammed the Estonians with a *distributed denial of service* (DDoS) attack—a preprogrammed flood of Internet traffic that shuts down or at least jams websites or computer networks. It is "distributed" because countless computers, distributed over a wide geographical area, are given electronic instructions to flood Internet traffic at targeted websites or networks. In this particular case, "one million computers from 75 countries were enslaved by a botnet to conduct a coordinated attack on Estonia's network."[10]

This kind of cyber attack is common today, so I'll provide a little backdrop before further addressing Russian cyber activity. The participating computers involved in this cyber attack are collectively called a *botnet*—a network of computers (*bot* stands for "robot," and *net* is short for "network") infected with malware that brings them under remote control.

Amazingly, these computers are all owned and operated by people who have no idea that their computers have been secretly hijacked and are being used in this way. They do not even know that instructions for launching a cyber attack against a targeted website have been loaded onto their computers. They are completely oblivious to what is going on.

The computer owner might notice that the computer seems to be running a little slower than normal, or perhaps it is taking a bit longer than normal to access websites. Almost everyone experiences these kinds of things at one time or another anyway, so people generally do not suspect foul play. While the instructions to send a flood of traffic are activated and running in the background, the computer user has no signal that something is going on. It all takes place in the background. (Is *your* computer running a bit slow this week?)

Where did those instructions to send a flood of traffic come from in the first place? It all takes place without the user knowing what has occurred. A person might be Web surfing one day, come across an interesting, innocent-looking website, click on an advertisement banner, and *zap*—malware (malicious software code) is automatically downloaded to the computer by stealth, completely in the background. That computer is now a robot, a slave-computer that has no choice but to follow the instructions sent to it by a remote user.

Or a person might receive an e-mail that says, "You've received a postcard—click here to read it." Simply clicking on the link initiates a download without the computer user even knowing it is happening. Cyber warfare includes a great deal of stealth and deception.

This zombie computer—infected by malware—then begins secretly seeking other computers to infect. This is known as a *worm* because the infection worms its way around the Internet from one computer to another until thousands and even hundreds of thousands of computers are infected. It happens insidiously and quickly.

Now then, back to the Russian attack against Estonian websites in the spring of 2007. Predictably, the Russian government denies responsibility. The Estonian government claims to have cyber proof, and most of the intelligence world agrees. Estonia's computer networks were able to recover relatively quickly following the attack because the United States and some European countries loaned them some highly trained technicians to counteract the worm. This cyber attack made the front pages of newspapers around the world and raised awareness of this new kind of warfare.[11]

The Russia–Georgia War (2008)

In 2008, Russia and Georgia (directly to the south of Russia) quarreled over some disputed territories. Soviet dominance of Georgia ended in 1991 as Russia was wrestling with its own internal problems. But in 2008, Russian Federation (RF) Armed Forces invaded Georgia, alleging that they were acting in self-defense against Georgian aggression. Russia's military strategy was interesting:

1. An initial series of cyber attacks took place several weeks before the invasion. This largely involved a distributed denial of service (DDoS), in which a preprogrammed flood of Internet traffic shut down or jammed key Georgian sites.

2. Twenty-four hours before the actual invasion, Russians launched a much larger wave of cyber attacks, prohibiting Georgians from connecting to any outside information sources or sending e-mails out of the country.

3. Then the physical invasion itself took place.

The cyber attacks appeared to be spontaneous attempts by solo

Russian hackers who were not affiliated with the military. All the while, however, the military was at work. Jeffrey Carr explains in his important book *Inside Cyber Warfare*: "I found myself becoming more and more intrigued by the pattern that was emerging. There were at least four other examples of cyber attacks timed with RF military actions dating back to 2002. Why wasn't anyone exploring that, I wondered?"[12] Russia engaged in a sophisticated cyber-based attack that coincided directly with a land, sea, and air invasion.

As might be expected, the Georgians sought to rectify their cyberspace woes, engaging in some cyber work-arounds. Russia, however, countered their every cyber move. Russian hackers were one step ahead of Georgian hackers every step of the way, with a notably superior cyber strategy.[13]

For example, Georgian banks shut down their servers and planned to lay low until the attack was over. They chose to suffer a temporary loss of online banking rather than risk data being stolen or having the banking infrastructure damaged. Unable to link in to Georgia's banking networks, Russian hackers responded by instructing their botnets to send a tidal wave of cyber traffic to the international banking community, disguised as a cyber attack from Georgia itself. In response, foreign banks automatically shut down connections with the Georgian banking sector. This effectively paralyzed all of Georgia's banking operations.[14]

Is a Russian–NATO War Coming?

Those in the know have pointed out that the Russian cyber attacks against Estonia and Georgia were relatively mild. We have not seen what Russia's cyber warriors are truly capable of. Might they be saving their best cyber weapons for more cyber-savvy opponents—NATO and the United States?[15]

NORTH KOREA'S CYBER WARFARE CAPABILITIES

We Americans like to celebrate our independence on July 4. But our government computers and networks were anything *but* independent during the July 4 weekend in 2009. Indeed, several dozen websites in the United States—including the White House website and those of some other government entities—came under a DDoS attack. South Korea's government and civilians, as well as some international companies, were also targets of this attack. It was strongly suspected that the cyber culprit was the Democratic People's Republic of Korea.[16]

The task was fairly easy for the North Korean government hackers. About 40,000 computers around the world had already been infected by a botnet virus. The owners of those computers were completely unaware that their computers had become robot computers awaiting cyber instructions from the North Korean hackers. Just before the July 4 weekend, a coded message instructed those many computers to begin flooding traffic to the targeted computer websites. Whenever those computers were on, they became a part of the assault force without their owners having any inkling about it. Their computers might have run a little slower for a while, and their Internet connections might have slowed down a bit, but aside from that they noticed nothing out of the ordinary.

As a result of these U.S. government sites receiving about a million hits per second, the websites became temporarily unavailable. The servers choked. No site can withstand that kind of cyber assault. Affected websites included those of the Treasury, the Secret Service, the Federal Trade Commission, and the Department of Transportation. Also hit were the websites of NASDAQ, New York Mercantile, the New York Stock Exchange, and *The Washington Post*.

U.S. intelligence has discovered a number of highly capable cyber attack units in North Korea. The Korean People's Army Joint Chiefs Cyber Warfare Unit 121 has more than 600 hackers. The Enemy Secret Department Cyber Psychological Warfare Unit 204 has 100 hackers. (Where do they come up with these names?) Apparently, computer hackers make up a healthy portion of North Korea's annual military budget. To the best of our knowledge, they have more than a thousand cyber warfare agents at their disposal.[17]

Training begins at a very early age. The North Korean government identifies elementary students who have obvious computer skills and begins grooming them to become government hackers. In middle and high school, they are trained in everything they will need to know about computers, and then they attend a specialized university to complete their training. The sole academic purpose of their training is to learn to break into enemy computers, networks, and websites—such as those in the United States and its allies.

CHINA'S TACTICAL CYBER WARFARE CAPABILITIES

China is a major player in the cyber war and is expanding traditional military capabilities as well. It has incredibly long-range radar systems, antiship missiles that are too fast to be intercepted, and thousands of missiles aimed at Taiwan. China is also constructing aircraft carriers and an impressive long-range missile that would provide a sea-based nuclear strike capability.

The Chinese government, like most other national governments, is also heavily involved in espionage. One of its goals seems to be to steal information on enemy technologies, dissect that information, and uncover flaws. It also seems intent on becoming increasingly adept at cyber warfare. China does not currently possess America's physical military capabilities, but adeptness in cyber warfare could even the playing field.

Leaders in the U.S. military received a wake-up call when a major publication ran an article titled "How the United States Lost the Naval War of 2015." The author of the article, James Kraska, speculated on how China could actually win in an encounter with the U.S. Navy, sneakily sinking the USS George Washington.[18]

China has also taken steps to increase its chances of disrupting networks inside the United States. For example, Chinese hackers copied the Cisco network router that is the backbone of networks and Internet service providers in the United States. Then these hackers began selling routers at greatly discounted prices all over the globe. The buyers for these bogus routers included the U.S. Pentagon, Marine Corps, and Air Force, as well as many defense contractors. If these specially designed routers include hidden malware, they could be used to disrupt our networks and render cyber damage to our country.[19]

Further, in 2009 a sophisticated computer program known as

GhostNet penetrated approximately 1300 computers at the embassies of several countries. GhostNet remotely activated the computers' webcams and microphones without alerting the users. This enabled the Chinese government—the source of GhostNet—to see and hear what was happening at these embassies. GhostNet remained active for almost two full years before being discovered. [20]

Richard Clarke comments on the extent of Chinese cyber espionage.

> The extent of Chinese government hacking against U.S., European, and Japanese industries and research facilities is without precedent in the history of espionage. Exabytes* of data have been copied from universities, industrial labs, and government facilities. The secrets behind everything from pharmaceutical formulas to bioengineering designs, to nanotechnology, to weapons systems, to everyday industrial products have been taken. [21]

As it turns out, GhostNet is not the only Chinese software that hid behind the scenes for a long time. U.S. intelligence agents also discovered that Chinese hackers successfully infiltrated the U.S. power grid computers and left behind logic bombs that can later be activated remotely to bring the grid down. The cyber threat continues to grow daily.

ISRAEL'S TACTICAL CYBER WARFARE CAPABILITIES

How did Israel's Air Force penetrate Syrian air space and accomplish its strategic bombing mission in Syria's own backyard without Israel's jets appearing on Syrian radar? Answer: Israel hacked into the Syrian radar system the night before so the Syrians would see only what Israel's Air Force wanted them to see—absolutely nothing! [22]

How did the Israelites pull off this cyber victory? No one knows for sure. Some suggest that Israeli aircraft may have detected Syrian radar and then utilized the same frequency to transmit computer code into the radar's computer system, thereby causing the radar to malfunction.

---

* An exabyte is equivalent to one billion gigabytes.

The packets of computer code may have instructed the radar system to simply play a loop of what the sky looked like prior to the attack.

Another possibility is that Israeli agents somehow slipped some lines of computer code—a *trapdoor*—into the Russian-designed software of Syria's radar system. It would be very hard to visually detect these new lines of computer code because the software itself has millions of lines of such code. This trapdoor could enable Israeli hackers to sign in to the system undetected and instruct it to "go blind" for a while.

However Israeli hackers did it, it was an impressive act of cyber warfare!

HACK-ATTACKS AGAINST ISRAEL

Not unexpectedly, Israeli websites also get attacked by hackers of various countries. Israel has plenty of cyber enemies out there. The most active hackers appear to be Moroccan, Algerian, Saudi Arabian, Turkish, Palestinian, and Iranian. The exact number of Israeli websites that are regularly disrupted by hackers is unknown, but the number is well into the thousands—up to 10,000 sites in a single week.

In one case, a group called DZ Team, made up of Algerian and Egyptian hackers, hacked the Bank of Israel over a Passover weekend. Following the attack, members of the group contacted the media and claimed that they were religiously motivated: "We do everything in the name of Allah."[23]

An Arabic group of anti-Israeli hackers say they want to inflict financial damage to Israeli businesses, government, and individuals: "Disrupt and destroy Zionist government and banking sites to cost the enemy not thousands but millions of dollars..."[24]

Israel sometimes retaliates by flooding blogs of enemy countries with pro-Israeli opinions. Israeli hackers have also penetrated into Hamas-owned TV stations and pro-Palestinian Facebook groups. The battle is ongoing. One creative tactic employed by Israel's supporters is the development of a "Help Israel Win" botnet, called Patriot, that is designed to attack anti-Israel websites.[25] The cyber war continues.

NIGHTMARE ON CYBER STREET

Much of our daily lives hinges in one way or another on computer technology and the Internet, so a potent cyber attack from one of these countries against the United States could have a catastrophic effect. Many aspects of our national life are directly tied into computerized information systems.

> The U.S. military, for example, relies upon information networks, including the global information grid, to conduct modern-era combat operations. Many civilian institutions, infrastructures, and essential government services are also highly dependent on the Internet and other information networks. Police, firefighters, and other emergency services providers, public health, education, transportation, banking and finance, water supply, sanitation, and energy systems all depend on computers and information networks, as do the air traffic control system, hydroelectric dams, nuclear power plants, traffic lights, water treatment facilities, and key private sector institutions such as colleges and universities, hospitals, stock markets, business corporations, shopping malls, and credit card companies.[26]

I know this. Now you know this. Our enemies know it too.

3

WE ARE BEING WATCHED: CYBER ESPIONAGE

Espionage has been around for a very long time. It took place in biblical times (Joshua 2:1; 6:23; 1 Samuel 26:4). It is still happening today, but these days it is much easier and faster—it can be done with a laptop computer in the convenience of one's own living room!

People are spying on other people. Companies are spying on other companies. Organizations are spying on other organizations. And countries are spying on other countries. Espionage has become more pervasive than ever, and a lot of it is happening through the portal of cyberspace. In the old days, people read each other's mail and peeked into their desk drawers. Today, people intercept and read each other's e-mail and peek inside their private computers and networks.

Cyber espionage is the new kid on the block when it comes to spying on each other. One cyber analyst defines cyber espionage as "the unauthorized probing of a target computer's configuration to evaluate its system defenses, or the unauthorized viewing and copying of data files."[1] *Fox Business News* adds a few more details.

> [Cyber espionage uses] secretive means to infiltrate a network and steal information to receive a competitive advantage. The spying could be aimed at gaining a technology

such as blueprints for a new type of micro processor, finding out strategic plans such as a potential acquisition, or confidential data from a lawsuit.[2]

The stealing of private information has become commonplace in cyberspace. At recent congressional hearings, Director of National Intelligence Dennis Blair was forthright. "Sensitive information is stolen daily from both government and private sector networks, undermining confidence in our information systems, and in the very information these systems were intended to convey."[3] Cyber espionage is a 24/7 reality in our day.

Even social networks, such as Facebook, MySpace, and Twitter, are regularly penetrated by hackers and used for devious purposes. As cyber war expert Jeffrey Carr puts it, "Commonly known as the Social Web, these services provide a heretofore unprecedented data store of personal information about people, companies, and governments that can be leveraged for financial crime, espionage, and disinformation by both state and non-state hackers."[4]

James Miller, principal deputy undersecretary of defense for policy, says that cyber espionage is so pervasive that "the United States is losing enough data in cyber attacks to fill the Library of Congress many times over, and authorities have failed to stay ahead of the threat… Our systems are probed thousands of times a day and scanned millions of times a day."[5] No one is really safe. A cyber watch group called *NetWitness* reports that during the past year, more than 2500 companies around the world were seriously and injuriously hacked by cyber criminals, stealing countless moving vans worth of sensitive corporate data. Security experts say China and Russia are running neck and neck for the title of worst offender of cyber espionage.[6]

CORPORATE CYBER ESPIONAGE

Corporate information theft has become a huge problem. Countless cyber criminals have sought to steal trade secrets, business strategies, information on product development, and other sensitive information from corporations—and then use that information to their financial advantage. Gaining access to this kind of information can give these individuals a competitive economic advantage or, in some cases, enable them to cause economic injury.

How pervasive is information theft among corporations? This is difficult to assess. Corporations that have experienced information theft often keep quiet about it in order to maintain public confidence in the corporation.[7] Because of this no-tell policy of many corporations, the problem may actually be much bigger than we are aware of.

So how does cyber espionage happen? A prime means is through the use of *spyware*. Spyware is most often installed on a user's computer by stealth, without the user's consent or knowledge. This installation occurs automatically when the user opens an infected attachment in an e-mail or clicks on a link in an e-mail. In some cases, the e-mail might contain a headshot of a seductive-looking girl, and the link might say, "Click here to see my naughty pictures." If the user takes the bait, the spyware secretly loads onto the computer in the background.

Spyware is specifically designed to gather information from a user's computer. This form of spyware utilizes a *keystroke logger*, which records everything typed on the keyboard of an infected machine. Corporations use this type of spyware to steal sensitive or proprietary information from the computers and networks of other companies. Corporate executives and employees must be especially cautious at business conventions and conferences where free thumb drives are handed out as gifts. These drives—once plugged into a computer—could load a secret keystroke logger. This enables the cyber spy to watch the user's every move. The net result would be the same if a thief broke into the corporate offices and accessed all of the file cabinets.

HARD-TO-DETECT CYBER CULPRITS

One of the reasons cyber espionage has become so commonplace today is that it is difficult to detect. "The problem with most hacking attacks is that the source of them is, fundamentally, unverifiable. Even if you can have an intelligent guess at the origin, you can't usually know."[8]

A talented hacker can penetrate the computer network of a corporation, poke around for a while, steal data, and then exit the network without anyone ever knowing he or she was there. One report I came across addressed the staggering volume of industrial espionage in this country: "Some estimates put the amount of stolen data in the thousands of terabytes, ten times the amount of information stored in the U.S. Library of Congress."[9] A single terabyte is equivalent to one trillion bytes or 1000 gigabytes. It's equivalent to ten copies of the *Encyclopedia Britannica*—all 32 volumes, all 44 million words. To steal one terabyte worth of data in the form of real books would require a forklift and a moving van.[10] Just imagine the number of moving vans required for stealing thousands of terabytes of data in book form!

GUARD YOUR THUMB DRIVE!

Corporate espionage also occurs when executives and employees are careless with physical media. Data that is lost by misplacing or losing such physical media can pose a risk to the company, company employees, or even consumers who purchase products from that company. This commonly happens when executives or employees travel with their laptop computers, thumb drives, and CD-ROMs. In the book *The Myths of Security: What the Computer Industry Doesn't Want You to Know*, John Viega explains it this way:

> In reality, lots of data gets lost or stolen. According to the Privacy Rights Clearinghouse, in the United States alone, there have been over 215 million electronic data records lost since the beginning of 2005. Now, most of the time, those records are not used in identity theft, because they are lost, not stolen. For example, McAfee once had an auditor leave a CD with employee data in an airplane seat pocket. The data almost certainly went out with the trash. But, it happens often enough that there is real risk to consumers.[11]

CD-ROMs, thumb drives, and other forms of media are popular items among airport pickpockets and thieves. Corporate travelers beware!

CYBER EXTORTION

Unscrupulous cyber criminals sometimes engage in extortion against corporations. This can work in several ways. Someone could engage in massive cyber espionage of a corporation—stealing data about employee records, customer records, product development, economic forecasts, and the like—and then threaten the executives of that corporation with making all that stolen data public…unless a payment is rendered.

Or someone might threaten to jam or shut down a corporation's website unless they pay some big money. More specifically, the hacker could threaten to inflict a distributed denial of service (DDoS) attack against the corporation unless the corporation pays.

How could a cyber criminal arrange to do this? First, he or she would develop a website that drew many visitors. As bait, the website might feature or list many articles by respected investors on how to invest in the stock market. As visitors click on links or banner advertisements at this website, malware—malicious computer code—secretly downloads to their computers in the background without the computer owners realizing that it is happening. Because of this secretly downloaded software, that computer can now respond to instructions from a remote user.

Let us say that a thousand computers are infected in this way. This constitutes a botnet. As I have noted previously in the book, the owners of computers that are part of a botnet have no idea that their computers have been compromised and are now receiving remote commands to engage in certain actions. The users are oblivious to the fact that their computers have become puppets and that the cyber extortionist is pulling all the strings.

This cyber criminal could easily send a remote command to these many computers to start flooding the targeted corporation website with perpetual Internet traffic. With 1000, 10,000, or even 100,000 computers doing this all at once, the website becomes overwhelmed. If this particular website is the Internet store of the corporation—the website where e-commerce sales take place—such a website jam or shutdown could have catastrophic economic consequences, especially if this flood of Internet traffic lasts for a week, which it easily could.

If customers cannot access the site, they cannot buy the products. If customers cannot buy the products, the business loses money. If this happens day after day, the business loses *lots* of money. Because the e-commerce website has experienced a botnet meltdown, the corporation is essentially closed for business.

Next, cyber thugs—especially those who live in different countries, where things are hard to police—could demand payment to prevent such a cyber shutdown, or in what sounds like a cyber mafia, they could promise to provide protection services for a price. If the payment is withheld, the cyber assault begins.

The textbook *Cyberpower and National Security* informs us that this type of extortion scheme proliferated between 2000 and 2010. "[Cyber extortionists were] first targeting online gambling and commercial pornographic websites, then small- to mid-sized mainstream e-commerce sites and financial services institutions. A variety of companies have paid under such threats; others have refused and may have suffered the consequences."[12] The lack of national and international cyber laws makes this difficult to police. Until such national and international laws are in place, and nations agree to enforce those laws, such extortions will likely continue.

CASE STUDY: CHINA'S MASSIVE DATA THEFT

Jeffrey Carr, in his eye-opening book *Inside Cyber Warfare*, reveals that acts of cyber espionage are far more pervasive than acts of cyber warfare, and the nation leading the way on a global scale is the People's Republic of China.[13] In recent years, Chinese cyber capabilities have become increasingly visible and troubling. Evidence is mounting that China has launched an unknown number of cyber reconnaissance and offensive events with unknown intent against a variety of countries—and with notable skill.

Dmitri Alperovitch, who heads Internet-threat intelligence analysis and correlation for McAfee, makes this open concession: "[The Chinese have] thoroughly pierced unclassified U.S. government networks…In the U.S. when you're sending an email over an unclassified system you might as well copy the Chinese on that email because they'll probably read it anyway because of their pretty thorough penetration of our network."[14]

For 18 minutes in April of 2010, China's state-controlled telecommunications company hijacked a whopping 15 percent of the entire world's Internet traffic, military and civilian. Cyber experts in the United States say the Chinese could have carried out eavesdropping on unprotected communications—including e-mails and instant messaging—and even manipulated or deleted data. One cyber security specialist commented that "this is one of the biggest—if not the biggest—hijacks we have ever seen." And it could happen again, anywhere and anytime. It is just the way the Internet works, he explained. "What happened to the traffic while it was in China? No one knows!"[15]

China has established two network spy stations in Cuba, with the permission of the Castro government, to spy on America. These spy stations enable China to monitor Internet traffic as well as Department of Defense communications.[16] The Chinese government has its ears right up against the door, as it were.*

One example of Chinese cyber espionage against the United States Department of Defense has been dubbed "Titan Rain." On April 21, 2009, the *Wall Street Journal* reported that the People's Republic of China successfully penetrated cyber security protecting the Pentagon's multi-billion-dollar Joint Strike Fighter F-35 project.

The security breach actually took place in 2005. Lieutenant General William Lord, the Air Force's chief of warfighting integration and chief information officer, confirmed that "China has downloaded 10 to 20 terabytes of data from the NIPRNet (DOD's Non-Classified IP Router Network)."[17] The stolen data, he indicated, was derived from the U.S. Army Information Systems Engineering Command, the Naval Ocean Systems Center, the Missile Defense Agency, and Sandia National Laboratories. Richard Clarke tells us that "General William Lord directly and publicly attributed the attacks not to Chinese hacktivists, but to the Chinese government."[18]

This is obviously a severe breach in U.S. national security. The F-35 is a fifth-generation fighter jet developed by Lockheed Martin and is

* My comments should not be misconstrued to be a negative reflection on Chinese people. They are directed solely at government officials and government-sponsored hackers affiliated with the People's Republic of China.

considered a key component of keeping America safe in future decades. It is replacing the aging F-16s and F-18s and is designed to serve the Navy, Air Force, and Marines. The U.S. military has ordered 2500 of these fighter jets at a cost of more than $300 billion. NATO countries have also ordered the fighter jet. Unlike its predecessors, this aircraft is specially designed for both electronic warfare *and* smart weapons technology. No wonder China wants to see the blueprints. This fighter is intended to provide air dominance over enemies of the United States, but security breaches like Titan Rain enable adversaries to look for vulnerabilities in the F-35, thus reducing potential U.S. air dominance.

The stolen data on the F-35 relates to the design of the aircraft and to its electronics systems. It is impossible, however, to ascertain the specifics of what the Chinese saw. Thankfully, some of the most important data on the aircraft was not available on the network.

China's cyber espionage activities did not end in 2005. Department of Defense officials indicated in 2006 that the Global Information Grid—the Pentagon network backbone—was the recipient of about three million daily scans, and China was one of the main culprits. China has also engaged in cyber espionage against various companies working on government contracts, such as Raytheon, Lockheed Martin, Boeing, and Northrup Grumman. All of these companies experienced significant data breaches in 2007, and the security traces pointed to China.

EVERY COUNTRY DOES IT

Strictly speaking, hacking into U.S. government computers or networks for political and/or economic reasons is criminal activity. However, the line between fair and foul play has become blurred because our technology has outpaced public policy. As we have seen, cyberspace is a relatively new phenomenon, so not enough national and international laws have been enacted to govern it. Besides, most countries today probably view cyber espionage as a necessary component of national defense. Experts tell us that every country does it![19] And every country will probably continue to do it regardless of laws that are eventually enacted.

WEAPONIZED SOFTWARE: A REAL AND PRESENT DANGER

I remember the day as if it were yesterday. I was writing a book titled *Find It Fast in the Bible*, making great progress, and decided to take a short break to check my e-mail. As I opened up Microsoft Outlook, I saw that someone had sent me an electronic postcard. "How nice," I thought.

With no hesitation, I clicked on the link to retrieve my postcard. My computer suddenly went berserk. Everything went haywire. I lost complete control of my computer, and all kinds of strange designs and characters began flashing across my screen. It caused an endless scrolling of gibberish on my screen that I could not stop. I had been victimized by a computer virus. Regardless of what I did, I could not regain control of my machine.

I worked for hours, trying to counteract the effects of the virus, but to no avail. This virus scrambled everything on my computer, and I couldn't do a thing about it. My only choice was to wipe my hard disk clean and reload all of my software. That little computer virus caused me one huge headache. I also learned a very good lesson: Trust nothing on the Internet. Always beware of computer viruses.

Though I lost a good morning's work on my book, I was glad I had created daily online backups just in case something ever happened to my computer.

VARIETIES OF MALWARE

Malware is malicious software that causes computers or networks to do things their owners do not want done—often injurious and disruptive things. There are a variety of kinds of malware, including viruses, worms, phishing scams, spyware, adware, and logic bombs, some of which I have briefly touched on previously but now want to discuss in greater detail.[1] I will provide a primer on the arsenal used by today's computer hackers. You will soon recognize that cyberspace is filled with land mines.

HOW MALWARE INVADES YOUR COMPUTER

You have surely already picked up on the fact that there are a number of ways malware can find its way onto your personal computer. For example, you might innocently visit a website and click on a link, and without you even knowing it, malware downloads to your computer in the background. Or you might visit a website offering what you believe to be a legitimate software program that you would like to have on your computer, such as a calendar program. You have no idea that by downloading that software program, you are also installing malware on your computer that eventually will either damage your computer or be used for devious purposes, such as spying on your keystrokes.[2]

Attacks using Internet pornography as bait are particularly effective with teenage and twentysomething males. For example, a teenage male clicks on a link to watch a pornographic video on his computer. But as he does, a window pops up that says a plug-in for Windows Media Player is needed in order to view the video. When he clicks on the link to obtain the plug-in, he inadvertently installs malware on his computer. The plug-in is also installed on his computer so the pornographic video can be viewed, but the malware is installed behind the scenes as well. This user has no idea that his computer has just been infected.[3]

Or someone may click on a banner advertisement. Unfortunately, malicious advertisements sometimes appear even on good websites. Because the website is trustworthy, users naturally assume that the advertisements on the website are trustworthy as well. This is a false and naive assumption. Some cyber criminals place several legitimate ads on a reputable website. Then they occasionally slip in an advertisement that has malware built into the computer code (such as spyware).

Advertising networks and websites do their best to keep infected ads out. Still, advertisements often contain computer code, and anything that contains computer code can also contain *infected* computer code. The moral of the story is this: Always be cautious of advertisements, regardless of where you find them.

People who fail to update their system software with security patches can also become infected with malware.[4] In fact, in 2005, a number of people who had not updated their system software visited MySpace and YouTube. While there, they clicked on a particular banner advertisement and inadvertently downloaded and installed malicious code that logged all their keystrokes so their sensitive data could be captured (such as their username and password for their online bank account). Had they simply updated their system software, this would have been prevented.

Malware can also find its way onto your computer through security flaws in programs, such as Microsoft Word. For example, someone could e-mail you a Microsoft Word document that has been infected. When you open that document on your computer, it installs malware on your computer. (I *never* open attachments unless I know the sender personally.)

Some malware-ridden websites exploit security flaws in Web browsers, such as Microsoft Internet Explorer. If you happen to browse an infected website with a vulnerable browser and operating system configuration, a piece of malware is likely to be downloaded to your computer without you even knowing it.

I have just scratched the surface of some of the ways that malware could find its way onto your computer. Cyber criminals are often clever, devising new and creative ways to sneak onto your system. Internet surfer, beware!

A CLEAR AND PRESENT DANGER

Malware presents no small problem, as the book *Cyberpower and National Security* makes clear.

During the first half of 2006, the Microsoft Security Team reported that it removed 10 million pieces of malicious software from nearly 4 million computers and Web servers. When analysts at Google examined several million Web pages for the presence of malicious software, they determined that 4.5 million of the Web pages examined were suspicious in nature. After further testing of those pages, over 1 million were found to launch downloads of malicious software, and more than two-thirds of those programs were *bot* software that, among other things, collected data on banking transactions, which it emailed to a temporary (and thus hard to trace) email account.[5]

People can actually hire malware services to do their dirty work. That is evidently how some Israeli network security employees launched an attack against a Hezbollah website in 2009, causing it to temporarily go off-line. They did it by hiring a botnet service. For about $20 a month, the botnet service provides the client with a small network of ten bots (robot computers). For $100 a month, the service provides a network of a thousand bots (robot computers). The service "offers a user-friendly interface that allows the operator to choose the type of attack, attack speed, and number of computers (bots)."[6]

So for a mere hundred dollars a month, malicious users can hire 1000 computers to overwhelm and shut down a target website. All the work is done by professional hackers, and everything is handled in a user-friendly way so that those who utilize the service are satisfied and become repeat customers.

STAYING HIDDEN

Of course, hackers design their malware in such a way that it remains hidden. This has not always been the case. In earlier years, if you had a virus infection on your computer, you immediately experienced a slowdown on your computer, and in some cases, a multitude of ads would continually pop up on your computer screen. Not anymore. Hackers eventually recognized that in the long run, they could make more money off unsuspecting users if the virus infection was not so blatantly obvious. Such malware might still cause an occasional ad to pop up, but not a multitude of them. As a result, many computer users have no idea that their equipment is infected.

Now let's zero in on some of the different kinds of malware floating around out there. This will give you a good handle on the damage that can be done in cyberspace.

Computer Viruses

Viruses are software programs that pass from one computer user to another through the Internet, through a network (such as at your workplace), or through hardware (such as thumb drives or CD-ROMs). Computer viruses can disrupt the normal operation of a computer (just as one did that fateful day when I was writing a book) and can even render it unusable. Such viruses can also provide hackers with hidden access to your system so they can copy or steal information from your computer, such as banking or credit card information.

Computer Worms

Computer worms are aptly named because they can spread viruses from one computer to another without the computer users doing anything. Worms can copy themselves from one computer to another by taking advantage of known vulnerabilities in other software programs. This form of malware literally worms itself through the Internet, from computer to computer. Worms can infect hundreds of thousands of computers. In fact, they can go global in a very short time. Expanding on the virus analogy, worm viruses are highly infectious and contagious.

Spyware

Like other forms of malware, spyware is installed on a user's computer without the user's consent or knowledge. It typically finds its way onto a computer when the user clicks on a link in an e-mail or opens a Microsoft Word document that has been attached to an email. (Do not click on links in e-mails or open attachments unless you know the sender.)

Spyware uses a keystroke logger, which records everything typed into the keyboard of an infected machine. The hacker uses this information to steal personal usernames and passwords or sensitive or proprietary corporate documents.

Phishing Scams

Phishing scams are especially devious. You may receive an e-mail that appears to be from your bank, such as the Bank of America or Wells Fargo. The e-mail graphics have been carefully copied so that the e-mail appears to be a legitimate communication from the bank.

The e-mail might request that you click on a link to the bank website, where you are then requested to provide your username and password. The website looks like your real bank website. It has the same graphics and the same logo. But it is actually a bogus website, designed by a hacker who wants your username and password, that provides access to your money. My innocent young niece fell for a phishing scam just like this. Money was sifted from her bank account, and she endured a nightmare experience with her bank in order to unravel the cyber mess and get her money back.

More than 100,000 phishing websites are currently on the Internet, and millions of phishing e-mails are sent out every day. It is one of the most effective scams out there.

Spear-Phishing Scams

Spear-phishing scams are also pervasive. These include e-mails that appear to be legitimate messages from friends or family members. Hackers obtain these names illegally from social networks such as Facebook or MySpace and then use them in spear-phishing attacks.

The e-mail message, seeming to be from a real friend, typically asks the recipient to click on a link or open an attachment. For example, the e-mail might say, "Hey John, I came across this article and knew you would want to see it too. Enjoy! Love, Ginny Nelson." Once John clicks on the article link—*zap*—malware is downloaded to his computer.

Logic Bombs

A logic bomb is a very nasty piece of malware. It is a software application or computer code that erases all the data on a computer or network of computers, or it may shut down the system completely. Once a logic bomb detonates on your computer or network, all that remains is useless hardware.

Some logic bombs are particularly malicious. Let's say, for example, that a hacker has tapped into computer networks that run electrical power grids. This hacker could infect these networks with logic bombs that can initiate power surges sufficient to fry the circuits of the transformers. Then the logic bombs could issue instructions for the computer networks to erase themselves.[7] If that happened, the electricity would go out throughout those grids—possibly for a very long time.

In fact, networks than run America's electrical grids have already been laced with such logic bombs. Richard Clarke, in his book *Cyber War: The Next Threat to National Security and What to Do About It*, notes that "there is good reason to believe that someone actually has already implanted logic bombs in the U.S. power grid control networks."[8] Russia and/or China are believed to be the culprits. Clarke implies that the United States has also engaged in such activity in other countries. (More on all this in a later chapter.)

Trapdoors

Once hackers penetrate private networks for the first time, they often leave behind *trapdoors* to permit easier and faster access in the future. These trapdoors allow hackers to gain *roots*. A black market of root kits has emerged, allowing hackers to trade or sell these to each other—often for a good price. Thus people can buy root access to a network or perhaps to a software program under development. This root access allows hackers to poke around on the network and erase any evidence that they were ever there. This is much like a criminal who steals a homeowner's key, lets himself in, and wipes his fingerprints before he leaves.

Botnets

As we have seen, a botnet is a network of robot computers that are controlled remotely by an unauthorized user (*bot* is short for "robot"; *net* is short for "network"). This usually takes place without any

knowledge of the computer's owner. Such a network of robot computers can be used to launch an attack against a target website, typically by
flooding the target website with relentless Internet traffic. This causes
the website to become jammed or to shut down altogether.

Some hackers are making a lot of money through use of botnets.
Here is how: First, the cyber criminal builds a website that contains
information about a topic people will be interested in. Let's say, for the
sake of illustration, that the site contains information on how to put
together a will. The site includes many helpful articles, so the site gets
heavy traffic.

This website also features a number of Google AdSense advertisements for the services of lawyers who specialize in writing wills. Just
click on an advertisement, and *voila*, you are at the lawyer's website.
The great thing about Google AdSense advertisements is that if you
have them posted on your own website, you get paid every time someone clicks on an advertisement. Many lawyers have allocated marketing dollars to pay every time someone clicks on an ad at *your* website
that takes that person to *their* website.

So far so good, but this is where the illegal stuff comes into the picture. After the hacker designs this apparently legitimate website with
apparently legitimate links, he will then set up a botnet—that is, a network of robot computers that must follow his remote instructions. In
this case, the hacker issues instructions for these computers (owned by
unsuspecting users) to visit his "learn about wills" website and click
on a Google AdSense advertisement that will take the person to the
unsuspecting lawyer's website. If there are, say, 10,000 computers in
this botnet, all clicking on the link that goes to the lawyer's website, the
hacker will generate some pretty significant revenue from the lawyer.
Many hackers are making tens of thousands of dollars using such devious methodology.[9] How ironic that lawyers become victims of such
rank illegal activity.

ANTIVIRUS SOFTWARE

Many people install antivirus software that they think will keep
them safe from computer viruses. Such software is intended to identify

malware and prevent it from being installed on the computer in the first place, or if it has already been installed, to remove it. Antivirus software can engage in *on-access* scanning, meaning that every time a software program runs or a file is accessed, it is examined to see if viruses are present. The software can also engage in *on-demand* scanning, in which a computer user simply instructs the program to look for viruses on his or her hard disk or in a particular folder.

But the sheer prevalence and pervasiveness of constantly new malware in cyberspace creates a huge challenge for the antivirus software. Because malware is so prevalent, the makers of antivirus software can hardly keep their programs updated fast enough to deal with the onslaught of new attacks.

You may not know that a new form of malware enters into cyberspace every 2.2 seconds. Does the maker of your antivirus software have the manpower to deal with a new virus every 2.2 seconds? Not likely. Some computer experts say that the major antivirus software companies find and fix about one out of every ten malware viruses that are discovered. Even then, antivirus providers can take days and sometimes weeks to design a fix and distribute it to users across the Internet. During the interim, everyone who accesses the Internet is vulnerable to that piece of malware. And if that malware finds its way onto someone's computer, the owner of that computer will be completely in the dark about it.

If the malware that downloads to your computer is spyware that contains a keyboard logger, it will log all of your keystrokes. That means the next time you sign on to your online bank account, typing in your username and password, that piece of malware will transmit that information to another computer. That computer could be anywhere in the world, including places where there are few if any cybercrime laws.

Thousands of new pieces of malware enter cyberspace every single day. A large antivirus company may have a hundred people working on the malware onslaught, but each individual employee is realistically able to provide a fix for only a few pieces of malware each day. That means no fixes are available for the majority of malware floating around in cyberspace.

Computer experts tell us that finding people with the necessary technical qualifications to recognize and then provide a fix for malware is no easy task. This essentially guarantees that the malware will succeed in infecting a large number of computers throughout cyberspace before a fix is provided.

This is unquestionably the primary reason why the detection rate for antivirus technology is so low—some estimates place it at 30 percent. Yet many people are under the illusion that their antivirus software is keeping them absolutely safe. Ignorance is bliss.

Additionally, hackers have copies of all the popular antivirus software, and they continue to tweak their malware until the antivirus software no longer recognizes it. Once they unleash this new version on cyberspace and antivirus companies recognize that it exists, several days or even a week will pass before a fix is available.

Finally, once a piece of malware reaches your machine, one of its first objectives is to secretly disable your antivirus software. If you are now thinking that perhaps you are not as safe as you once thought you were, you have taken your first baby steps toward cyber wisdom.

STUXNET: CYBER APOCALYPSE NOW

Stuxnet is a highly virulent computer worm that was the weapon of choice for the most potent cyber attack ever launched, and many believe it gives us a portent of the future. It's name is formed from keywords buried in the code. Following Stuxnet's initial assault in 2009, one reporter assessed what could lie ahead:

> Future wars will be fought from a desk in a closed-up room. No missiles will be fired, no drone attacks will be launched on civilians, and no soldiers will die. Nuclear weapons will be of no use. Yet nations will be brought to their knees by the press of a button. Yes, it is all but official that the era of cyber warfare has begun.[1]

At the time of this writing, this attack has been worming its way through cyberspace for more than a year and is now ravaging computers and computer network systems around the world, with some countries being hit much harder than others. As a worm, Stuxnet copies itself and then sends itself to other computers connected to a network. Because of the damage Stuxnet has done, the media has given it unprecedented attention on television shows and in magazines, newspapers, and blogs, all speaking about it in sensational terms:

- "cyber shot heard around the world"[2]
- "first-of-its-kind guided cyber missile"[3]
- "cyber superweapon"[4]
- "the best malware ever"[5]
- "This is what nation states build if their only other option would be to go to war."[6]
- "a working and fearsome prototype of a cyber-weapon that will lead to a new arms race in the world…this time it will be a cyber arms race"[7]
- "could produce the kind of damage only seen in Hollywood disaster films"[8]

THE TARGET OF THE GUIDED CYBER MISSILE

Cyber analysts in the United States tell us that the Stuxnet worm was specifically designed to infiltrate heavy-duty industrial control programs. These are computer systems—"programmable logic controllers" (or PLCs)—that monitor and manage such things as oil pipelines, factories, power plants, nuclear reactors, and other industrial facilities.

> Industrial computer systems deliver instructions to real pieces of hardware on pipelines and electrical grids opening valves and flipping switches. This is work that used to be done by human beings, much like telephone calls used to be completed by real operators at switchboards. PLC computers take people out of the loop; they collect data from sensors and then activate resources in response.[9]

Therein lies the danger of Stuxnet. Indeed, Stuxnet is feared by experts around the globe as it can break into computers that control machinery at the heart of industry, allowing an attacker to assume control of critical systems such as pumps, motors, alarms, and valves. "It could, technically, make factory boilers explode, destroy gas pipelines, or even cause a nuclear plant to malfunction."[10]

Another engineer lamented that "this malware is specially designed to sabotage plants and damage industrial systems."[11] Stuxnet is capable of reprogramming parts of software that control such things as robot arms, elevator doors, climate control systems, and other industrial components. The worm can thus alter the way hardware is supposed to work. It has affected a nuclear reactor in Iran, so many people are nervous about what might malfunction there. In fact, Iranian nuclear reactors appear to be a primary target of this virulent worm.

PRECISION TARGETING

Just prior to the publication of this book, analysts discovered that Stuxnet was specifically targeting the PLCs manufactured by German electronics giant Siemens, which has supplied large amounts of industrial control hardware and software to Iran. More specifically, the Stuxnet worm targets only two models of the Siemens PLCs—the S7-300 and the S7-400. Moreover, U.S. cyber experts tell us that the computer code is so narrowly targeted that it allegedly will not infect the PLC unless it first finds a specific network card in the computer system— that is, the CP-342-5 network card. [12]

Once a computer system is infected, Stuxnet simply sits and waits— checking every five seconds to see if its exact "attack parameters" are found on the system. After it enters a network, this super-intelligent program figures out what kind of computer system it has penetrated, and then it decides whether or not to attack, based on specific parameters—Siemens programmable logic controllers and a specific network card. If parameters are met, the worm activates a sequence that causes the industrial process to self-destruct. [13] If it does not find those exact parameters, it is not supposed to do anything.

In view of the precise nature of Stuxnet, the designers of the worm may have felt that the danger of self-infection would be minimal because they do not use Siemens products themselves. Perhaps the country that is responsible for Stuxnet "knew that their own critical infrastructure wouldn't be affected by Stuxnet because it's not using Siemens PLCs," one cyber expert mused. [14]

DIGITAL WARHEADS AGAINST IRAN'S NUCLEAR REACTORS

Senior U.S. cyber security experts now say that Stuxnet is "essentially a precision, military-grade cyber missile deployed early last year

[2009] to seek out and destroy one real-world target of high impor-tance."[15] "The worm's probable target was Iran, possibly the systems in its budding nuclear power program."[16] Ralph Langner, a well-known computer security researcher, performed a forensic analysis of the Stux-net worm in action. "[He concluded that] the worm's purpose is sab-otage and suggested that the sabotage may have already taken place at Iran's Bushehr reactor."[17]

In his analysis, Langner said Stuxnet contained two distinct "digital warheads" that are specifically designed to attack uranium enrichment plants and the Bushehr nuclear power plant in Iran. He said that the part of the worm targeting uranium enrichment plants manipulates the speeds of mechanical parts in the enrichment process. This would "result in cracking the rotor, thereby destroying the centrifuge."[18]

Tens of thousands of Iranian-owned Windows PCs were infected with Stuxnet, including PCs at the nuclear power plant in southwest-ern Iran. Following the Stuxnet invasion, Mahmoud Liayi, head of the Information Technology Council at the Ministry of Industries in Teh-ran, said that "electronic war has been launched against Iran."[19]

With much bravado, Iranian officials have claimed the cyber attack did not damage any of their facilities. But cyber experts say it is impos-sible that the worm has not rendered severe damage there.[20] The hard evidence is that virtually tens of thousands of IP addresses* in Iran have been infected.

Iranian analysts have tried to fix the Stuxnet worm problem, but things have gotten worse.

> The Iranians are getting desperate. Not only have their own attempts to defeat the invading worm failed, but they made matters worse: The malware became more aggressive and returned to the attack on parts of the systems damaged in the initial attack... The Iranians have been forced to real-ize that they would be better off not "irritating" the invader because it hits back with a bigger punch.[21]

---

* An *IP address*, or Internet Protocol address, is a numerical label that is assigned to devices such as computers that participate in a computer network.

Iranian officials have understandably given outward signs of being alarmed and frustrated. "It has dawned on them that the trouble cannot be waved away overnight but is around for the long haul." Indeed, "after their own attempts to defeat Stuxnet backfired, all the Iranians can do now is to sit back and hope for the best, helpless to predict the worm's next target and which other of their strategic industries will go down or be robbed of its secrets next."[22]

At the time of this writing, Iran has sent out a call for help in solving this cyber catastrophe.

> [Tehran has] secretly appealed to a number of computer security experts in West and East Europe with offers of handsome fees for consultations on ways to exorcize the Stuxnet worm spreading havoc through the computer networks and administrative software of its most important industrial complexes and military command centers.[23]

Meanwhile, the success of Stuxnet in disrupting Iran's nuclear reactors made it seem like Christmas had come early to the White House, according to some reports.[24] The United States, of course, has long opposed Iran's development of nuclear technology.

Tehran is bent on military action to settle scores with those responsible for the worm, and Iran suspects both Israel and the United States.[25] It is unclear what form Iran's retaliation will take.

Meanwhile, Stuxnet has also hit China very hard. One report reveals that the worm has "wreaked havoc in China, infecting millions of computers around the country."[26] One cyber security analyst warns that "once Stuxnet successfully penetrates factory computers in China, those industries may collapse, which would damage China's national security."[27] And what has happened to Iran and China has also happened to other countries, though to a somewhat lesser intensity.

WHO DONE IT?

As we have seen, cyber attackers can do their devious work and leave no traces behind so that victims do not know who attacked them. That is certainly the case with Stuxnet, for many experts are saying that the identity of its makers may never be known.

There are some, however, who believe that the evidence points to Israel as the culprit—and certainly Israel has hackers who are talented enough to pull it off. They also have a motive for doing it, for they want to stop Iran's nuclear activities. *National Public Radio* reported that many cyber experts are convinced that Israel's hackers may have developed the cyber weapon as an alternative to a physical attack on Iran. [28]

More recently, researchers have claimed that secret messages may be embedded in Stuxnet's computer code, making the software worm somewhat Dan-Brown-like. Cyber experts tell us that one of the files in the worm is called Myrtus, which may be a reference to the Old Testament book of Esther, in which Jews thwart a Persian plot against them. [29] Some people believe this adds credence to the idea that Israel is behind the worm. (Ancient Persia is modern Iran.)

Still others have pointed out that the number 19790509, which appears often in Stuxnet code, is significant. It is suggested that this number alludes to the date May 09, 1979, which was "the day that Jewish-Iranian businessman Habib Elghanian was executed in Tehran after being convicted of spying for Israel by the new government of Iran." [30] Is this too perhaps a clue?

Of course, we must be very cautious, for it is certainly possible that some other country is responsible for Stuxnet but deliberately left clues in the malicious code of the worm pointing a finger at Israel. Perhaps Israel is being framed for this cyber crime. It may be that decoys and misdirection were programmed into the computer code itself. Myrtus may be little more than a red herring deliberately planted to put investigators off the scent.

ISRAEL DENIES INVOLVEMENT

Shai Blitzblau, technical director of the Israeli-based Maglan security firm, dogmatically states that the Jewish state had absolutely nothing to do with Stuxnet. [31] Wherever it came from, he says, it was not from Israel.

In Tel Aviv, cyber-security expert Gadi Evron likewise denied that Israel created the worm. But he did concede that the project would have "required the resources on the level of a nation-state. Taking into account the intelligence needed to attack a specific target, it would be impossible that this is the work of a lone attacker sitting at home."[32] So if it was not Israel, it was some other techno-savvy country with talented hackers and a major budget for launching cyber attacks.

Despite Israel's denial, it is interesting—and somewhat amusing— that *The Jerusalem Post* praises Stuxnet as "a great achievement" because of what it has done to Iran, Israel's enemy.[33]

Regardless of the source of Stuxnet, three cyber experts affiliated with Symantec discovered in the code a *kill date*—that is, a date on which the worm is allegedly programmed to shut down. That termination date is June 24, 2012.[34] We will see.

A SOPHISTICATED, WELL-FINANCED CYBER MISSILE

Cyber analysts in the United States agree with Israeli analysts that a massive expenditure of time, money, and software engineering talent were required to identify and exploit vulnerabilities in industrial control software systems the way Stuxnet does.[35] The more Stuxnet is studied, the more it becomes clear that this was no weekend hacker that put together the worm. Because of this worm's incredible sophistication, it is impossible to avoid the conclusion that it was masterminded and constructed by a well-financed, large team of government-sponsored hackers. One cyber expert commented, "the worm is so polished and complex it must have required a lot of resources, suggesting it was created by a nation-state."[36] Security software firm Symantec estimates that Stuxnet would have taken between five and ten specialists around six months to compile—a resource not within the means of the average Internet criminal.[37] Well-known cyber analyst Ralph Langner, however, said "it is obvious that several years of preparation went into the design of this attack."[38] Yet another report compiled by U.S. cyber analysts says that traces of more than 30 programmers were found in the Stuxnet worm source code.[39] We are talking about a mega-expensive cyber assault strategically designed by PhD-level computer software engineers.

THE STUFF OF CYBER NIGHTMARES

Roel Schouwenberg, a senior antivirus researcher at Kaspersky Lab (one of the two computer security companies that has spent the most time analyzing Stuxnet), now says that Stuxnet has quite obviously "spread beyond its intended target or targets."[40] In other words, it has wormed its way into far more targets than originally intended and rendered significant damage to them. So far, Stuxnet has infected at least 45,000 industrial control systems around the world.[41] That indeed is an "apocalypse now" for the global industrial sector.

If Stuxnet was aimed at a specific target list of computer systems (such as Iran's nuclear reactors), why has it spread so infectiously to thousands of computers outside of Iran, including such countries as China, Germany, Kazakhstan, and Indonesia? This has baffled computer security officials.

Liam O Murchu, operations manager with Symantec's security response team, makes this assessment: "Even though the Stuxnet makers obviously included measures to limit its spread, something went amiss...It is clear that the attackers did not want Stuxnet to spread very far...They wanted it to remain close to the original infection point."[42] This corresponds with the fact that the original infection was communicated through USB drives.

According to cyber analysts who have dissected the Stuxnet worm, it has a "21-day propagation window," meaning that the worm was intended to migrate and infect other computers in a network for only three weeks before calling it quits. And yet, despite this built-in limitation, Stuxnet has continued to spread on its own—on a global basis—almost as if it has a mind of its own. This is the stuff of cyber nightmares. Something went wrong—very wrong!

TWO VERSIONS

The best evidence indicates that there was an original version of the Stuxnet worm that began circulating in 2009. But this version—which made staying hidden (operating behind the scenes) a high priority—apparently did not accomplish what the creators desired. It did not spread aggressively enough and did not penetrate the target computers and networks.

The new, more-virulent version was released in March 2010 and abandoned all hopes of stealth. It propagated much more aggressively. This is the version of the worm that has now made headlines around the world. And as both versions continue to be examined, it has become quite clear that the worm evolved over time, adding more "infective" ways to spread on networks and thus affect the targeted hardware systems. [43]

BOOMERANG EFFECT?

Because Stuxnet has become much more infectious than apparently intended (spreading virulently around the globe), one must wonder whether the host country that sponsored this worm has itself been hit (or *boomeranged*) by it. One might note parallels between Stuxnet and biological germ warfare. Sometimes those involved in the design of deadly biological agents to be used in germ warfare themselves become contaminated and suffer injury or even death.

Did those who designed Stuxnet feel that the target result of the worm—disrupting Iran's nuclear reactors—would be worth the risk? Did they feel that if it accomplished the purpose for which it was created, that in itself is worthy of releasing it into cyberspace, even if the worm did boomerang and affect computer systems in the host country?

A CYBER WAKE-UP CALL

What can we conclude about Stuxnet? Michael Assante, who has for years been involved in cyber security research, observes that Stuxnet "is the first direct example of weaponized software, highly customized and designed to find a particular target." [44] Jonathan Pollet, CEO of Red Tiger Security, said "I'd agree with the classification of this as a weapon." [45]

Numerous top cyber security experts are now saying that Stuxnet's arrival heralds something blindingly new: a cyber weapon created to cross from the digital realm to the physical world—to destroy something. No other malware program has ever managed to move from cyberspace to the real world. And this is what makes Stuxnet so revolutionary. It is not a tool of industrial espionage. It is a weapon of war. [46]

Derek Reveron, a cyber expert at the U.S. Naval War School, thus suggests that "the Stuxnet worm is a wake-up call to governments around the world...It is the first known worm to target industrial control systems."[47] We now have firsthand evidence of what a cyber attack can do to hardware in industrial contexts. It is hard to get a handle on just how much a threat such worms can be. Patrick Fitzgerald, senior intelligence officer with Symantec, describes Stuxnet as "a serious threat with huge world-wide implications. It has changed everything."[48]

A PORTENT OF THINGS TO COME?

Stuxnet is scary enough in itself. But there are even scarier scenarios on the horizon. Some are now warning that "the one certainty is that having succeeded, Stuxnet's creators will produce even more threatening software."[49] Stuxnet may be the first of many such viruses and worms to appear in the future. We probably have not seen the last of this phenomenon. Stuxnet could become a template—a working model—for attackers wishing to launch a digital strike at physical hardware in the future.[50]

"Quite honestly you've got a blueprint now," said security expert Michael Assante. "A copycat may decide to emulate it, maybe to cause a pressure valve to open or close at the wrong time. You could cause damage, and the damage could be catastrophic."[51] "The big fear is that Stuxnet provided a road map for malicious actors who can copycat it to launch similar attacks against other industrial control systems" in the United States.[52] Sean McGurk, director of the National Cyber-Security and Communications Integration Center at the U.S. Department of Homeland Security, said "the concern for the future of Stuxnet is that the underlying code could be adapted to target a broader range of control systems in any number of critical infrastructure sectors."[53]

Americans must resist the temptation to feel invulnerable regarding cyber threat. Indeed, the head of the Pentagon's newly inaugurated U.S. Cyber Command, General Keith Alexander, said just prior to the publication of this book that it is only a matter of time before America is attacked by something like the Stuxnet worm.[54] And since there is no overnight fix for such troublesome cyber attacks, they could have long-lasting consequences for the American way of life.

HARD LESSONS LEARNED

The Stuxnet invasion demonstrated the important lesson that our military must be a leader rather than a follower in cyber technology. The first to deploy a new technology on the battlefield has always had an enormous advantage over rivals. That advantage may be enough to win a war. That is one reason why many believe that the United States must take whatever steps are necessary to attain military cyber dominance, just as it already has military dominance on land, on the seas, and in the air.

Stuxnet also reminds us that a monopoly in a new weapon system is always fleeting. One cyber analyst explains it this way:

> The U.S. nuclear monopoly at the end of World War II allowed it to defeat Imperial Japan and bring the war to an end in allied victory. Once the U.S. exposed its nuclear arsenal, however, the Soviet Union's race to acquire nuclear weapons of its own began. Just four years after the U.S. used its nuclear weapons, it found itself in a nuclear arms race with the Soviets. America's possession of nuclear weapons did not shield it from the threat of their destructive power. The risks of proliferation are the flip side to the advantage of deploying new technology. [55]

Unlike nuclear technology, cyber technology is economical—in fact, downright cheap. Practically any country can afford to form a cyber attack unit. An official with the McAfee computer security company thus observes that "we're seeing a cyber arms race that is alive and well…The cost barrier for countries to enter this race is very low… How much does it really cost to hire ten really good engineers to break down a system and find a technological advantage on, say, the smart grid in the United States?" [56] Lord, deliver us from cyber insanity!

THE CYBER THREAT AGAINST THE U.S. INFRASTRUCTURE

One of the most vexing problems about the Internet is that it was not developed with security in mind. Instead, the Internet was developed with transparency in mind. It was developed to be open and free, accessible to anyone, anywhere. Those attributes are great as long as it is used for good. But because people also use it for evil, those same attributes do not lend themselves to good security—especially for the infrastructure of the United States.[1]

When I refer to infrastructure, I am referring to the facilities and services that our society requires in order to function. This includes ground transportation, banking, telecommunications, pipelines, railroads, aviation, energy (such as electricity), and so on. Our political leaders are becoming increasingly aware that the critical infrastructure of our country is highly vulnerable to cyber attacks. This is one of the most disconcerting aspects of the possibility of a cyber war.[2]

Of course, infrastructure attacks in themselves are nothing new. In nearly all wars, attackers have sought to cut off their enemy's water supply, transportation, and other foundational needs. In modern times, however, attackers can damage the infrastructure much more quickly and easily because much of the infrastructure is now connected to cyberspace.[3] An article published in *The National Interest* magazine affirms that "offensive cyber attacks have the potential to reach out from cyberspace into the physical dimension, causing giant electrical generators to shred themselves, trains to derail, high-tension power-transmission lines to burn, gas pipelines to explode," and much more.[4]

Several countries around the world are currently reporting massive cyber attacks on their infrastructure. McAfee produced a 2010 report titled "In the Crossfire: Critical Infrastructure in the Age of Cyber War." Some 600 IT (information technology) and security executives from critical infrastructure enterprises in 14 different countries anonymously answered an extensive series of detailed questions about computer and network security issues. Their responses were highly revealing of an increasing global problem, and the report has profound implications for the United States' posture on infrastructure protection.

This report tells us that critical infrastructure business owners and operators concede that their IT networks are under repeated cyber attack, often by high-level adversaries. Who are these adversaries?

> A majority of executives believed that foreign governments were already involved in network attacks against their country's critical infrastructure...Assaults run the gamut from massive [denial of service] attacks designed to shut down systems all the way to stealthy efforts to enter networks undetected.[5]

The impact of such attacks is often quite severe, and their cost is high. They typically cause "critical operational failures," and "the reported cost of downtime from major attacks exceeds U.S. $6 million per day."[6]

In the book *Cyberpower and National Security*, we are warned that the kinds of lethal cyber attacks that have afflicted and even crippled other countries could likewise afflict the United States in the near future. The CIA in particular has warned of the threat of a cyber attack against our nation's electrical utilities, noting that "cyber attackers have hacked into the computer systems of utility companies outside the United States and made demands, in at least one case causing a power outage that affected multiple cities." The CIA was unable to ascertain who executed these attacks and why, but every one of the attacks involved intrusions through the Internet.[7]

No nation depends on cyber systems and networks for the operation of its infrastructure as much as the United States does. Our own Energy Department laboratory has confirmed, by extensive cyber tests, that "a cyber attack from the Internet could weave its way into the digital control system of a generator and cause the device to self-destruct."[8] Think of it—electrical generators on our own soil could be shut down by a foreign country through cyberspace. Our own tests prove it!

Most Americans have gotten used to the fact that when the electricity goes out in their neighborhoods, the lights are back on in an hour or two. That is most certainly *not* what would happen in the event of a cyber attack against our electrical grids.

Scott Borg, director and chief economist of the nonprofit U.S. Cyber Consequences Unit, warns that such cyber attacks can render "horrendous damage." He warns that "cyber attacks on a large number of electricity generators could have a lasting effect, with little U.S. capability to support new parts for damaged generators." Indeed, "most of the parts for electricity generators come from China and India." Would China be motivated to quickly send parts for our electrical generators if its own hackers launched the cyber attack in the first place? (Current evidence indicates that China is an A-list cyber threat to the United States.) Borg lamented, "We can't figure out a way to replace them that doesn't take months."[9]

Experiencing a prolonged outage of electricity would definitely not be pleasant. "For the millions of people thrown into the dark and perhaps the cold, unable to get food, without access to cash, and dealing with social disorder, it would be in many ways the same as if bombs had been dropped on their cities."[10]

Borg warned that the loss of electricity over an extended time would render irreparable damage to the U.S. economy. He notes that for the first couple of days, an area with a loss of electricity generally functions fairly well. However, "after eight to ten days, 72 percent of all economic activity in an area without electricity would stop." He thus warns, "Shutting down the electricity in a large area of the U.S.

for months, it would have a similar level of damage to the economy of a nuclear attack."[11]

Deputy U.S. Defense Secretary William Lynn agrees, noting that any major future conflict inevitably will involve cyber warfare that could knock out power, transport, and banks, causing massive economic disruption.[12] It is almost impossible to measure how long a full recovery from such an attack would take.

THE IMPLANTING OF LOGIC BOMBS

We have seen that a *logic bomb* is malware or computer code that contains instructions that erase the data on a computer or network or causes it to shut down. Once a logic bomb activates, a computer becomes a useless piece of hardware until it is wiped clean and software is reinstalled.

Logic bombs can also inflict physical damage on hardware. For example, a hacker could infect a computer network that runs an electrical power grid with a logic bomb that initiates instructions to cause a power surge sufficient to fry the circuits of the transformers.

Cyber experts are currently warning government officials about Chinese and Russian penetrations of our country's electricity grids, which depend on the Internet to function. China, especially angry because the United States sold arms to Taiwan, has "laced U.S. infrastructure with logic bombs," according to former National Security Council official Richard Clarke. China denies this, but the evidence is pervasive.[13] Is this an indicator of China's long-range intentions?

> The only reason to hack into a power grid's controls, install a "trapdoor" so you can get back in quickly later on, and leave behind computer code that would, when activated, cause damage to the software (and even the hardware) of the network, is if you are planning a cyber war. It does not mean that you have already decided to conduct that war, but it certainly means that you want to be ready to do so.[14]

As we have seen, when hackers access a private network, such as one that controls a power grid, they can leave behind what is called a trapdoor. This is malicious software code that hides in the background and permits easy and fast access to that same network in the future. It enables the hacker to easily access that network at will.

This means that at some point in the future, hackers affiliated with China's government could utilize these trapdoors, already within our power grids, to cause the components of power generators across the country to fry, thereby knocking out our much-needed electricity. The United States is so power dependent that such a cyber attack would render incalculable damage. Assuming we would not recover for months, the economic damage to the country would be truly catastrophic.

WARNING SHOTS ACROSS THE BOW

We have already experienced some "warning shots across the bow" that should serve as wake-up calls to each of us regarding the vulnerable infrastructure in the United States. For example, a 2008 report in a security magazine tells us that "the Slammer worm [a self-replicating virus that spreads from computer to computer] penetrated a private computer network at Ohio's Davis-Besse nuclear power plant...and disabled a safety monitoring system for nearly five hours, despite a belief by plant personnel that the network was protected by a firewall."[15]

Could the same worm that infected this particular nuclear plant also infect multiple other nuclear plants around the country? You bet it could. The previous chapter, which discusses the Stuxnet worm, dispels all doubt.

VULNERABILITIES OF U.S. BUSINESSES

How would a lethal cyber attack impact small businesses in our country, including distribution companies, transportation companies, communications companies, and the like? A 2009 National Small Business Cybersecurity study reveals a very heavy dependence of U.S. small businesses on computers, computer networks, and the Internet.

- Sixty-five percent of small businesses store customer data electronically.

- Forty-three percent of small businesses store financial records electronically.

- Thirty-three percent of small businesses store credit card information electronically.

- Twenty percent of small businesses store intellectual property and other sensitive corporate content online.

- Sixty-five percent of small businesses say the Internet is critical to their business success.[16]

If a lethal computer virus wormed its way through the U.S. infrastructure, countless small businesses in our country would suffer a catastrophic loss. They would be unable to continue business in a meaningful way until the infrastructure is repaired, data is recovered, and business systems are back up and running. Such recovery might require months!

U.S. LACK OF PREPAREDNESS

As an American patriot, I hate to say it, but the hard facts reveal that the current ability of the United States to defend its infrastructure against a cyber attack ranks far behind the preparedness level of other countries.

> Some countries, like China, have implemented plans allowing them to shut the limited number of portals that connect their cyberspace to the outside world. Other nations, like North Korea, have such limited cyberspace and cyberdependence that there is almost nothing to defend. America's connectivity to the rest of the world is unlimited and controlled by no plan or agency.[17]

So if the United States' infrastructure were hit by a lethal cyber attack, our ability to repel the attack and rectify the damage in a timely manner would be positively dismal. This is one of the reasons why U.S. officials who participated in *Cyber Shock Wave* and *Cyber Storm III* (exercises that measured U.S. readiness for a cyber attack) concluded that time is of the essence in bolstering U.S. cyber defenses. In fact, some said the possibility of a cyber attack must receive the same urgent attention we give to the possibility of a nuclear attack.

MILITARY PROTECTION OF THE INFRASTRUCTURE

Protecting the infrastructure of the United States from cyber attack has now become a priority issue with the U.S. military. Deputy U.S. Defense Secretary William Lynn explains that "the best-laid defenses on military networks will matter little unless our civilian critical infrastructure is also able to withstand attacks."[18]

During the Middle Ages, vital resources were protected behind castle walls and surrounded by moats. Entrance required crossing drawbridges and passing armed guards. Today, many of our national security planners are proposing that we do something similar with our critical infrastructure.

Presently the Pentagon is pushing to put all civilian infrastructure under its own wing by creating a cyber realm that is walled off from the rest of the Internet (surrounded, as it were, by cyber moats). "It would feature 'active' perimeter defenses, including intrusion monitoring and scanning technology."[19]

Army General Keith Alexander, the head of the military's new Cyber Command, suggested that setting things up this way would be straightforward from a technological perspective. He refers to it as a "secure zone, a protected zone." Others have christened the idea "dot.secure."

The proposal has many critics, however. Among the concerns is that such a scenario might cause more problems than it solves. This new secure perimeter might become the new prime target. As General Electric's director of incident response Richard Bejtlich puts it, "Dot.secure becomes new Target One...I can't think of an easier way to help an adversary target the most critical information on industry computers."[20]

Critics point out that this type of scenario would only be as strong as its weakest link. They suggest that the arrangement is vulnerable to compromise in many ways. Bejtlich suggests, for example, that "users will want to and need to transfer information between their normal company Internet-connected computers and 'dot.secure'...Separation is thus a fool's goal." Besides, critics note, moving all infrastructure traffic off of the existing Internet and onto a separate independent computer network would be phenomenally expensive and would not be able to guarantee security.

Dan Sheflin, a vice president at Honeywell International, represents many when he affirms that "even a private network is only so secure…A big threat is that employees walk in, unknowingly or knowingly, with (an infected) thumb drive, plug it in, put their kids' pictures on their PC and, oh boy, something's on the network. Those are things that even a private network could be subject to." [21]

Critics thus suggest that instead of erecting a new separate network, perhaps we should simply improve the security of the existing systems. Some cyber experts suggest that we should focus on keeping foreign hackers from penetrating private networks to begin with. If they are able to get in, however, the secondary goal should be to provide many layers of security through which the hackers must pass before they can do any real damage.

Meanwhile, the U.S. government is also investigating the feasibility of expanding NATO's collective defense posture to include the domain of cyberspace. [22] This in itself might deter a nation-state from launching a cyber attack against a member-nation of NATO.

In a later chapter, I will discuss specific steps that cyber experts suggest our government should take in protecting the U.S. infrastructure.

CYBER THUGS AND THEIR CYBER CRIMES

Symantec conducted a comprehensive survey of 7000 users in 14 countries about the issue of cyber crimes. The findings of the study reveal how pervasive cyber criminal activity is around the world.

- Seventy-three percent of respondents said they had experienced some form of cyber crime.

- Sixty-five percent said they were victimized by some type of cyber foul play.

- Fifty-five percent were victims of a computer virus or malware.

- Only 13 percent said they felt "very safe" online.

- Ninety-seven percent expect to be victims of cyber crime at some point in their lives.

- Of those who had been victimized, 58 percent felt angry, 51 percent were annoyed, and 40 percent felt cheated.

- The average cost of resolving a cyber crime is $334 globally and $128 in the United States.

- It takes about a month and a lot of headache to get things resolved.

- Thirty-one percent of global respondents and 25 percent of Americans said their cyber crime problems were never resolved.[1]

A *cyber crime* is any crime that involves a computer and a network. In this chapter, I will demonstrate that people can fall prey to a variety of cyber crimes. Cyber criminals are creative. And unfortunately, cyber crime pays. Committing a cyber crime—and getting away with it—is much easier than committing a traditional crime.

Why? First, cyber crimes can be committed far from the scene of the crime. The perpetrator and victim could live in separate countries. This emboldens cyber criminals because they have little chance of being caught. Also, cyber crime laws are very weak in many countries around the world, and this is good news for cyber criminals. Punishing them is hard to do.

Cyber criminals can also commit their crimes without leaving any evidence behind. This is unlike physical crime scenes, where CSI agents uncover physical evidence that can be used to identify traditional criminals. Smart cyber criminals know how to cover their tracks—at least most of them.[2] They know how to wipe their digital fingerprints clean.

HOW CYBER CRIMINALS TAKE YOUR MONEY

As an illustration, let's say you are a cyber criminal. You send out a spam e-mail to thousands of people around the Internet that says something like this: "Someone you know has sent you a Hallmark postcard. Click here to open it." The e-mail appears to be legitimate because it features Hallmark graphics (without Hallmark's authorization, of course).

Most people will not be gullible enough to click on the link, but you know that some will be naive enough to fall for your trick. When they do so, a keystroke logger will be downloaded to their computer. This particular form of malware records all the victim's keystrokes and transmits that data back to your computer. The victim does not know that her every keyboard move is now being watched by this malware. Therefore, when she signs onto an e-commerce website and makes a purchase, inputting her credit card number (complete with validation code), she is completely oblivious to the fact that you now possess those numbers.

At this point, you have several choices. Every month, you could make some purchases that were small enough to go undetected when she receives her monthly statement. (Many people do not carefully check their credit card statements as long as the total is in the general ballpark of their previous statements.) The more you can operate by stealth, the better. If you managed to get the credit card information of a hundred people, you could make a hundred small purchases each month, and many of those folks would never notice it.

Some cyber criminals choose not to do it this way. Instead, they will make an initial small charge to the credit card just to make sure that it works. Following that, they continue to use the credit card in ever-increasing amounts over a short time period until the antifraud division at the bank deactivates the card. They get all the goodies they can out of that card and then move on to prey on new victims.

Other cyber criminals opt to sell the credit card information to other identity thieves. Interested buyers are plentiful, as we will see below.

ORGANIZED CYBER CRIME

You will probably not be surprised to learn that cyber crime entices not only solitary practitioners but also organized crime syndicates. Such crime syndicates exist in Russia, Japan, Hong Kong, the United States, and other countries. To be sure, law enforcement officials have been able to find and lock up some of these cyber criminals, but only a small minority.

> Although law enforcement agencies are making sustained progress in cyber crime detection and enforcement—such as Operation Dark Market, an FBI sting that resulted in the arrest of 56 individuals worldwide, more than $70 million in potential economic loss prevented, and recovery of 100,000 compromised credit cards—cyberspace is still a

crime syndicate's dream environment for making a lot of money with little to no risk.[3]

Unfortunately for small and midsize companies in the United States, organized cyber gangs in Eastern Europe have been increasingly successful in engaging in cyber crimes here. This multimillion-dollar crime wave has now gotten the attention of America's largest financial institutions.

At the height of this crime wave, the following alert was distributed to members of the Financial Services Information Sharing and Analysis Center, an industry organization that shares data about critical threats to the financial sector. The Center is underwritten by many major corporations.

> In the past six months, financial institutions, security companies, the media, and law enforcement agencies are all reporting a significant increase in funds-transfer fraud involving the exploitation of valid banking credentials belonging to small and medium sized businesses.[4]

Because only small to midsize businesses have been affected by this crime wave, it has not been widely reported in the news, as is the case when major security breaches occur with billion-dollar companies. But some of these smaller companies have lost staggering amounts of money.

- A school district not far from Pittsburgh was robbed online of $700,000 by cyber criminals.

- A company in Texas lost $1.2 million due to cyber crime.

- A Baton Rouge electronics firm lost almost $100,000 due to cyber crime.

How did the cyber crimes occur? The process was actually relatively easy, using the same kind of keystroke logger malware I described earlier. Typically, the cyber criminal sends an e-mail to the treasurer of the company (or whoever controls the money) with a virus-ridden link or attachment relating to the business. When clicked on, the link or attachment automatically downloads malware to the victim's computer. This malware records and transmits keystrokes back to the cyber criminal, enabling him or her to derive usernames and passwords of bank accounts. The cyber criminal signs on to these bank accounts and arranges wire transfers to another account—generally outside of the United States. Most of this money ends up in the hands of cyber gangs in Eastern Europe.

The FBI is working hard to stem this increasing problem. However, as we have seen, cyber criminals are often adept at erasing evidence that implicates them, which makes convictions difficult to obtain. Also, the sheer volume of cyber crimes can overwhelm the resources of the FBI. Cyber criminals far outnumber the FBI agents looking for them.

The Financial Crimes Enforcement Network, a division of the Treasury Department that tracks fraud, said that wire-transfer fraud rose by 58 percent in 2008 alone. But many cyber incidents go unreported, so the actual percentage is undoubtedly much higher. As well, the problem has gotten notably worse since 2008.

LESS LEGAL PROTECTION FOR BUSINESSES

Small to midsize companies do not have the same legal protections for online banking that individual consumers enjoy. Consumers have up to 60 days to dispute unauthorized charges on their bank statements, but businesses have roughly two business days to spot and dispute such unauthorized activity. That is enough to make any business owner paranoid, wondering if hourly monitoring of the business bank accounts is necessary.

Why such different bank policies for individual consumers versus small businesses? Brian Krebs, who has done significant investigative reporting on this issue for *The Washington Post*, explains. "The banks spend a lot of money on protecting consumer customers because they owe money if the consumer loses money. But the banks don't spend the same resources on the corporate accounts because they don't have to refund the corporate losses."[5] No wonder many small businesses are suing their banks these days.

IDENTITY THEFT ON THE RISE

Utilizing techniques like those described above, many cyber criminals have successfully stolen the identities of multitudes of people. Here are a few other common tactics to watch out for.

Identity Theft Through Phishing

Cyber criminals can engage in identity theft through phishing. As we have seen, phishing involves a deception in which people receive an e-mail that is apparently (but not really) from their bank or credit card company, with the same logo and other graphics affiliated with that bank or credit card company. The e-mail recipients are asked to click on a link to go to the bank or credit card website and sign on with their username and password so their data can be updated. The website looks like the genuine bank or credit card website, with the same graphics and the same logo. In reality, it is a bogus website designed by a hacker who steals people's usernames and passwords and sifts money from their accounts. Some phishing scams seem so real that even savvy computer users are occasionally fooled.

Some cyber criminals are very creative phishers. One particularly effective scam used an e-mail message informing the recipients that they had a UPS package that could not be delivered. The graphics in the e-mail made it look genuine. The e-mail requested personal details so the package could be delivered. Many people fell for this scam, and the phisher stole many identities.

John Viega, in his book *The Myths of Security: What the Computer Industry Doesn't Want You to Know*, warns that you might even get an e-mail message that seems to come from your employer's IT department, asking you to log in to a Web portal to change your password because it is about to expire.[6] These cyber criminals are very sneaky. Plenty of people would not think twice about logging on to a Web portal to change their password if their own IT department asked them to. And once they do, they become victimized.

Identity Theft Through Spear Phishing

Another technique I documented earlier in the book is spear

phishing—a technique that has proven to be a gold mine for adept cyber criminals. This technique involves e-mail messages that appear to be from someone you actually know. These messages use real names of friends, family members, acquaintances, or coworkers. The perpetrators acquire these names from social networks like Facebook or MySpace, where they can click on a button to view people's friends. This apparently trustworthy e-mail message typically asks the recipient to either click on a link or open an attachment. The e-mail message might say, "Hey Harry, I found this old photo of you and me. Check it out. Love, Sarah Hawkins." Once Harry clicks on the link to view the photo, malware is downloaded to his computer, and he is victimized.

Of course, people can go to the preference page of Facebook and hide their friend lists from strangers. But users have to go out of their way to do this, and very few people actually do it.

The good folks at Facebook also try to detect people who are sifting too much information from Facebook and shut them down. However, smart hackers sift just a little information at a time. They rarely get caught, and the crimes continue.

Identity Theft by Penetrating Companies

Some cyber criminals are not satisfied with going after one identity theft at a time. Why use a fishing rod to catch a single fish at a time when you can use a net to catch hundreds of fish at once?

These hackers tap into the private networks or computers of business offices. For example, a cyber criminal might gain access to a private network at a company and steal the personnel records of thousands of employees. Cyber experts tell us that up to a million computer users are victimized by such security breaches each week. One report I came across revealed that more than 1500 records of employees of the National Nuclear Security Administration had been stolen in a network intrusion.[7] You would think a Security Administration would be secure!

Identity Theft Through Worms

I noted earlier that worms are computer viruses that do not require the computer user to necessarily do anything to spread the virus from one computer to another. Rather, computer worms can copy themselves from one computer to another by taking advantage of known vulnerabilities in other software programs. This form of malware worms its way through cyberspace from computer to computer.

The Conficker worm has been used for extensive identity theft and credit card fraud. Many leaders in the software world have made great efforts to stop this worm. Microsoft has even offered a $250,000 reward for information that leads to the arrest and conviction of Conficker's authors. Cyber expert Jeffrey Carr, however, says that this bounty is laughably low, considering the fact that some cyber criminals make more than ten times that amount annually.[8]

The Black Market for New IDs

Once cyber criminals obtain private information—whether through phishing, worms, or some other means—they often sell this information online.

> Attackers can sell credit card account information on the black market. Card-selling exchanges on the Internet are hosted in a variety of countries, especially in Eastern Europe...Stolen credit card numbers and bank account information are now traded online in a highly structured arrangement involving buyers, sellers, intermediaries, and service industries. Services offered include changing the address of a stolen identity through manipulation of stolen personal identification numbers or passwords.[9]

An identity that includes a bank account number, credit card number, date of birth, and government-issued ID number sells for up to $18. Thieves who purchase new identities use this information to create their own identity documents using modern digital technology. For example, they could easily make realistic-looking driver's licenses, birth certificates, or bank statements by using a digital camera and a laser color printer. Thousands of identities have been stolen in such a manner.

FRAUDULENT CLICKS ON GOOGLE

The primary way Google makes money is through pay-per-click advertising. As might be expected, cyber crime activity occurs even here, for some of the clicks are fraudulent. Based on its own internal research, Google says that less than 10 percent of its clicks are fraudulent and that Google workers discover the great majority of such fraudulent clicks before sellers get charged for them. However, Click-Forensics—an independent firm—has estimated that more than 28 percent of the ad clicks were fraudulent, and that more than 16 percent of the clicks that sellers paid for were fraudulent. Clearly, Google's estimates do not coincide with those of independent evaluators.[10]

Earlier, I briefly explained how such fraudulent clicks can be automated by cyber criminals. Sellers pay Google every time their ad is clicked on. Other websites agree to show Google ads because Google pays the owners of those sites each time an ad is clicked on. By setting up a botnet (robot network), a cyber criminal can instruct thousands of robot computers out in cyberspace to click on ads at a website previously set up by the cyber criminal. Some cyber criminals make regular incomes this way.

COPY-MACHINE CYBER CRIMES

Who would ever have thought that a copy machine could become a tool used by a cyber criminal? Most office workers are unaware that their copy machines are connected to cyberspace and that almost anything connected to the Internet can be hacked.

The copy machine is not only connected to the Internet but also has software inside it, just like a normal computer, and this software can be hacked. Cyber experts point out that a cyber criminal could hack the software of a business copier, causing the copier to overheat, which in turn activates the fire sprinklers inside the building. From the convenience of their own homes, cyber criminals could use a laptop computer to do tens of thousands of dollars of damage to a company![11]

SHREDDER CRIMES

Did you know that shredder machines can be used to commit cyber crimes? They are not connected to cyberspace themselves, but the data derived from them could ultimately find its way online.

Here is the way it works. A high-tech cyber criminal designs and markets a special shredder that also has a scanning camera inside of it—which, of course, the company that bought the shredder is completely unaware of. As sensitive documents are fed into the shredder to be cut into a million pieces, they first pass by the scanning camera, and the images are electronically recorded to a data card secretly embedded in the shredder.

Later, that data is retrieved by someone—perhaps a person on the cleaning crew who doubles as a corporate spy. That data can then be sold and transmitted online.[12]

WILL THINGS EVER GET BETTER?

Many people wonder whether things will ever get better in cyberspace. A few comments might help. First, the FBI and other law enforcement officials continue their efforts to find and prosecute cyber criminals. They will no doubt have some success.

Second, if there is anything positive that has come about as a result of the preponderance of cyber criminals and their scams, it is that the more common they become, the less successful they will be. John Viega uses the analogy of traditional fishing to make this point. The more fishermen there are in a pond, the fewer fish there are to catch—and the harder each fisherman must work in order to catch any fish. "Once people have been phished, not too many of them get thrown back into the pond (meaning that people who have been phished before are generally more wary and less likely to be phished again)."[13]

Third, as we will see, the ultimate solution probably lies in our coming one-world economy and cashless society, which the ancient biblical prophets predicted.

PROTECT YOURSELF!

Meanwhile, you can take some definite steps to help keep yourself as safe as reasonably possible from cyber crimes.

You can begin by installing a program called SiteAdvisor on your Web browser. This program identifies safe and unsafe websites. So, for example, if you do a search on Google for a list of sites relating to software purchases, Google will give you a list of links, and on that list of links, SiteAdvisor will add either a green check mark or a red *X*. You should stay away from any website that has a red *X* (it is a site at which malware has been detected). Only visit websites that have a green check mark. After you have used SiteAdvisor for a while, you will become truly appreciative for having installed it. I have been using it since it first came out years ago.

Always keep your system software updated, and run updates as soon as they become available. This is true whether you use a PC or a Macintosh. Both Microsoft and Apple issue system updates, not only to make their software run better with new features but also to fix security flaws they discover. Your first line of defense is to always keep your system software updated.

The same is true for the other software on your computer. Always install the latest updates. It is especially important to update extremely popular software programs like Microsoft Word, Microsoft Excel, and Microsoft Internet Explorer.

Malware can often be downloaded to your computer when you download software from a file-sharing application (such as Limewire, Kazaa, or Bearshare). Malware is also often downloaded to your computer when you use a program that allows you to download music from the Internet. To be sure, plenty of good music services are available on the Internet, including iTunes and the MP3 files you can purchase and download from Amazon.com. But beware of smaller programs you have never heard of.

As a general policy, do not click on advertisements at websites. Ads are a favorite tool among cyber criminals for downloading malware to your computer. The exception, of course, is if you are very familiar with a particular website and have learned to trust it over a long period.

Be cautious about sharing any kind of personal information on Internet websites.

Never, ever open e-mail attachments from people you do not know.

Use common sense and do not click on links in e-mail messages with invitations like these: "Click here to see my new pictures." "Someone has a crush on you. Click here to find out who."

Antivirus software is not foolproof, but install it and keep it up-to-date anyway. It will at least keep you safe from some of the long-standing viruses. The program I personally recommend is NOD32 by ESET. This program not only does a good job of protecting against viruses but also uses very little of your computer's CPU power. (Some antivirus programs can drain up to 11 percent of your computing power, making your computer run noticeably slower.)

Beware of downloading software bundles. Hackers sometimes hide malware in them without the manufacturers' knowledge.

Never, under any circumstances, give your usernames or passwords to anyone. Bank and credit card companies will never ask for these by e-mail.

Consider purchasing and installing spy-software detectors, such as Spybot.

Consider installing a biometric password manager, which blocks anyone from logging on to your computer without your physical fingerprint.

THE MILITARIZATION OF CYBERSPACE

an initially fought all his battles on land. As technology increased, he added another domain—the sea. Eventually he developed the technology to engage in battle beneath the sea. Still later, after a quantum leap forward in technological advancements, another physical domain for battle was added—the air. And still later, after further technological gains, man attained the capability of going into outer space, creating satellites with military applications. With each new technology, human beings have discovered new ways to do battle against each other.[1]

Today, yet another domain for doing battle has emerged—only this time, it is not a physical domain. I am talking, of course, about cyberspace.[2]

Earlier in the book, I noted that cyberspace includes more than just the Internet. As various networking technologies began to develop, the Department of Defense quickly began using them for military purposes.[3] In the Gulf War, America had a plan in place to bring down Iraq's air defense system through cyber warfare. Not long after this, the United States Air Force set up its Info War Center. Then, in 1995, the National Defense University graduated its first class of officers technologically trained to engage in cyber warfare.[4] The militarization of cyberspace had arrived!

Cyber warfare is so new that it is difficult to define precisely. The international community does not yet have a standard agreement as to what constitutes an act of cyber war. Certain kinds of cyber activity may be considered acts of war by some countries but not by others. More than 140 nations are "leveraging the Internet for political, military, and economic espionage activities,"[5] so we might expect the international community to come together and hammer out some kind of agreement on the rules of engagement in cyber warfare. But such has not yet happened.

Broadly, cyber warfare involves "the art and science of fighting without fighting; of defeating an opponent without spilling their blood."[6] Lieutenant General Keith Alexander, serving in the Department of Defense, suggests that "the focus of cyber warfare is on using cyberspace (by operating *within* or *through* it) to attack personnel, facilities, or equipment with the intent of degrading, neutralizing, or destroying enemy combat capability, while protecting our own."[7]

Richard Clarke, the author of *Cyber War: The Next Threat to National Security and What to Do About It*, affirms that one goal in cyber warfare is to penetrate enemy networks and either gain control of them or crash them. If the enemy network can be controlled, the attacker could injure or destroy its infrastructure, including electrical generators, air traffic control centers, transportation, financial institutions, communications, and missile systems. If the enemy's network cannot be controlled but only crashed, that would wipe all the data from their computers and networks, collapse their financial system, disrupt all their communications, and wreak general havoc.[8]

Of course, the United States itself is vulnerable in this regard. We have seen that computers and computer networks play a large role in running the infrastructure of our country—including our electrical grid, our transportation, our banking and financial institutions, and much more. The networks that control these various aspects of our infrastructure can be penetrated and exploited from overseas locations.

Consequently, cyberspace makes the traditional understanding of war obsolete. "Now war means that any group can fight any other group, anywhere in the world, by any number of methods, instantly."[9]

ATTAINING MILITARY DOMINANCE IN CYBERSPACE

The United States prides itself in having the most powerful military ever seen. However, cyber warriors in this country are wondering whether any country can attain overwhelming military superiority in cyberspace. More than a few brilliant strategic thinkers believe that attaining such cyber dominance may be impossible.

We might define *cyber military strategy* as the development and employment of strategic capabilities to operate effectively in cyberspace, to integrate and coordinate with other operational domains—the Army, Navy, Air Force, and Marines—and to achieve or support the achievement of the objectives of our government. In keeping with that overall strategy, a prime goal of our government is to ensure that "the U.S. military [has] strategic superiority in cyberspace." This strategic superiority will enable "freedom of action" for America's military and will at the same time "deny the same to our adversaries." ("Freedom of action" means none of our military's actions will be thwarted by a cyber attack.) In order for this to be the case, the United States must have strong cyber offensive capabilities. "Offensive capabilities in cyberspace [are needed] to gain and maintain the initiative."[10]

The U.S. strategy for cyber warfare recognizes a number of critical factors. First, unlike land battles, cyber warfare can be engaged anywhere a connection to the Internet is available. Also, a cyber attack will undoubtedly affect not only another country's military but also civilians. After all, the critical infrastructure of most countries is tightly integrated to the Internet. In physical battles, the U.S. military tries to avoid injuring innocent civilians. But civilian targets in cyberspace are not necessarily off-limits.

The U.S. military also recognizes that cyber war moves at a much faster pace than traditional warfare. Therefore, one must be ready to "do unto others" before they "do unto you." Because cyber attacks against thousands of targets can take place instantly, one must be prepared to take the initiative to strike first, recognizing that waiting a few seconds can make one a few seconds too late. If cyber adversaries manage to attack the United States first, they could disable our cyberspace capabilities, and we would be unable to engage in cyber warfare.

Timing is everything. Cyber attacks take place at incomprehensibly fast speeds. Our military leaders say that waiting too late can take one out of the battle in an instant. If the United States waits for the other side to shoot first in cyberspace, we may find that our ability to return fire has been greatly impeded or even shut down altogether.

FLEXING OUR CYBER MUSCLES

The book *Cyberpower and National Security* defines *cyberpower* as "the ability to use cyberspace to create advantages and influence events in all the other operational environments and across the instruments of power."[11] It is clearly an objective for any country's military.

The United States wants not only to possess cyberpower but also to be able to use it before the rest of the world does. At present, most nations around the world would not consider physically attacking the United States because of its overwhelmingly powerful military. If they tried to physically attack the United States, they would be repelled with overwhelming force. Our powerful military serves as a deterrent to physical attack.

Our military leaders say it would be ideal if the same were true of cyber attacks. In other words, we would like other countries to know that if they launched a cyber attack against the United States, our country would respond with such overwhelming cyberpower that the attack would be utterly self-defeating and self-destructive. If other countries knew the United States had overwhelming cyber superiority, that in itself might serve as a deterrent to cyber attacks against our country.

Herein lies the problem. Attaining such a position of overwhelming cyber superiority is difficult if not impossible. The United States has many talented cyber hackers on the military payroll, but other countries have talented cyber hackers as well. In some ways, cyberspace levels the playing ground because a country with a weaker and smaller physical army could have a team of a hundred talented computer hackers who could render great cyber damage to any country in the world.

Therefore, many smaller nations may be able to inflict cyber damage on the United States that is equal to the United States' ability to inflict cyber harm on them. The United States may actually suffer more harm from such attacks because of its greater dependence on cyberspace.

AIR FORCE CYBER COMMAND

Despite the difficulty in achieving cyber superiority, the United States took a big step in that direction by establishing the Air Force Cyber Command in October of 2009. This is a military organization with about 1100 personnel and an annual budget of $150 million. Its goal is to use information technology and the Internet as a weapon. In effect, cyberspace has been weaponized by Cyber Command.

The United States is not the only country with a cyber command center. Russia, China, Britain, Israel, Iran, and 30 other nations have set up similar organizations.

John A. Serabian Jr., information operations issue manager at the Central Intelligence Agency, provides this warning: "Foreign nations have begun to include information warfare in their military doctrine, as well as their war college curricula, with respect to both defensive and offensive applications. They are developing strategies and tools to conduct information attacks."[12]

In 1982, Israeli prime minister Menachem Begin revealed that a secret but massive cache of Russian weaponry had been discovered in deep underground cellars in Lebanon, apparently prepositioned for later use in a Russian invasion of Israel and perhaps other Middle East nations. This cache included massive quantities of ammunition, armored vehicles, tanks, small arms, heavy weapons, communications devices, and other paraphernalia useful to military forces. Much of the equipment was highly sophisticated. Removing it all required hundreds of trucks. Begin admitted that Israel's leaders had no idea that such extensive plans had been made for a future ground assault into Israel. Secretary of Defense Caspar Weinberger said that the Soviet arms cache took the Pentagon off guard because of its volume as well as its secrecy. The United States had been carefully observing movements of the Soviet military.

In like manner, the cyber command centers in various countries—including the one in the United States—are busy today prepositioning cyber weapons throughout cyberspace. For example, logic bombs are being prepositioned for the cyber wars of the future.

> Imagine a world where other countries hack into your IT systems to plant defective code in that product you are designing for the military, so that it will not work during a future crisis. Imagine hackers planting logic bombs in the electricity grid and Internet backbones to shut them down as a strike against the military's command-and-control structure—catching your business in the cyber-crossfire. [13]

This is not just a possible future fiction; such things are happening *now*! Preparations are now in motion for the cyber wars of the future.

These various international cyber command centers are also planting trapdoors in the enemy networks they have penetrated (including U.S. networks). Again, a trapdoor is malicious software code that hides in the background and permits easier and faster unauthorized access to that network. This enables the cyber command in one country to easily access enemy private networks at will.

Logic bombs and trapdoors have been planted in private networks across the United States. Perhaps now you understand why our government is presently spending so much money on the military—including preparing for possible cyber war. How much have we been spending?

> In 2008, 41.5 percent of all the military expenditures in the entire world belonged to the United States. We spent more on national defense than China, Japan, Russia, Europe, and several other nations combined. In 2009 our defense budget was $642 billion, second only to Social Security at $677 billion. Our defense costs were 36 percent of the total income from taxes in fiscal year 2009. [14]

With each year that passes, an increased portion of that money has been allocated to cyber defenses.

The cyber goal of the U.S. military is to have combat-ready forces that are trained and equipped to conduct "sustained cyber operations" that coordinate with air and space operations. This may sound like something from *Star Wars*, but this is the current cyber strategy of the United States. It is not the future—it is now!

To meet these objectives, the 24th Air Force has aligned some 5300 military and civilian personnel to conduct or support round-the-clock cyber operations. This unit maintains and defends Air Force networks.[15] According to the book *Cyberpower and National Security*, "the Air Force considers cyberspace superiority an imperative and establishes the proposition that it is the prerequisite to effective U.S. military operations in all other war-fighting domains."[16]

The Navy has added into the mix some 14,000 active duty military and civilian personnel who serve in information operations, network defense, and space and telecommunication facilities around the world. They are now aligned operationally under the U.S. Cyber Command.[17]

The Army has also contributed some 21,000 soldiers and civilians—including the Army Intelligence and Security Command—to participate in cyber-related activities. As well, the Marine Corps has assigned 800 of its forces purely to cyber work.

The U.S. Air Force Space Command has proposed the establishment of a graduate-level course for network warfare operations. This class will last almost half a year, and its objective is to produce officers capable of providing "in-depth expertise throughout the air, space, and cyberspace domains focused on the application of network defense, exploitation, and attack."[18]

U.S. VULNERABILITIES

The U.S. military is taking all of this seriously because of perceived vulnerabilities in the United States. After doing a great deal of research on the subject, I can tell you that our military is tightly integrated with the Internet (command and control, the positioning of fleets, targeting, and much more). If the Internet became obliterated through some kind of lethal cyber attack, that would greatly impede the coordinated efforts of our military in all domains (land, sea, air, and space). Therefore our military is taking unprecedented steps to beef up our capabilities in cyberspace.

One reason that many U.S. officials sense vulnerability is that our own cyber geniuses have discovered hard evidence that logic bombs and trapdoors have already been planted in U.S. networks. *They are already there.* We are like sitting ducks, just waiting to be cyber slammed. Many analysts believe that both China and Russia are responsible for these preplanted cyber weapons.

THE USE OF SOCIAL NETWORKS

Social networks are also being used for devious purposes. Foreign intelligence agencies can derive significant actionable intelligence information on government and military personnel, in the United States and overseas, by their postings on such social networks as Facebook and MySpace. "According to a recent study conducted for one of the U.S. Armed Services, 60% of the service members posting on MySpace have posted enough information to make themselves vulnerable to adversary targeting." Such information has already been used to facilitate kidnapping and ransoming of government officials overseas, military and intelligence officers being blackmailed, and much more.[19] U.S. cyber defense strategy must include preventing social networks from being used against us.

DEFENSE READINESS CONDITION FOR CYBERSPACE

Cyber strategist Jeffrey Carr has suggested a five-stage framework to delineate the Defense Readiness Condition (DEFCON) for cyberspace.[20]

- Cyber DEFCON 5 represents normal peacetime conditions.

- Cyber DEFCON 4 becomes activated when cyber reconnaissance appears against the backdrop of existing political tensions between the United States and its adversaries.

- Cyber DEFCON 3 becomes activated in the aftermath of cyber reconnaissance and some kind of initiating event (a cyber attack).

- Cyber DEFCON 2 becomes activated after an initiating

event occurs and the mobilization of enemy cyber militias is definitely detected.

- Cyber DEFCON 1 becomes activated when actual attacks appear imminent or are ongoing.

All of this assumes that cyber attacks will be used either in parallel with kinetic (physical) armed attacks or as the sole means of attack between adversaries.

IS THERE NO DEFENSE?

ountries all around the world are spending truckloads of money to beef up their cyber defenses. Some governments are actually hiring teenagers and twentysomethings to engage in their cyber defenses. MI5, the British Security Service, has "hired 50 computer-savvy youngsters—some only in their late teens—to work in a top-secret Cyber Operations Command," according to British reports. Lord West, the Security Minister, described the key members of the command. "[They are] youngsters who have been naughty boys until we caught them. Now we use their talents to stop other naughty boys from trying to shut down this country…We needed those youngsters who are deep into this hacking business. Hacking is a young person's game and we need to fight fire with fire."[1]

SECURITY BREACHES WILL OCCUR

Even if everyone on the Internet takes security measures, security breaches will occur. If 1.6 billion Internet users take security measures that are 99.9 percent effective, and there is an attempted virus attack against every one of these users at least once a year, then 1.6 million users per year will succumb to a computer virus.[2]

Of course, our security measures are not 99.9 percent effective (far from it!), nor does every computer user on the planet experience only one attempted virus attack each year. The truth is, building security into the Internet is a monumentally challenging task. Eugene Kaspersky, leader of an antimalware company, is probably right when he quips that the only safe computer is one that is shut off, disconnected from any networks, and locked in a vault.[3]

The problem is exacerbated by the fact that some of today's most popular software packages have vulnerabilities that allow viruses to find their way onto computers. For example, even though Microsoft has spent billions of dollars to fight this problem, it has not been able to completely rid its software of security flaws.

Every year, security companies release dozens of security alerts regarding Microsoft software—often 70 or more. Those security flaws are like doorways that enable talented hackers to design malware that can make its way onto your computer.

Microsoft made a bold attempt to make the Vista operating system the most secure product they had ever released, and it was heavily advertised as being secure. Yet, the same year it was released, three dozen security vulnerabilities were announced. That is much better than the track record of the XP operating system—it had about three times as many vulnerabilities—but Vista's record is nothing to brag about.[4]

Remember, hackers are relentless in their pursuit of finding ways to infiltrate your computer. As long as vulnerabilities remain in popular software packages, hackers will be able to virally contaminate your computer.

If there is any benefit to the cyber attacks we have experienced in recent years, it is that public awareness is now higher—and that is a good thing. Mark Cohn, a vice president at the security firm Unisys, made this comment:

> [Public awareness has] grown tremendously over the last year or two. Cyber-security affects us all from national security to the mundane level of identity theft and fraud. But that means society as a whole is more receptive to many of the things we need to do that would in the past have been seen as politically motivated.[5]

DETERRENCE DIFFICULT IN TODAY'S WORLD

Back in the cold war days, deterrence seemed so much easier. For many years, the "Mutual Assured Destruction" (MAD) policy served as a deterrent for the United States and the Soviet Union not to launch nuclear missiles at each other. If the Soviet Union had launched an attack against the United States, the United States would have retaliated by launching an attack against the Soviet Union. The fact that each superpower could blow up the other served as a good deterrent.

By contrast, deterrence in modern times is exceedingly difficult. This is true in terms of warfare in physical domains (land, sea, air, and space) as well as the cyber domain.

In terms of physical domains, consider deterrence as related to Muslim countries. Islamic theology teaches that any Muslim who loses his or her life in service to Allah is guaranteed entrance into Paradise (Hadith 9:459). Muslim tradition attributes this quote to Muhammad:

> The person who participates in (holy battles) in Allah's cause and nothing compels him to do so except belief in Allah and His Apostles, will be recompensed by Allah either with a reward, or booty (if he survives) or will be admitted to Paradise (if he is killed in the battle as a martyr) (Hadith 1:35).

It is not clear how radical Muslims view the MAD policy, as Al Venter, author of *Iran's Nuclear Option*, notes.

> If Iran were to acquire nuclear weapons, it is unclear how the concept of martyrdom—now glorified in the Islamic world—would come into play. According to Cold War logic, the fact that America could react to a hundred thousand of its own dead by inflicting ten million on the enemy served as a sufficient deterrent to the other side not to attack. But against a culture that glorifies death in "Holy War," the principle of deterrence dissolves. If millions of martyrs are created in order to eradicate the state of Israel, or severely damage the United States, they might be honored for having made the supreme sacrifice.[6]

Walid Phares, author of *Future Jihad*, agrees.

> The jihadists are Islamists, and one of their major doctri-
> nal pillars is sacrificing for the other life. Suicide bombers
> are a chilling reminder of this ideological reality—which
> directly leads to one conclusion: Unlike the Soviets or even
> the Chinese or North Koreans, the jihadists do not fear
> death, let alone fear mass death. Fear of nuclear retaliation
> is not a determining factor in a jihadi state of mind.[7]

Phares also suggests that there are clear signs that radical Muslims
would indeed be willing to detonate a nuclear device. First, he notes
that in 1993 such radicals exploded a truck inside the World Trade
Center's underground parking garage with the hope that at least one
tower might collapse, thereby killing tens of thousands. Then, in the
2001 attack against the Twin Towers, Osama bin Laden hoped for tens
of thousands of casualties. Both these egregious attacks aimed at casualties of a nuclear magnitude and thus indicate that these terrorists—
should they ever attain a nuclear weapon—would not hesitate to use
it in the furtherance of their radical cause.[8]

Deterrence in the cyber domain is a different problem altogether.
Martin Libicki, a senior management scientist specializing in cyber
security at Rand (a nonprofit think tank), represents many in his asser-
tion that it will be difficult for the U.S. government to voice and follow
through with a policy of cyber deterrence. There are a number of reasons for this. First, and most foundational, precisely identifying cyber
attackers is exceedingly difficult. Cyber hackers can do their dastardly
work and then erase their tracks. Libicki also suggests there is some evidence that some countries seem to be underwriting private hackers to
do their work—which makes it more difficult to pin a cyber attack on
the country itself.[9]

Another issue relates to the perceived possibility among some countries that the United States' cyber retaliation may be weak. Many countries would not necessarily be dissuaded from launching a cyber attack
against the United States because, frankly, they are not sure the United
States' cyber retaliation would be prohibitively bad. Even U.S. cyber

experts say it could be difficult to follow through with threats of a counter cyber attack, especially if we have been hit first. For this reason, some countries may be willing to gamble in launching a cyber attack against the United States.

> Any deterrence policy is designed to scare people away… The problem is, though, if you cannot execute it, you are bluffing. It is possible to believe people will call our bluff. If it turns out we can't do what we say, we not only look embarrassed for ourselves, but we end up calling all of our other deterrents into question.[10]

That puts our government into a real dilemma: "On the one hand," Libicki says, "you shouldn't go around saying you're not going to deter, and you're not going to retaliate…On the other hand, actually going out and saying it can lead to a lot of problems."[11]

CYBER DETERRENCE IS MORE THAN CYBER RETALIATION

In view of the problems delineated above, a number of cyber strategists in this country suggest that the U.S. response to cyber attacks cannot be limited to cyber retaliation alone. Our deterrence policy, they say, must be broader—the government must be free to decide what kind of response is appropriate for whatever attack is launched against us. One strategist described a U.S. cyber response this way:

> [It] would be based on all elements of national power so that, for example, any retaliation would not necessarily be by cyber but could be by diplomatic, economic, or kinetic means, depending on the circumstances. Retaliation, when and if it occurred, would be at a time, place, and manner of our choosing.[12]

The word *kinetic* refers to a physical response, using things like guns, tanks, and bombs. The idea, then, is that if the United States should be on the receiving end of a lethal cyber attack, all options are on the table. If the cyber attack were significant, one option on the table would be for the U.S. Army, Navy, and Air Force to use whatever physical force is necessary to make a very loud point to a watching world—that a cyber attack may well draw more than a cyber response.

A DECLARATORY POSTURE

A number of cyber strategists have suggested that the United States must publish a formal *declaratory posture*. The purpose of such a declaratory posture is to inform any nation-state contemplating launching a cyber attack against the United States of how the United States would specifically respond. This might cause some combatant nation-states to think twice before launching such an attack.

At present, our country does not have such a declaratory posture. Many believe that developing one would obviously be in our best interests. Strategists say this declaratory posture should note the possibility of a physical, kinetic response—involving Army, Navy, and Air Force. The idea to communicate would be this: If you attack us with your malicious computer software, we very well may respond with our destructive military hardware.

PROTECT THE IMPORTANT STUFF

When professional football players go out on the field and entertain us on Sunday afternoons, they are always careful to protect the most important parts of their bodies. For example, they wear helmets to protect their heads because head injuries can be catastrophic. That is a wise defense strategy.

Likewise, cyber strategists say we should take steps to protect the most important components of our cyber capabilities because certain kinds of cyber injuries could be catastrophic to our society. They suggest that our government differentiate between "indispensable," "key," and "other" cyber capabilities.

- Indispensable cyber capabilities include our military and intelligence capacities, without which we would become vulnerable to further attack.

- Key cyber capabilities include important things like the electrical grid and financial institutions. These are functionalities the country could not do without for a significant amount of time, but for which short-term workarounds might be available in the event of a cyber attack.

- The other capabilities include the great majority of cyber functionalities which, though of lesser priority than the other two, still have security requirements that need to be met.[13]

With this kind of differentiation, the government can strategically plan on how to best allocate funds in building America's cyber defenses. All three areas would be allocated government funding, but the higher priority items would obviously receive the stronger funding.

AN ALTERNATE LAYERED APPROACH

An alternate layered approach has been suggested by Richard Clarke, who prioritizes things a bit differently.[14] His approach is to protect the Internet, protect the power grid, and protect the Department of Defense.

First, the backbone of the Internet must be protected. There are hundreds of Internet providers in the United States, but the real backbone of the Internet involves only half a dozen of the larger Internet providers, including AT&T, Verizon, and Sprint. Companies such as these own the thousands of miles of fiber optic cables running across the country that make the Internet possible. Here is the important point: Attacking either government or private-sector networks requires first accessing this Internet backbone. So it makes good sense to detect and prevent an attack from entering the backbone before it even has a chance to harm a targeted government or private-sector network. This ought to be a top priority.

Second, we must protect the power grid of the country. After all, without energy, nothing else works—not even the Internet. An enemy cyber attack could easily target our power grid, so perhaps we should reconsider whether the power grid should be connected to the Internet at all.

Third, the Department of Defense must be protected against cyber attacks. It is a foregone conclusion that if a major cyber attack were launched against the United States, the Department of Defense would be targeted. After all, the nation-state launching the cyber attack would be aware of the possibility that the United States would respond not only with a cyber retaliation but also with physical force. To thwart or at least hinder this, the Department of Defense would surely be a prime cyber target. Therefore, protecting the Department of Defense—with its networks and its communication capabilities—must remain a high priority. Clarke is convinced that if our country's president and congress…

> were to agree to harden the Internet backbone, separate and secure the controls for the power grid, and vigorously pursue security upgrades for Defense IT systems, we could cast doubt in the minds of potential nation-state attackers about how well they would do in launching a large-scale attack against us.[15]

WILL ANTIVIRUS SOFTWARE SAVE THE DAY?

I touched on antivirus software earlier in the book. Here I will address how such software actually works and why it is not a foolproof solution to our cyber problem.

Antivirus software is intended to detect and protect against computer viruses, worms, botnet malware, Trojan horses, spyware, adware, and other forms of malware. If the antivirus software can do all that, I want it on my computer! But alas, nothing is perfect, and antivirus software definitely has its limitations.

The antivirus software depends on data files or *signature files* in order to discover viruses on the computer. By itself, the software is not very "smart"—it cannot determine what is and what is not a virus. That is why it needs the signature files, for those files tell the software what to look for on your computer.

Imagine a police officer looking for an escaped convict. The police officer takes a piece of the convict's clothing and lets a trained dog smell it. He then says to the dog, "Okay, Rover, go find him." The dog runs off, and based on his keen sense of smell, he finds the convict.

Signature files are akin to that piece of clothing. These files tell the software what to look for.

Of course, no analogy is perfect. Some of these signature files not only tell the software what to look for but also contain embedded information about what action the software should take once a virus is discovered.

Most antivirus programs download and install new signature files at least once each day. Of course, that assumes that the computer is continually connected to the Internet. Some antivirus software products check for new files more often than that, sometimes even on an hourly basis.

Ideally, when antivirus software discovers a bad file, it notifies the user—a window typically pops up with an alert. Then the antivirus software engages in an action, such as removing the file or moving the file to a quarantined area of your disk where it will not be able to run. In the best of all worlds, such software would find virtually all viruses, and cyberspace would be much more secure.

However, computer virus experts themselves tell us that antivirus software does not do a good job of finding or protecting against a lot of the cyber bugs that are a threat against your computer. Why? The answer is simple: The technology is not perfect. A common problem with antivirus software packages is that they often give false positives—that is, they falsely classify something as a virus when it is not really a virus at all. It is kind of like your police dog leading you to the wrong person—someone who is not a convict at all. In 2006, a popular antivirus software package classified Microsoft Excel as a virus and subsequently deleted it from machines. I imagine Bill Gates did not appreciate that. Computer security firms are trying hard to solve the false positives problem, but for now, we must all recognize and deal with it. The technology is simply not perfect.

To minimize the possibility of false positives, companies that produce antivirus software do lots and lots of testing. This takes lots of personnel and lots of time. Combine that with the company's goal of updating your signature files at least once each day, and it becomes reasonable to expect a delay of a day or two between the time a piece of malware hits the Internet and the time your antivirus software downloads a signature file for it.

But in reality, it can often take one to three weeks before a signature file for a new piece of malware downloads to your antivirus software. For example, for one threatening virus that hit the Internet some time ago, McAfee (a first-rate antivirus software company) took ten days to send out a signature file to their users, and Symantec (another first-rate antivirus software company) took thirteen days.[16] In the interim—that is, between the time the virus first hit the Internet and the time users were able to download a signature file for it—many computers became infected by that piece of malware.

Another problem is noted by Alex Shipp, a pioneer of online security. He tells us that some of today's hackers are adept at disabling the antimalware products on your computer. In other words, some hackers can bring down your cyber defenses.[17]

Yet the experts say that despite the so-so competency of today's antivirus software, some malware protection is better than none. Indeed, "even a bad AV [antivirus] technology can be valuable, because protection against, say, 30% of all threats is still a lot better than protection against 0% of all threats."[18] So the bottom line is that it is definitely a good thing for you to have antivirus software on your computer—but do not for a minute think you are thereby absolutely safe from virus invasions!

The aggravating thing about all this is that in order to get this limited amount of virus protection, people have to put up with the antivirus software slowly loading every time they turn on the computer, and then—depending on how the preferences have been set—there is also typically a slow-down as the software checks individual files when they are launched. For those with a need for speed, this can really cramp their style. I noted earlier that the single best antivirus software I have found—one that is fast and has a minimum speed drain on the computer—is NOD 32 by ESET. (By the way, I do not own stock in ESET.)

WHAT ABOUT PERSONAL FIREWALLS?

Many people wonder whether personal firewalls should be a part of their cyber arsenal. Many others have no idea what a personal firewall even is.

Let's say that someone has sent you an e-mail that says, "Click here to buy Rolex watches cheap." You click on a link, and without knowing it, your computer downloads some malware—the kind that records all your keystrokes and then transmits them over the Internet to a cyber criminal. (Oops—your antivirus software did not work!)

A personal firewall can stop *outbound* Internet traffic. The difficulty is in configuring your personal firewall to not restrict applications you like (such as your Web browser, or perhaps Skype), but disallow keyboard loggers. You want your firewall to allow the reputable applications to interact with the Internet while disallowing the invasive applications from interacting with the Internet.

To do this, you set the firewall preferences such that it disallows *everything* unless you specifically instruct it to allow a particular software program—and that can get tedious real quick. People often forget to readjust their firewall every time they load a new application on their computer that might utilize the Internet. And if they forget to readjust the firewall, their application may not work right, which causes a lot of frustration, especially for computer users who are not too computer savvy.

When a software application wants access to the Internet but is blocked, most firewalls display a little window asking you to choose to allow or deny access to the Internet. For example, if you install Skype (for video conferencing) and launch the application, a window will pop up and say, "Do you wish skype.exe to access the Internet?" In this case, you would allow access.

But when this window pops up, you may not recognize the name of the application that wants access to the Internet. You may not be sure whether it is a reputable application or a dangerous one. One cyber malware expert noted, for example, that the pop-up window might say something like, "GCONSYNC.EXE would like to use the Internet. Do you wish to allow it?" Because you do not recognize the name, you immediately think to yourself, "Oh no, I've downloaded some malware that's trying to communicate with some cyber criminal out there." So you deny that application access to the Internet. In reality, however, you have just blocked a necessary component of iTunes. The point I am making is that it is very easy to block applications that you do not want to block. And because it can be difficult for you to determine what is safe and what is dangerous just by the application's name, you might wrongly end up giving the benefit of the doubt to a piece of malware that has a name similar to the iTunes component.

What can we conclude? On the one hand, personal firewalls can be a benefit to you and keep you safer if you know what you are doing. If you are unfamiliar with the names of files that applications use, you may save yourself a lot of frustration, making "denial" choices that make certain software applications not work right because one of the needed components was denied access to the Internet. Here's my advice: If you install a firewall and it displays a window asking whether to allow a strange-sounding file to communicate to the Internet, open your Web browser and do a quick Google search for the name of the file you are not sure about. (For example, a Google-search of GCONSYNC quickly reveals that it is an iTunes file.) If the Google search reveals that the file is related to a new software package you just installed, you are probably safe in allowing it to access the Internet. If the Google search reveals that it is malware, however, you obviously should deny it access to the Internet and then take steps to eradicate the malware from your computer.

FOR MAC USERS

Macintosh users may be somewhat safer than their PC counterparts. Easy-to-use malware creation tools are available for PCs, whereas at present, no such malware creation tools exist for the Macintosh platform. This means that if a hacker wants to write malware for the Macintosh, he must first learn how to program for the Macintosh, and that takes a great deal of effort.

Furthermore, Macintosh computers usually cost a lot more money than PCs, and not every hacker has that kind of money. Because Windows machines are traditionally much cheaper, more hackers write malware for that platform.

So Macintosh users may not be in as much danger as Windows users, but their computers are not invulnerable to attack. As the Apple market share continues to grow, as it has consistently over the past decade, the influx of malware for the Macintosh is expected to increase.

REBOOTING THE INTERNET

As I was writing this book, information began to surface in news reports regarding the possibility of turning off and rebooting the Internet. According to these reports, seven individuals have been given "smart cards" or "keys" that contain a portion of the DNSSEC root key (the "master key" to the whole system). This root key would be necessary to reboot the Internet if connections to it were severed in order to stem off a cataclysmic cyber attack. (During a major international cyber attack, key Internet servers might be disconnected in order to contain or minimize the damage.)

"A minimum of five of the seven key-holders—one each from Britain, the U.S., Burkina Faso, Trinidad and Tobago, Canada, China, and the Czech Republic—would have to converge at a U.S. base with their keys to restart the system and connect everything once again." They received their keys "while locked deep in a U.S. bunker."[19]

This almost sounds like something from a Dan Brown novel, but it is not fiction. One day in the not-too-distant future, a cyber attack could be launched that is so lethal, a reboot of the Internet might be the only possible solution. We are living in exciting but strange days!

PART 2

WHO ARE YOU?
WHERE ARE YOU?

BIOMETRICS

In addition to the cyber technologies I have addressed up to now, two other technologies also have great relevance to biblical prophecy—biometrics and GPS. I will focus on these two cutting-edge technologies in this chapter and the next.

Biometrics is an amazing technology that has the potential to be both an incredible blessing and an incredible curse. The term itself derives from two Greek words: *bios* (life) and *metrikos* (measure). Biometrics is a technology that enables the identification of people by measuring and analyzing biological data and/or behavioral traits. More specifically, it verifies people's identity by measuring and analyzing one of their bodily characteristics, such as their fingerprints, voice patterns, facial patterns, scent, hand geometry, palm print, iris recognition, retina recognition, or even DNA. Behavioral traits used for identifying people include typing rhythms, gait, and speaking patterns.

A person's voice may seem like a physiological trait instead of a behavioral trait, but this aspect of the science studies the way a person speaks. Some have coined the term *behaviometrics* to refer to the behavior-trait aspect of biometrics. Experts note that a biometric system based on a physiological characteristic is usually more reliable than one based on a behavioral characteristic.

In a later chapter, I will relate this technology specifically to our coming cashless society. We will see that this technology goes hand in hand with a no-cash lifestyle. After all, this technology guarantees that I am who I claim to be so that instant monetary transfers from my bank account to a vendor are secure and trustworthy. In this chapter, however, I will focus on the technology itself.

ALREADY IN WIDE USE

Biometric technology is already used in a variety of contexts around the world. For example, some laptops and PCs have fingerprint scanners that allow only the owner to use the computer. The technology is also being used to control access to private corporate networks containing confidential data. As well, it is being used to seek out and identify individuals in groups that are under surveillance.

In the United Kingdom, some students pay for meals with a thumbprint. They simply put their thumb on a scanner, and funds are withdrawn from an account already set up by the students' parents. The parents also receive nutrition reports of the food the students have purchased.

Australia uses biometrics in connection with visas and passports. Canadians use it for border security and immigration purposes. Israelis use it in connection with a new high-tech ID card. The Dutch use it in connection with both passports and ID cards.

Finger imaging is presently being used in different parts of the world to provide identification verification at ATM machines and to prevent check-cashing fraud. Hand-scanning biometrics is being used in various parts of the world to verify credit card purchases, to prevent welfare fraud, and to process immigrants at airports.

The United States and the European Union are now both considering new biometric methods for border-crossing procedures. Biometrics may play an increasing role in travel in the coming years for many countries around the world. The science of biometrics appears to be here to stay.

REQUIREMENTS OF BIOMETRICS

In order for a personal characteristic to be useful in a biometric context, certain things must be true regarding that characteristic.

- *Universal.* The characteristic must be common to all people (everyone has an iris or thumbprint).

- *Collectability.* The characteristic must be easy to measure (for example, with a thumbprint or retinal scanner).

- *Uniqueness.* Each person's measurement must be unique.

- *Permanence.* People must retain the characteristic as time passes (for example, one's thumbprint does not change over time).

- *Performance.* The technology must be fast and accurate.

- *Acceptability.* The technology must be widely accepted by people as reliable.

Any personal characteristic that fits these criteria might be suitable for biometric purposes.

GENERAL APPLICATIONS OF BIOMETRICS

There are two primary applications of biometrics: identification and verification.

Identification involves a "one to many" comparison—that is, the measured characteristic (a thumbprint, for example) is compared to a massive database of other fingerprinted individuals in order to identify the person.

Verification, on the other hand, is a "one to one" comparison—that is, the measured characteristic (a thumbprint, for example) is compared to the person's previously recorded and stored thumbprint to verify that the person is who he or she claims to be. Obviously, verification is faster than identification because it does not require a massive database search.

The first time a person utilizes a biometric device, biometric information about that person is permanently stored. For example, when a thumbprint is taken or an iris or a hand is scanned, a biometric profile (or *template*) for that person is created and stored electronically. Subsequent biometric scans are compared against this initial profile data.

Unique body characteristics cannot easily be borrowed, stolen, or forgotten, so one's biometric identity cannot usually be forged. This makes biometrics ideal for personal identification and verification.

VARIETY OF BIOMETRIC TECHNOLOGIES

There are a variety of biometric technologies, some in widespread use, others in an experimental phase. Here is a small representative sampling.

Infrared thermogram. This technology measures the pattern of heat radiated in some part of the human body—for example, one's face, hand, or vein. The radiated pattern of each person is unique. This technology can be used without the person realizing he or she is being scanned.

Gait. This technology measures the peculiar way each person walks. Gait is not as distinctive as, say, a fingerprint or iris, but it is sufficiently unique for low-security applications. Of course, as a person grows older, he or she might walk a bit differently. Gait is considered a behavioral biometric.

Keystroke. This technology measures the way a person types on a keyboard. Every person types in a characteristic way, so this mode of identification is sufficient in lower-security applications. This too is considered a behavioral biometric.

Ear. A person's ears are also distinctive.

> Just like finger printing, passport photos, and eye recognition, our ears too can be scanned at airports to prove our identity…Researchers have discovered that every person has uniquely shaped ears and have formulated a way to scan them to compare them with images already compiled in a database…There are a whole load of structures in the ear that you can use to get a set of measurements that are unique to an individual…The ear scan system is said to be 99.6 percent accurate. It maps the curves and wrinkles of the skin, cartilage, and lobes.[1]

Hand geometry. This technology measures the dimensions of

fingers in conjunction with finger joints and the overall shape and size of the hand. This biometric measure has been used for four decades. Because hand geometry is not highly distinctive, it is best used for verification of identities as opposed to identifying people from a large population.

Fingerprint. Sensors on a reader device can easily provide a digital image of a fingerprint, and because fingerprints are unique, they constitute a good biometric. Fingerprint biometric devices cost less than $20, so this is a popular biometric device and is often used for computer security.

Face. This nonintrusive biometric method is suitable for both covert and overt identity checks. A popular facial biometric recognition approach measures the location and shape of such facial attributes as the eyes, eyebrows, nose, lips, and chin as well as their spacial relationships to each other. The combined effect of these features makes for a unique biometric. Some experts question whether a person's face alone is sufficient to identify him or her from a large population of faces with an "extremely high level of confidence." And of course, a person's face can change due to weight gain or loss, aging, or expressions, thereby possibly invalidating the biometric process.

New software has brought facial-recognition technology to mobile phones. The software is fast and accurate, and it is now being touted as something that will soon replace passwords and PIN numbers to log on to Internet sites from a mobile phone. [2]

Retina. Retina recognition—which requires a retina scan—is based on the fact that each person has a unique vascular configuration in the retina. This is a very secure biometric because people can't change their vascular configuration.

Iris. Each iris has a complex and unique pattern with many distinctive features. Iris scans are easier than retina scans because a retina scan requires looking into a lens, whereas an iris scan can be accomplished from several yards away. Increased verification is possible by measuring the iris in light conditions (irises change in light). This is a very reliable biometric.

Palm. Palm prints are unique to each person, and because they are larger than fingers, they can be even more reliable than fingerprints—measuring ridge and valley features, principal lines, and wrinkles in the palm.

Voice. People have unique voices, based on physical characteristics such as their mouths, lips, nasal cavities, and the like. Voice recognition distinguishes a person by measuring the voice against a voice profile or template stored in a database. Obviously, the first time the system is used, the individual must go through a training period (sometimes more than one) until the voice template is complete.

Signature. The way a person signs his or her name is generally unique. Signatures are thus a behavioral biometric. But peoples' signatures can change over time, they can purposefully write differently, and other people can copy their writing, so this is not a premium biometric.

DNA. DNA contains the genetic blueprints of life, and because DNA is unique to each person, it is probably the most reliable biometric. There are a few problems to note, however. First, one could feasibly steal DNA from another person. Second, tests are not always practical because they require complex chemical procedures performed by experts. At present, then, this biometric technology has limited applications.

PEOPLE'S PREFERENCES

Some experts in biometrics believe that voice-based authentication seems to engender less resistance among real users than other forms of biometric security. After all, voice recognition is easy and nonintrusive, and it involves no physical contact. A recent survey revealed these preferences:

- About one-third of the American public prefers voice recognition technologies.

- About one-fourth prefer fingerprint technologies.

- About one-fifth prefer facial scan technologies.

- About a tenth prefer hand geometry technologies and iris scan technologies.[3]

Though the majority of Americans opt for voice recognition

biometric technology, some experts have noted that there is actually a higher percentage of error with this biometric technology than other such technologies. Peoples' voices can change due to such things as a respiratory illness.

BETTER FOR LAW ENFORCEMENT

Some people believe that facial recognition technology could be a great benefit to law enforcement efforts. A large crowd of people could be scanned, and facial images could be measured against a master database. This would provide a quick readout of names and addresses of people in the crowd and would also flag individuals that the authorities are looking for. The obvious downside is the huge invasion of privacy. If you were in a crowd, would you want your face to be scanned and measured against a master database of criminals?

Nevertheless, with terrorism on the rise, such technology could make the world safer for all of us. Biometrics, some people argue, could save lives. Facial recognition technology, for example, could allegedly make all our airports much safer.[4] Advocates in favor of this technology for law enforcement reasons point out that it has already been used to keep German Olympians safe. If the technology works in this context, it can work in any context. So, some people say, get over your privacy paranoia and get with the program!

MILITARY APPLICATIONS

Biometric technologies are widely used in foreign military contexts. For example, "within minutes of knocking down the door of a suspected bomb maker in Iraq, U.S. troops can fingerprint everyone they find inside, send the scans across a satellite link, and find out if the subjects are suspected terrorists."[5]

Through biometric technology, the U.S. military has put a damper on terrorists who are building explosive devices. "Biometric tools, when used on raids on suspected bomb makers' safe houses, have helped to kill or capture individuals who are involved in the construction of improvised explosive devices at the average rate of two per day for the last two years."[6]

How does it work? Collector ID kits are utilized to gather finger-prints and photographic mug shots. Those records are sent by means of a small satellite dish to three databases at the Defense Department's Biometrics Fusion Center, the Army's National Ground Intelligence Center, and the FBI's automated fingerprint identification system. Presently the Defense Department has about 2.2 million files, and the FBI has a whopping 58 million. Once data is sent off by satel-lite, the goal is to have a response back in no later than fifteen min-utes (the average is less than five minutes). This makes operations fast and smooth.

THE USE OF RFID CHIPS

Another emerging technology uses RFID (Radio Frequency Iden-tification) chips, which could potentially be injected directly into human beings with a syringe, a good target area being the fatty part of the palm. This biometric application has the potential use of effort-lessly proving that a person is, in fact, who he or she claims to be. For example, if a person was at a store and was writing a check to pay for a product, the RFID chip in his or her palm could instantly provide proof that the checks actually belong to him or her. This is like a built-in ID system. These chips could potentially also contain critical medi-cal information about a person.

RFID technology is actually already in wide use in toll booths. I have a little transponder at the top of my windshield that enables me to drive on tollways in the Dallas–Fort Worth area, and money is auto-matically withdrawn from my personal bank account so I do not have to stop to pay toll fees manually. Just as this technology identifies my car as belonging to me, it can also be used to verify the identity of indi-vidual human beings. You may think that is pretty cool, but I person-ally want nothing to do with it. It is just one more technology that could be exploited for watching and controlling us all.

Some businesses monitor employees by requiring them to carry company ID cards with RFID chips planted in them. The technol-ogy enables employers to keep an eye on employee activities and have an objective measure of their productivity. Employers can easily track where their employees go and how long they stay there. For example, they can track how long employees are in the lunch room or snack room each day.

RFID technology can easily be placed in devices that we carry around with us, such as our cell phones or smart phones. They can also be placed in smart cards. I would not be surprised if one day we see RFID-equipped watches or jewelry!

Christian prophecy scholar Mark Hitchcock tells us that the technology involves three primary components: an antenna or coil, a transceiver (with decoder), and a transponder (RF tag) that is electronically programmed with unique information.

- The antenna emits radio signals to activate the tag and to read and write data to it.

- The reader emits radio waves in ranges of anywhere from one inch to 100 feet or more, depending upon its power output and the radio frequency used. When an RFID tag passes through the electromagnetic zone, it detects the reader's activation signal.

- The reader decodes the data encoded in the tag's integrated circuit (silicon chip), and the data is passed to the host computer for processing.[7]

Now, here is something to think about: Technology experts tell us that in the future, products in stores will likely have RFID tags. If you have a smart card or a cell phone that contains RFID technology, and your banking information is stored on the RFID chip, you can pay for that product in an instant. It will be a fully automated process. "It is entirely possible that one day soon you could load up your weekly groceries and walk through a virtual checkout without stopping."[8] The items in your basket would be instantly totaled up and the amount deducted from your bank account.

I don't know about you, but I would be uncomfortable with such a system. I would always be concerned about potential flaws. For example, I could go to a store to buy a shirt, and then, by some strange digital accident, the store system charges me for everything in the store and drains my bank account. No thanks!

What if such a chip were implanted in the human body? Thomas Ice and Timothy Demy make this note: "A chip implanted some-where in our bodies might serve as a combination credit card, pass-port, driver's license, personal diary, and you name it. No longer would we worry about losing our credit cards while traveling."[9] Such an implant would also make it much easier for someone to track your every move.

Researcher Stewart Watkins suggests that "RFID tags can be used to track vehicles, passengers, hospital patients, and even pets. The U.S. military widely deploys their forces using RFID technology. Children who play truant could even be tagged—though I'm sure civil liberty groups would have a word or two to say about that!"[10]

THE USE OF SMART CARDS

I have already made reference to smart cards. They are so impor-tant that they deserve a bit more discussion. In our day of smart tech-nology (including the smart phone in my pocket), it makes sense for people to have one smart card they could use to make purchases at any store. The card would be secure, so it could not be used by any unau-thorized persons. The technology already exists to make this a reality—including iris scans and fingerprints.

Such a card would be just like your MasterCard, Visa, or Ameri-can Express card except that it would be a tad thicker. It is called *smart* because it would contain a microchip (like a computer with memory) that contains large amounts of information about you.

There are two varieties. One form of the smart card requires that its owner stick it into a smart card reader at the point of sale. The other form only requires that the owner be in the immediate proximity to the point of sale. One merely has to wave the card in front of the reader, and *voila*, the purchase is instantaneous.

Smart cards are presently being used in a variety of contexts. For example, college students can purchase them for use with laundry machines, soda machines, and photocopy machines. In Europe they are used for public phone booths. Many believe that smart cards will become the standard currency of the future.

DANGER IN THE AIR

Many people are concerned that biometric technology could be used for purposes other than identification and verification of identity. A person may consent to biometric measurements only for identification purposes, but that same biometric data could later be used, for example, to infringe upon a person's privacy.

Though the 2002 movie *Minority Report* was strictly fictional, it illustrated what could happen in the future as a result of biometric technology. In the movie, biometric iris scanners were scattered throughout the city, keeping track of people wherever they went. That biometric data, tied into a master database containing lots of information about each person (including personal tastes), triggered customized advertisements in the person's vicinity, typically at the point of sale. John Anderton (played by Tom Cruise) changes his biometric identity by having an eye transplant. In the movie, going anywhere without being watched was difficult.

When facial recognition technology improves to the degree that surveillance cameras over widespread areas could recognize individuals, and if that technology is put to use, privacy becomes a thing of the past. Even in our present day, many people in the United States who work in major cities are concerned because they are recorded about 60 times daily by various surveillance cameras scattered about the city.

In my research, I came across this information in an article titled "Biometric ID that 'gives Big Brother a passport to your privacy'":

> Perhaps your firm already has your fingerprints on file so you can get into the office without any hassle. But although you may think nothing of it, giving over this type of information could be leaving you open to Big Brother–type surveillance...Volunteering fingerprint and DNA information, and even eye scans, could lead to racial or social profiling and invasion of privacy...Biometrics are put forward as a way of enhancing personal security, but the use of

biometrics requires people to give up pieces of their body, effectively. The ubiquity of biometrics begs the question whether any of us can lead truly private lives anymore.[11]

When a person makes a credit card purchase, the information regarding that specific purchase becomes a part of that person's personal profile—a profile that provides details on that person's tastes, interests, and activities. Since this information is electronically stored in computer systems, people could potentially find out a lot more about you than you are comfortable with. All electronic purchases leave electronic footprints, and those footprints can be traced.

In London (a city I like a lot), cameras are now being used to scan the faces of people who enter parks to check them against a crime database. Understandably, this has not gone over well with many people. After all, those who live in the UK are already the most watched people on the earth. The average person is caught on camera some 3000 times each week (surveillance cameras are just about everywhere).

Some worry that innocent people could be convicted of a crime. As one person put it, "If you are an innocent person who happens to look a bit like a criminal, I would be worried about what the response would be. What would happen if you were wrongly added to this database?... It's overthrowing the presumption of innocence from the start."[12]

Biometric systems could also lead to personal attacks and mutilation. For example, a burglar could kidnap an executive and force him to yield to a fingerprint scan to allow the burglar entry. In one case already on file, a perpetrator cut off the finger of an executive so the perpetrator could access the corporation's offices.

In still another dangerous scenario, technology designed to make things more convenient for people could be used to control them. In chapter 12, I will explore this possibility and investigate what the book of Revelation reveals about the antichrist and the false prophet usurping economic control over all who live on the earth. They will undoubtedly accomplish this through technologies similar to the ones we are discussing in this chapter. Clearly, these technologies can be a blessing, but they can also be a curse.

GPS TECHNOLOGY

A few days before I wrote this chapter, I was driving in a part of Dallas I had never been in before. A new acquaintance at Dallas Theological Seminary asked me to meet him at a restaurant for lunch. After our meeting, I started out on my journey home. Apparently, I was not paying very close attention, because in no time I found myself on the wrong road. I turned right to see if I could get back to where I was before. It turned out to be a one-way street, and I had to keep going a long way until I could turn right again. By then, I was utterly lost.

No problem. I pulled over to the side of the road, turned on my iPhone, and activated a little program called GPS-Drive. *GPS*, of course, refers to the Global Positioning System. My iPhone immediately detected my exact location and promptly provided visual graphics as well as a voice that guided me back to my house. Technology can sure be a big help!

When I walked in the door of our home, our two cats—Sam and Ruby—were asleep on their luxurious cat beds. My iPhone and GPS program must have still been on my mind. As soon as I saw the two cats, I thought of a pet service I recently read about that will, for a fee, insert a biochip into your pets so wherever they go, their location can always be determined with the Global Positioning System. Those who opt for this procedure now have pets that will never again be lost. (Our cats remain GPS free.) Prophecy scholars Thomas Ice and Timothy Demy, authors of *The Coming Cashless Society*, raise the obvious question.

> When you hum "Home on the Range," the images that pass through your mind may be of the campfire at night, the cowboys at roundup, and the wide-open spaces where the buffalo roam. But in today's world, though the buffalo may roam, we still know where they are. Tracking wildlife, pets, livestock, and even fish has become commonplace. Many such creatures no longer have brands, they have bio-chips…If we can put chips in chimps, why not in people?[1]

HOW DOES GPS WORK?

The GPS is a space-based radio-navigation system that provides free, continuous, and reliable positioning and navigation guidance to anyone. The system also provides the exact time for wherever you are. It was originally intended for the U.S. military but was made available to everyone in the 1980s. The Global Positioning System hinges on three primary components.

First, a network of 24 satellites orbit the earth at an altitude of about 12,000 miles and speeds of roughly 7000 miles an hour (close to two miles per second). They are solar powered but also have backup batteries in case of a solar eclipse. Each satellite has small rocket boosters that can make course corrections to keep it going in the right direction.

These satellites were put into orbit by the U.S. Department of Defense and orbit the earth twice a day. They are designed to last about ten years, so eventually, they will need to be replaced. As technology continues to improve, replacement satellites are built and launched into orbit. These techno-marvels are 17 feet across with their solar panels fully extended and weigh in at 2000 pounds each.

Second, control and monitoring stations on the ground are in direct contact with the satellites in space.

Third, GPS receivers are built into many recent-model cars, smartphones, watches, and other electronic devices. They can also be purchased as separate handheld units—typically small enough to slip into your pocket.[2]

Through this technological triad—and through a process called *triangulation*—GPS receivers are able to provide your location in three dimensions (latitude, longitude, and altitude).

> A GPS receiver must be locked on to the signal of at least three satellites to calculate a 2D [two dimensional] position (latitude and longitude) and track movement. With four or more satellites in view, the receiver can determine the user's 3D position (latitude, longitude, and altitude). Once the user's position has been determined, the GPS unit can calculate other information, such as speed, bearing, track, trip distance, distance to destination, sunrise and sunset time, and more.[3]

Of course, you and I do not have to be aware of all the technology that goes on behind the scenes as all these calculations take place. Most of us only care that a device can tell us and show us visually how to get to where we want to go. Whether we are hiking, boating, driving, or flying, GPS receivers can guide us to the places we need to be.

Understandably, the Global Positioning System has become a mainstay of transportation systems all around the world. I am amused that one of my brothers recently said to me, "Remember the old days, when we had to pull out paper maps?"

IS GPS ACCURATE?

Some people may be tempted to wonder how accurate GPS really is. It is extremely accurate. Keep in mind that the U.S. Department of Defense created this system as a benefit to the military. This was a megabucks endeavor. You and I have the privilege and convenience of buying a GPS device that can easily tap into an incalculably expensive system and show us where we are and how to get to where we want to be. (Of course, you and I also helped pay for the entire GPS system with our tax dollars.)

Though your GPS device will be extremely accurate the great majority of the time, experts tell us that a few things can impede accuracy.

- Bad atmospheric conditions can mess things up. But most of the time, the atmospheric conditions are not a big concern.

- If you are downtown, a GPS signal could reflect off of buildings, and that could confuse your GPS receiver. Dense foliage can also impede the signal and cause an error.

- Every once in a while, there could be an orbital error in one of the satellites. However, GPS technicians are constantly monitoring and aligning them.

- Older GPS devices often do not work if you are indoors, underwater, or underground. If you go through a tunnel, you will probably lose the signal.

- The geometry between different satellites can, on occasion, become less than optimal. (It is best for them to be at wide angles relative to each other.) If this happens, things will not function right on your GPS receiver. Again, however, the GPS technicians keep an eye on all this, and course corrections are made to keep the satellites on track.

- Finally, apparently, the U.S. Department of Defense can intentionally degrade the GPS signal so enemy combatants cannot use the system to attack us.

ABUSES OF THE SYSTEM

GPS technology has many obvious benefits, but it could possibly be adapted for evil purposes. Most newer smartphones have built-in GPS technology. This can enable emergency personnel to find you in the event that you call 911 and then pass out. As well, several companies, such as AT&T Wireless, also offer services in which family members can log on to a website to track where a phone's location is. (Parents might want to know where their teenage children are, for example.) It does not take much imagination, however, to figure out how such technologies could also be used for devious purposes, including stalking.

One article published in *Popular Science* grabbed my attention: "Every Step You Take...Every Move You Make...My GPS Unit Will Be Watching You." Underneath the title, we read the following ominous words: "Technology may be ushering in a golden age of stalking, in which predators use GPS, cell phones, and other devices to track and terrorize."[4]

In this article, author Michael Rosenwald documents a man and a woman near Boulder, Colorado, who divorced after years of marriage. During the time of the divorce proceedings, the husband came across an advertisement for the TravelEyes Tracking Unit, which, once installed in a car, could enable a computer user to track its every move. He purchased the device and then invited his wife to his house to talk about the divorce proceedings. While they were chatting inside, he had his sons go outside to change oil in the car she was driving—and secretly install the unit.

This man was later brought up on stalking charges. In court, one of the sons testified that he installed the unit in her car, hidden away from plain sight, using Velcro. It turned out to be a simple installation, especially for techno-savvy teenagers.

How did the wife catch on? After she had moved out of the house, the husband suddenly appeared and confronted her, asking her why she had been at a particular place for 30 minutes. After a number of such interrogations, she said she started to look over her shoulder but never saw any sign of him.

She eventually moved to a new home and tried to keep the location a secret. "I had just been there half an hour, starting to take the few things I had with me into the duplex, and he came to the door and made some threats," she recalled during his stalking trial. "I didn't know that he knew where I was moving to. I had been real cautious, trying to make sure nobody was following me—watching in my rearview mirror, taking alternate routes to get places, going to a different grocery store."

She began to feel paranoid. She looked in her purse to see if there was a bug. On the witness stand, she gave this testimony:

> To know somebody knows where you are every second of
> the day and how many seconds you are at each stoplight

and to yet not know how they were able to figure it out—it's a frightening feeling…You are always constantly being watched and under surveillance. It gave me stomachaches; it made me not sleep really well. It's not a comfortable feeling.[5]

The husband also often harassed his wife on the phone. She eventually went to the police. While there, her phone rang again. It was him. A police officer took the phone and asked him to come in. While there, he admitted to having installed a GPS device in his car. He claimed it was not illegal at all, for he was the owner of the car his wife was driving around. That was technically true, but the police officer pointed out that using such technology to harass his wife was illegal, so he was charged with stalking. As a result of his trial, he was found guilty, and the judge in the case commented on how frightening it would be for *any* person to feel they were being monitored 24/7 without knowing how it was being done.

The stalker received a three-year suspended sentence, serving 57 days in jail and then being on probation for four years—what amounts to a slap on the wrist. Many people believe the laws against such crimes need to be substantially stiffened.

Rosenwald says that in this case, "we are faced with a classic technology dilemma, as perfectly legal and useful devices are turned to less savory ends."[6] Such GPS technology has been a great benefit in many ways, including tracking rental cars, Alzheimer's patients, children who wander off, cattle on large farms, and the like. But the same technology can be used by high-tech stalkers.

In the old days, stalkers had to do things the hard way—they had to be in the physical vicinity of their victims. That is no longer the case. GPS technology is readily available and can be installed by stealth. Also, anyone's complete address history is available on the Internet for the cost of a single dinner. And for even less money, anyone can download aerial satellite photos of a person's neighborhood. Technology has made things much easier for today's stalkers. In fact, if you type *track* and *spouse* into Google, you will find a list of high-tech services that will track and catch your cheating spouse.

Stalkers can often engage in their deviousness without being caught in the act. (Most are not as obnoxiously aggressive as the husband described above.) Because many such high-tech stalkers are not caught, law enforcement officials are unsure how many of them actually exist.

Some stalkers take things a step further. They launch secretive cyber attacks against their victims—perhaps sending an e-mail saying, "You've received a postcard from Sarah Johnson" if the victim actually knows a Sarah Johnson. (The stalker can potentially derive this personal information off the victim's Facebook account.) Once the victim clicks on the link in the e-mail, a bogus postcard from Sarah pops up, and malware is downloaded to the victim's computer that enables the stalker to watch every single keystroke, including all of the victim's e-mails, banking transactions, and online credit card transactions.

Some high-tech stalkers manage to gain access to the victim's property while the victim is not home. In some cases, law enforcement personnel have reported that sprinkler heads in the lawn have been replaced with new sprinkler heads that also have microcameras on them. Moreover, some high-tech stalkers who have gained access to victims' houses replace smoke detectors with new smoke detectors that have microcameras. These camera images are then transmitted to the stalker. (I cannot imagine what kind of person would be sick enough to do such things, but law enforcement officers assure us that some people do.)

BIG BUSINESS

A huge market has emerged for products that rob victims of privacy. Some companies actually market the products by saying they are designed to help you spy on your spouse. One Internet store is described as a "7-Eleven for jealous mates." The store offers all kinds of GPS devices and spy cameras—such as clock radios with cameras in them—to enable people to keep an ever-present eye on others. A GPS device similar to the one used in the husband-wife case mentioned above retails for almost $500.

Some of these clock radios have been purchased at a discount from Walmart and then altered by installing a microcamera. Then they are sold at a greatly increased price ($379), which many people are willing to pay. The spy camera is advertised to take high-quality images even in low-light conditions, such as a bedroom.

Such spy stores also sell countermeasure devices so users can detect whether cameras or bugs are being used against them. Business at such stores is brisk.

NEW PRODUCT LINES

New products with hidden GPS components continue to be developed. Some wristwatches have GPS microtechnology hidden in them. One could easily give such a wristwatch to someone as a gift and then track that person's whereabouts on a computer. Some pens contain microcameras and transmitters. Many privacy advocates are understandably concerned about the wide variety of such products hitting the marketplace.[7]

CONCLUSION

Many have pointed out that technology in itself is neutral—that is, it is neither good nor bad. But modern technologies can be used for good or for evil, to do good things or bad things. Modern technologies make it much easier for perpetrators to do bad things without getting caught. This might entice would-be criminals to accelerate down the path of evil far faster than they would have without such technologies.

Might such technologies be used against Christians by the forces of the antichrist in the end times during the future tribulation period? I will make that precise case later in the book.

PART 3

THE ROLE OF CYBER TECHNOLOGIES IN END-TIMES BIBLE PROPHECY

CYBER ECONOMICS AND OUR COMING CASHLESS SOCIETY

We are headed toward a cashless society. The technologies in place today will no doubt be utilized by the forces of the antichrist to bring about this cashless reality. To be sure, the text of Scripture does not come right out and say that the world in the end times will be cashless, but this is a clear and unmistakable inference in prophetic Scripture.

In Revelation 13, we read about two beasts: the antichrist and the false prophet. This diabolical duo will subjugate the entire world so that no one can buy or sell who does not receive the mark of the beast. We read that the false prophet...

> causes all, both small and great, both rich and poor, both free and slave, to be marked on the right hand or the forehead, so that no one can buy or sell unless he has the mark, that is, the name of the beast or the number of its name. This calls for wisdom: let the one who has understanding calculate the number of the beast, for it is the number of a man, and his number is 666 (verses 16-18).

Clearly, the book of Revelation reveals that the false prophet will force people to worship the antichrist, the man of sin. His "squeeze play"—demanding the mark of the beast on people worldwide—will effectively force them to make the following choice: Either receive the mark of the beast and worship the antichrist, or starve because you cannot buy or sell.

Later, in Revelation 14:1, we read, "Then I looked, and behold, on Mount Zion stood the Lamb, and with him 144,000 who had his [the Lamb, Jesus Christ's] name and his Father's name written on their foreheads." It would seem that the antichrist's mark is a parody of God's sealing of the 144,000 witnesses of Revelation 7 and 14. Prophecy experts Thomas Ice and Timothy Demy make this suggestion: "God's seal of His witnesses most likely is invisible and for the purpose of protection from the antichrist. On the other hand, antichrist offers protection from the wrath of God—a promise he cannot deliver—and his mark is visible and external." They note, "For the only time in history, an outward indication will identify those who reject Christ and His gospel of forgiveness of sins."[1] Receiving this mark is a serious business, as we read in Revelation 14:9-10.

> If anyone worships the beast and its image and receives a mark on his forehead or on his hand, he also will drink the wine of God's wrath, poured full strength into the cup of his anger, and he will be tormented with fire and sulfur in the presence of the holy angels and in the presence of the Lamb.

We are likewise told in Revelation 16:2, "The first angel went and poured out his bowl on the earth, and harmful and painful sores came upon the people who bore the mark of the beast and worshiped its image."

Such words are sobering. Any who express loyalty to the antichrist and his cause will suffer the wrath of our holy and just God. How awful it will be for these to experience the full force of God's divine anger and unmitigated vengeance! (See Psalm 75:8; Isaiah 51:17; Jeremiah 25:15-16.) Revelation 20:4 tells us, by contrast, that believers in the Lord Jesus Christ refuse the mark of the beast.

> I saw the souls of those who had been beheaded for the testimony of Jesus and for the word of God, and who had not

worshiped the beast or its image and had not received its mark on their foreheads or their hands. They came to life and reigned with Christ for a thousand years.

WHAT IS THE MARK?

What kind of mark will be placed on human beings? Apparently, people in that day will somehow be branded, just as animals today are branded—and just as slaves were once branded by their slave owners. We cannot be certain how the number 666 relates to this personage or the mark.

Bible interpreters have offered many suggestions as to the meaning of 666 down through the centuries. A popular theory is that inasmuch as 7 is the number of perfection, and 777 reflects the perfect Trinity, perhaps 666 points to a being who aspires to perfect deity (like the Trinity) but never attains it. (In reality, the antichrist is ultimately just a man, though influenced—and possibly indwelt—by Satan.)

Others have suggested that perhaps the number refers to a specific man—such as the Roman emperor Nero. It is suggested that the numerical value of the letters in the Hebrew translation of Nero's name is 666. Some suggest that the antichrist will be a man *like* Nero of old. Of course, all this is highly speculative. The truth is, Scripture does not clearly define what is meant by 666. Interpreting this verse involves some guesswork.

One thing is certain. In some way that is presently unknown to us, this number will be a crucial part of his identification. It is sobering to realize that receiving this mark of the beast is apparently an unpardonable sin (Revelation 14:9-10). The decision to receive the mark is an irreversible decision. Once made, there is no turning back.

Receiving the mark reveals an implicit approval of the antichrist's leadership and his purpose. No one takes this mark as an accident. One must choose to do so, with all the facts on the table. The choice will be deliberate and will have eternal consequences. Those who choose to receive the mark will do so with the full knowledge of what they have done.

The choice will cause a radical polarization. There is no possible middle ground. One chooses either for or against the antichrist, for or against God. Today, people think they can avoid God and His demands on their lives by feigning neutrality, but no such neutrality will be possible during the tribulation, for one's very survival will be determined by a decision for or against God. One must choose to either receive the mark and live (being able to buy and sell) or reject the mark and face suffering and death. One must choose to follow the antichrist and eat well or reject the antichrist and starve.

In the pages that follow, I will examine some current ideas of prophecy scholars on the mark of the beast and its relationship to the global economy. I will then relate my findings to the coming cashless society that will surely emerge during the future tribulation period.

THE MARK OF THE BEAST: A COMMERCE PASSPORT

The mark of the beast will be a commerce passport during the future tribulation period. Prophecy scholar Arnold Fruchtenbaum expands on this idea.

> [The mark of the beast] will be given to all who submit themselves to the authority of the antichrist and accept him as god. The mark will serve as a passport for business... They will be able to neither buy nor sell anything unless they have the mark...Only those who have this number will be permitted to work, to buy, to sell, or simply to make a living.[2]

This mark will apparently be required during the second half of the tribulation period.

Prophecy scholar Mark Hitchcock suggests that there is ancient historical precedence for such a mark. For example, he points to Ezekiel 9:4: "The LORD said to him, 'Pass through the city, through Jerusalem, and put a mark on the foreheads of the men who sigh and groan over all the abominations that are committed in it.'" In this context, the mark on the forehead was one of preservation, just as blood marked the Israelites' doorposts and spared them from death during the tenth plague that was inflicted on the Egyptians (see Exodus 12:21-29).[3]

Such a mark was also used in connection with pagans and false deities in ancient times. Robert Thomas explains it this way:

> The mark must be some sort of branding similar to that given soldiers, slaves, and temple devotees in John's day. In Asia Minor, devotees of pagan religions delighted in the display of such a tattoo as an emblem of ownership by a certain god. In Egypt, Ptolemy Philopator I branded Jews, who submitted to registration, with an ivy leaf in recognition of their Dionysian worship (cf. 3 Mace. 2:29). This meaning resembles the long-time practice of carrying signs to advertise religious loyalties (cf. Isa. 44:5) and follows the habit of branding slaves with the name or special mark of their owners (cf. Gal. 6:17). *Charagma* ("mark") was a [Greek] term for the images or names of emperors on Roman coins, so it fittingly could apply to the beast's emblem put on people.[4]

John MacArthur makes a similar note.

> In the Roman Empire, this was a normal identifying symbol, or brand, that slaves and soldiers bore on their bodies. Some of the ancient mystical cults delighted in such tattoos, which identified members with a form of worship. The antichrist will have a similar requirement, one that will need to be visible on the hand or forehead.[5]

THE FALSE PROPHET: AN ECONOMIC AND RELIGIOUS LEADER

Prophetic Scripture reveals that the false prophet will be a leader of both economics and religion. These two domains will become merged so that one depends on the other during the future tribulation. The mark of the beast ties them together. As David Jeremiah puts it, "The mark will allow the antichrist's followers to buy and sell because it identifies them as religiously orthodox—submissive followers of the beast and worshipers of his image. Those without the mark are forbidden to buy because they are identified as traitors."[6] So, though receiving the mark is essentially a spiritual decision, it will have life-and-death economic consequences.

THE MARK ITSELF IS NOT HIGH TECHNOLOGY

Please note this very important point. Though modern technology will enable the antichrist and false prophet to bring about a cashless society and control all commerce on earth, we must differentiate between this technology and the mark of the beast, for the technology itself is not the mark. I make this point because a number of prophecy expositors have claimed that the mark will be a chip inserted under the skin, a barcode on the hand or the forehead, some kind of universal product code, or some other such technology.

This is not the case. The mark itself will identify allegiance to the antichrist, but that is separate and distinct from the technology that enables him to enforce his economic system. My former prophecy mentor John F. Walvoord comments on how technology will pave the way for such economic control, based on whether or not people have received the mark.

> There is no doubt that with today's technology, a world ruler, who is in total control, would have the ability to keep a continually updated census of all living persons and know day-by-day precisely which people had pledged their allegiance to him and received the mark and which had not.[7]

Having said that, it is also highly likely that "chip implants, scan technology, and biometrics will be used as tools to enforce his policy that one cannot buy or sell without the mark."[8]

In keeping with this, notice that this mark will be *on* people, not *in* them (like some kind of microchip). It will be on the right hand or head and will be plainly visible (perhaps like a tattoo), not hidden beneath the skin. It will be universally rejected by Christians but universally accepted by non-Christians.

END-TIMES INFLATION AND FAMINE

I would be remiss to discuss the economics of the end times without noting the prophetic revelation that the tribulation will include war, severe inflation, and famine. People will be strongly yearning for some-one to emerge to take leadership who can solve these and other prob-lems. That person will be the antichrist. As a backdrop, let us briefly consider the four horsemen of the apocalypse.

The First Horseman

The four horsemen of the apocalypse relate to the seal judgments that are poured out on humankind during the tribulation (see Revela-tion 6). We first see a person riding a white horse (6:2). Some have spec-ulated that perhaps the rider is Jesus Christ because He rides a white horse in Revelation 19:11. However, the contexts are entirely different. In Revelation 19 Christ returns to the earth as a conqueror on a horse at the end of the tribulation. By contrast, Revelation 6 deals with a rider on a horse at the beginning of the tribulation, he is joined by three other horses and their riders, and they are all associated with the seal judgments. Most scholars believe the rider of the white horse in Revela-tion 6:2 is none other than the antichrist (Daniel 9:26). The crown sug-gests that the individual is a ruler. The bow without an arrow signifies that the antichrist's world government will be accomplished without warfare. His government seems to begin with a time of peace, but it is short-lived, for destruction will surely follow (see 1 Thessalonians 5:3).

The Second Horseman

The second horse, mentioned in Revelation 6:3-4, is red—a color that represents bloodshed, killing with the sword, and war (see also Matthew 24:6-7). The rider carries a large sword. These verses sym-bolize that man's efforts at bringing about peace will be utterly frus-trated, for peace will be taken from the entire earth. As bad as this will be, however, it will only represent the initial birth pangs of what is yet to come upon the earth (see Matthew 24:8; Mark 13:7-8; Luke 21:9). Of course, history tells us that war always brings economic instability and food shortages.

The Third Horseman

The third horse, mentioned in Revelation 6:5-6, is black. The rider is carrying a pair of scales in his hand. This apparently symbolizes famine (with subsequent death) as prices for wheat and barley soar extravagantly high, requiring a full day's wages just to buy a few meals (see Lamentations 5:8-10). Such a famine would be expected following global war.

There will be runaway inflation during this time. The buying power of money will drop dramatically, as John Walvoord explains.

> To put it in ordinary language, the situation would be such that one would have to spend a day's wages for a loaf of bread with no money left to buy anything else. The symbolism therefore indicates a time of economic devastation and famine when life will be reduced to the barest necessities. [9]

Things will get so bad that people will be looking to anyone who can solve the dilemma, and that someone will be the antichrist.

Black is an appropriate color here, for it points to the lamentation and sorrow that naturally accompanies extreme deprivation. That black can represent hunger is illustrated for us in Lamentations 4:8-9: "Now their face is blacker than soot; they are not recognized in the streets; their skin has shriveled on their bones; it has become as dry as wood. Happier were the victims of the sword than the victims of hunger, who wasted away, pierced by lack of the fruits of the field."

Such famine is in keeping with Jesus' own words regarding the end times. He affirmed that the first three birth pangs of the end times will be false messiahs, war, and famine (Matthew 24:5-7). Some of this famine will be due to the outbreak of war (the second horse), but some famine may also relate to the fact that those who refuse to take the mark of the beast will not be permitted to buy or sell, which means they will have much less food than everyone else. As economic outcasts, believers during the tribulation will experience much hunger. These will be black days indeed.

The Fourth Horseman

A fourth horse, mentioned in Revelation 6:7-8, is pale—literally, "yellowish green," the color of a corpse. The rider of this horse is appropriately named Death. The death symbolized here seems to be the natural consequence of the previous three judgments. The death toll will be catastrophic—a fourth of earth's population.

Woe to those who dwell on the earth during this time!

THE JUDGMENT OF THE NATIONS

Another issue that relates to end-time economics is the judgment of the nations, which takes place after the tribulation. This judgment directly relates to the fact that one will not be able to buy or sell in the tribulation period without receiving the mark of the beast (Revelation 13:16-17). I am referring specifically to the "brothers" mentioned in connection with the judgment of the nations in Matthew 25:31-46.

> When the Son of Man comes in his glory, and all the angels with him, then he will sit on his glorious throne. Before him will be gathered all the nations, and he will separate people one from another as a shepherd separates the sheep from the goats. And he will place the sheep on his right, but the goats on the left. Then the King will say to those on his right, "Come, you who are blessed by my Father, inherit the kingdom prepared for you from the foundation of the world. For I was hungry and you gave me food, I was thirsty and you gave me drink, I was a stranger and you welcomed me, I was naked and you clothed me, I was sick and you visited me, I was in prison and you came to me." Then the righteous will answer him, saying, "Lord, when did we see you hungry and feed you, or thirsty and give you drink? And when did we see you a stranger and welcome you, or naked and clothe you? And when did we see you sick or in prison and visit you?" And the King will answer them, "Truly, I say to you, as you did it to one of the least of these my brothers, you did it to me."

> Then he will say to those on his left, "Depart from me, you cursed, into the eternal fire prepared for the devil and his angels. For I was hungry and you gave me no food, I was thirsty and you gave me no drink, I was a stranger and you did not welcome me, naked and you did not clothe me,

sick and in prison and you did not visit me." Then they also will answer, saying, "Lord, when did we see you hungry or thirsty or a stranger or naked or sick or in prison, and did not minister to you?" Then he will answer them, saying, "Truly, I say to you, as you did not do it to one of the least of these, you did not do it to me." And these will go away into eternal punishment, but the righteous into eternal life.

Notice the basis of the judgment of these people. One's destiny—entering Christ's kingdom or entering into punishment—hinges on how one treated Christ's brothers. Who are these brothers? A comparison of this passage with the details of the tribulation as recorded in Revelation 4–19 suggests the possibility that the term *brothers* may be referring to the 144,000 mentioned in Revelation 7, Christ's Jewish brothers who bear witness of Him during the tribulation. Bible expositor Stan Toussaint, one of my former professors at Dallas Theological Seminary, notes, "It seems best to say that 'brothers of Mine' is a designation of the godly remnant of Israel that will proclaim the gospel of the kingdom unto every nation of the world."[10] Bible expositor Merrill F. Unger writes this concerning the brothers:

> They are Jews saved by the preaching of "the gospel of the kingdom" after the Rapture of the church (Mt. 24:14). During the tribulation period, God will sovereignly call and save 144,000 Jews…So glorious and wonderful will be the ministry of the 144,000 saved Jews and so faithful will be their powerful testimony, the King on His throne of glory will not be ashamed to call them "My brothers." More than that, He will consider Himself so intimately united to them that what was done or not done to them is the same as being actually done or not done to Himself…
>
> The fact that the Lord's brothers endured hunger, thirst, homelessness, nakedness, sickness, and imprisonment suggests their fidelity to their newfound Savior and Lord. They proved their willingness to suffer for Him amid the terrible persecutions and trials of the tribulation through which

they passed. They proved their loyalty to their King. He attests His identity with them.[11]

Bible expositor J. Dwight Pentecost, another of my former professors at Dallas Theological Seminary, agrees.

> That phrase [*my brothers*] may refer to…the 144,000 of Revelation 7, who will bear witness of Him during the Tribulation. Such ones will be under a death sentence by the beast. They will refuse to carry the beast's mark, and so they will not be able to buy and sell. Consequently, they will have to depend on those to whom they minister for hospitality, food, and support. Only those who receive the message will jeopardize their lives by extending hospitality to the messengers. Therefore what is done for them will be an evidence of their faith in Christ, that is, what is done for them will be done for Christ.[12]

Bible scholar Herman Hoyt also agrees, noting that "an unconverted person would not risk his life to befriend a Jew during the great tribulation; these acts of mercy are therefore evidence of salvation."[13] *The Bible Knowledge Commentary* provides this summary:

> The expression "these brothers" must refer to a third group that is neither sheep nor goats. The only possible group would be Jews, physical brothers of the Lord. In view of the distress in the Tribulation period, it is clear that any believing Jew will have a difficult time surviving (cf. 24:15-21). The forces of the world dictator will be doing everything possible to exterminate all Jews (cf. Rev. 12:17). A Gentile going out of his way to assist a Jew in the Tribulation will mean that Gentile has become a believer in Jesus Christ during the Tribulation. By such a stand and action, a believing Gentile will put his life in jeopardy. His works will not save him; but his works will reveal that he is redeemed.[14]

So then, here is the main point: Prophetic Scripture reveals that even though the antichrist and the false prophet will wield economic control over the world during the tribulation period, God will still be at work. Indeed, God's redeemed will come to the aid of Christ's Jewish brethren as they bear witness to Christ all around the world. Many will still suffer famine and many will die, but there will be a great harvest of souls during this time.

THE COMING GLOBAL CEO

We are currently witnessing major steps toward globalism. We see banks merging and financial regulations becoming more centralized. Even in the United States, we have witnessed steps away from national sovereignty and toward globalist solutions to problems. Is the antichrist waiting in the wings, ready to fill his role as the ultimate CEO of the end times and to control the world and its economy?

When he emerges on the scene in the tribulation, the world will embrace him with open arms. He will appear to have solutions to many of the problems that afflict humankind. He will promise stability and order, and he will appear to have the power and wisdom to follow through. But then his iron hand will fall on humanity, and during the last half of the tribulation, a policy will be enforced in which no one will be able to buy or sell without taking his mark.

The antichrist and his team will no doubt use the technology that is now in place to enforce his global dominion for the world's money. We are headed toward a cashless society, made possible by today's technologies, including biometrics, radio frequency identification, smart cards, and the like.

THE ANTICHRIST IS NOT IDENTIFIED IN OUR DAY

We do not currently know who the antichrist is. The antichrist will emerge during the future tribulation period, which follows the rapture of the church.[15] For this reason, Christians today should not be about the business of trying to identify the antichrist. Christians will be long gone before his identity is revealed.

A CASHLESS SOCIETY ON THE HORIZON

Certain aspects of our society are already cashless. If you take a flight on American Airlines, as I do dozens of times each year, flight attendants will offer you sandwiches, but you cannot use cash. "American Airlines has gone cashless," travelers are informed. Other airlines have also gone cashless, including Southwest, Alaska Airlines, JetBlue, AirTran, Virgin America, and Midwest Airlines.

On toll roads, smart technologies automatically charge credit cards or bank accounts so drivers don't have to stop for cash transactions at tollbooths. It all happens behind the scenes, and people are not even cognizant of the instant financial transactions that take place as they traverse those toll roads. Note this comment by Joel Kurtzman, executive editor of the *Harvard Business Review*.

> Few people realize that money, in the traditional sense, has met its demise. Fewer still have paused to reflect on the implications of that fact...[Money is] no longer a thing, an object you can dig up at the beach or search for behind the cushions of a sofa; it is a system. Money is a network that comprises hundreds of thousands of computers of every type, wired together in places as lofty as the Federal Reserve—which settles accounts between banks every night that are worth trillions of dollars—and as mundane as the thousands of gas pumps around the world outfitted to take credit and debit cards.[16]

Meanwhile, economists tell us that the amount of real cash in circulation continues to wane. In fact, the amount of cash being used today is about half that used in the 1970s. Why is this so? Because more and more people are using cashless options, such as credit and debit cards. That is the wave of the future. Even checks today are often read by scanners that instantly transfer money from your bank account to the vendors to whom you write the checks.

More than 70 percent of all consumer payments are now electronic. Meanwhile, the writing of checks continues to plummet. More than 2 billion credit cards are in use in the United States alone. "There are about seven credit cards for every person over the age of 15. The nature of how we pay for things is already changing drastically, but this is just a fraction of what's to come."[17]

Robert Samuelson, an economic columnist for the *Washington Post*, makes a similar affirmation. "The long-predicted 'cashless society' has quietly arrived, or nearly so. Electronic money is cheaper than cash or checks…[and] it is more convenient…We have crossed a cultural as well as an economic threshold when plastic and money are synonymous."[18] And here's the perspective of Peter Ayliffe, the chief executive of Visa in Europe:

> Paying for goods with [dollars] and coins could be consigned to history within five years…and some retailers could soon start surcharging customers if they choose to buy products with cash…It is likely that in the near future, no actual money will exchange hands at all. Even your paycheck will be electronically credited to your bank account, like that of 83 percent of all Social Security recipients—if it isn't already.[19]

MODERN TECHNOLOGIES AND THE FULFILLMENT OF BIBLICAL PROPHECY

Bible prophecies are often quite specific, but people living during the time of the prophets usually had no awareness of the providential circumstances that would one day emerge to bring about the fulfillment of those prophecies. For example, Micah 5:2 prophesied that the Messiah would be born in Bethlehem. But Joseph and Mary lived in Nazareth—why would they be in Bethlehem? Luke 2:1 gives us the answer: "In those days a decree went out from Caesar Augustus that all the world should be registered." Luke 2:3 then tells us that people had to register for this census in their original hometown. Bethlehem is Joseph's hometown. While they were in Bethlehem at government request, Mary gave birth to Jesus. But in Micah's day, people had no idea that this government census would enable the prophecy to be fulfilled. Only God Himself knew that detail.

We might say the same thing about Zechariah 12:10, which speaks of the Messiah as "him whom they have pierced." But how would the Messiah be pierced? This prophecy was written hundreds of years before crucifixion was Rome's chosen method of execution. So people in Zechariah's day were unaware of the providential circumstances that would one day emerge to bring about the fulfillment of that prophecy (execution by crucifixion).

Likewise, when the Bible predicts a one-world economy under the antichrist's control in the tribulation period, it doesn't mention computers or cyberspace or the Internet or biometrics. But clearly these new technologies, for the first time in human history, make it possible for these prophecies to be fulfilled. Now all becomes clear.

It now seems apparent that a cashless system will be the means by which the antichrist will control who can buy or sell. After all, if the world economy were still cash-based, people anywhere who possessed cash could still buy and sell. It would be impossible for the antichrist to enforce who can buy or sell in such a cash-based society. Only in a cashless world—with a centralized electronic transaction system, where all is controlled electronically—would such control be possible.

> It is becoming increasingly apparent that today's developing cashless system will become the instrument through which the antichrist will seek to control all who buy or sell, based upon whether they are a follower of Jesus Christ or a follower of the European ruler, and thus, Satan. It is obvious that any leader wanting to control the world's economy would avail themselves of the power that an electronic cashless system holds as a tool for implementing total control. [20]

Someone once said that prophetic events cast their shadows before them. David Jeremiah explains:

> We are on the cutting edge of having all the technology that the antichrist and false prophet would need to wire this world together for their evil purposes. Right now it is well within the range of possibility for a centralized power to gain worldwide control of all banking and purchasing...As we see things that are prophesied for the tribulation period beginning to take shape right now, we are made aware of the fact that surely the Lord's return is not far off. [21]

BIOMETRICS AND CHIPS

Biometrics, discussed earlier in the book, is increasingly being implemented for tighter security. Israel's airport is presently testing its biometric security system to supposedly make air travel safer and security screening more efficient. The new system creates a personal smart card for each participating traveler by scanning his or her passport, fingerprints, and facial image in a one-time registration process. Checkpoints are scattered throughout the airport. The first one scans people's passports and smart cards to verify their identities. Once cleared, travelers go to a machine with a touch screen, where they answer some security questions. Following that, the smart card is scanned at luggage, check-in, and carry-on checkpoints. Such technology might indeed make things faster and safer, but there is also great potential for this technology to be abused so that individuals lose personal control and privacy (as will happen under the antichrist during the tribulation).

RFID CHIPS AND TAGS

Small chips can now be injected or implanted beneath the surface of the skin—say, in the fatty part of the palm—so that wherever people go, the information stored in that chip is accessible. Such RFID (Radio Frequency Identification) chips consist of micro integrated circuitry that records and processes data, as well as an antenna that can receive or transmit a signal. Financial data stored on such a chip would make it easy to simply wave the hand to pay for a bus fare, a toll fare, or a product in a store.

Kevin Warwick, professor of cybernetics at England's University of Reading, is distinguished as the first person on the earth to be voluntarily implanted with such a chip. This chip enables him to transmit signals to the university's communication system. The device is only three millimeters wide and 23 millimeters long.[22] These chips can be implanted in a variety of convenient items.

> Many military intelligence agencies, government agencies, and large corporations have introduced sophisticated security systems requiring employees to wear a badge

containing a radio frequency identification microchip. This RFID chip enables companies, agencies, and organizations to monitor the location and activity of every worker during every moment that he or she is on the premises... RFID scanners can be imbedded in the ceilings, floors, and doorways of buildings in order to monitor the movements of people inside. [23]

Such technology used to be considered unattainable—the stuff of fantasy. In our day, however, the technology for all this already exists. One might therefore surmise that this may be among the technologies that will be used during the antichrist's end-times economic global order. Again, the one thing that will make possible the antichrist's economic control over people in the end times is that the world will be cashless. All your bank data will be stored on RFID chips. If you have the mark of the beast, bank transactions and purchases will be electronically enabled for your account. If you do not have the mark of the beast, bank transactions and purchases will be electronically disallowed. The technology will make it easy for the antichrist to maintain economic control over the world.

CELL PHONES

As noted previously, smartphones will reinforce the trend away from cash. Your cell phone may well be your digital wallet of the future, for it will probably have an implanted RFID chip with all your bank account information. People generally have their cell phones with them 24/7, so this seems to be an ideal means of making purchases. Shoppers merely need to hold their phones over an item in order to purchase it. The purchase is confirmed by entering a quick pin number—no need to go stand in line at a checkout. The purchase is a completed transaction.

RFID chips (and GPS technology) in cell phones will surely be part and parcel of the technology used in the end times to enforce a globalized economy. Those who have the mark of the beast will be allowed to make such easy and automated purchases, but those without the mark will not.

Because of such technologies, our world is rapidly becoming more and more interdependent and globalized. And virtually every aspect of our lives—making purchases, investments, communications, travel, and more—are technology dependent. But the more we depend on technology, the easier we can be controlled by it. And that is precisely where we are headed—toward a techno-world ruled by the antichrist.

SUPERCOMPUTERS

Science fiction shows created in the 1970s are laughable now. By the 1990s, home computers were much faster than the computer portrayed on the original Star Ship Enterprise, which displayed green words about as fast as an old teletype machine. The Enterprise computer appears even more comical compared to the super-fast computers that exist today. Current computing speeds are hard to describe in words. IBM has developed a supercomputer—the Sequoia—that can do 20,000 trillion calculations per second. How fast is that? Well, look at it this way: If you had billions of people on earth all using electronic calculators to work together on one massive calculation—and they were all working 24/7, 365 days a year—they would take more than 300 years to do what Sequoia does in an hour.[24] Of course, technology is now exploding so fast that in ten years, the equivalent of my MacBook Pro might be able to do that!

The obvious application is that plenty of computer power is currently available to control a global economy. We do not need to invent anything new to make it all possible. The technology that exists today is more than sufficient for the antichrist's future control of the world.

ADVANTAGES OF GOING CASHLESS

Technological advances almost always makes things easier. Calling someone on a telephone is easier than yelling down the street. Going to the store is easier in a car than on foot. Flushing a toilet is easier than using an outhouse. Air conditioners are much more comforting than handheld fans. Likewise, going cashless is easier and more convenient than carrying around paper bills and coinage. Consider some of the other benefits of going cashless.

- Very few places will not accept credit or debit cards. The great majority of grocery store purchases are now put on cards. Internet purchases are put on cards. Many bills are paid for through online banking. Cashless options are already widely available because they are so convenient, and that will only increase in the future.

- At present, more than $100 million of counterfeit money is removed from circulation by federal authorities every year. Once society goes entirely cashless, counterfeiting will become a thing of the past.

- Cash that has been circulating who knows where can carry all kinds of germs. Who knows what disease has contaminated the ten-dollar bill the cashier just handed you at Target? *Scientific American* tells us that dollar bills can be veritable reservoirs for flu viruses—and such viruses can survive on the dollar bill for as long as 17 days.[25] Going cashless would stop the transfer of all those germs.

- We sometimes lose our wallets or our purses. When that happens, we lose the cash inside them. That would no longer happen in a cashless society. Canceling and replacing a lost smart card is easy.

- Intelligent vending machines are easy to use—just wave your RFID-enabled credit card in front of the machine, and *voila*, your purchase is complete. Tax fraud could become a thing of the past in a cashless society. The government could already have an exact record of virtually all of your income and expenditures.

- Finally, some say, going cashless (and paperless) would save time and trees!

I FEEL A CHILL COMING ON

What is your reaction to our trend toward a cashless society? How does it make you feel? I have had enough computer crashes—and I know enough about cyber crimes—that this whole proposition makes me feel very uneasy. If little computer systems can crash and be manipulated, so can bigger computer systems. And the bigger they are, the bigger they fall.

To add balance, however, I should probably repeat something I said earlier in the book. Though these technologies will enable the antichrist to gain economic control over a cashless world in the tribulation, these technologies are not evil. They can be used for good or for evil, so they are morally neutral. It is fine for you to use smart phones and credit cards and online banking and the like. Simply recognize, however, that the stage is now being set for what the ancient prophets predicted. These are unquestionably days for discernment.

A NEW WORLD?

Joel Kurtzman, in his book *The Death of Money*, says that the new electronic form of money is a game-changer—we are entering a new world.

> For the last twenty years or so, the world and its economy have been in the midst of a wrenching change. What has changed? *Money.* Not the dollars in our pockets or the coins in our hands. That money—tangible money, old-fashioned money—now accounts for only the tiniest fraction of all the money that is in circulation around the world today. It is a phantom form from the past, an anachronism. In its place, traveling the world incessantly without rest and nearly at the speed of light, is an entirely new form of money based not on metal or paper but on technology, mathematics, and science. And like Einstein's assumption that a photon of light creates the universe wherever it goes, this new "megabyte" money is creating a new and different world wherever it proceeds. [26]

Whether Kurtzman realizes it or not, the coming "new and different world" he speaks of will one day be headed by a mighty leader that the Bible calls the antichrist. The stage is now being set. As Tim LaHaye and Jerry Jenkins put it in their book *Are We Living in the End Times?*, "Mark-of-the-Beast technology is already here!" [27]

CYBER CONTROL AND THE EMERGENCE OF A GLOBAL GOVERNMENT

The prophetic Scriptures are clear that during the future seven-year tribulation period, a one-world government and a one-world economy will emerge, all under the leadership of the antichrist, in association with his first lieutenant, the false prophet. The technology required to run a globalized government and economy exists today. On many different levels, the stage appears to be set for what will transpire in the prophetic end times.

In the previous chapter, we saw how the antichrist will be able to control our coming cashless society. Now I will focus on the antichrist's rise to world dominion and his instigation of a one-world government. The first part of the chapter will be largely theological; in the latter part of the chapter, I will summarize how modern technologies will serve to make it all possible.

THE ANTICHRIST: A GLOBAL LEADER

Revelation 13:1-3 refers to the antichrist as a beast. He is personally empowered by the dragon, or Satan. Apparently, God chose the symbol of the beast to designate the vicious, predatory nature of the antichrist. This "man of lawlessness" (ESV and others) or "man of sin" (KJV, NKJV) will display an ungodly and anti-God character (2 Thessalonians 2:3-12). (Notice that sin *is* lawlessness—see 1 John 3:4.)

Sin and lawlessness are already at work in our own day (verse 7), but Paul indicated that in the future tribulation period, a specific individual will rise to power who will be the embodiment of sin and lawlessness (see also 1 John 2:18; Revelation 11:7; 13:1-10). This lawless one will lead the entire world into rebellion against God (2 Thessalonians 2:10). He will even exalt himself and oppose God by moving into the Jewish temple, declaring himself God, and demanding to be worshipped as God.

The antichrist will perform counterfeit signs and wonders and deceive many people during the future tribulation period (verses 9-10). This Satan-inspired individual will rise to political prominence in the tribulation, seek to dominate the world, attempt to destroy the Jews, persecute all true believers, and set up his own kingdom (Revelation 13). He will speak arrogant and boastful words in glorifying himself (2 Thessalonians 2:4).

The antichrist's assistant, the false prophet, will entice the world to worship the antichrist (Revelation 13:11-12). These three—Satan, the antichrist, and the false prophet—form a counterfeit trinity. People around the world will be forced to receive the mark of the beast, without which they cannot buy or sell. The antichrist will thereby control the global economy (verses 16-17). However, to receive this mark ensures one of being the recipient of God's wrath.

The antichrist will eventually rule the whole world (verse 7), with his headquarters in a revived Roman Empire (Revelation 17:8-9). He will seem to have all the answers for a troubled world. He will seem to be the solution to a world seemingly out of control. But his ultimate agenda is self-glorification.

In recent days, a flood of books and articles have been published that present speculative ideas about the antichrist. For example, some have argued that he will be a Jew. Others have argued that he will be a Muslim. Still others suggest he is one and the same as Gog, the leader of the Ezekiel invasion into Israel. Before addressing the coming one-world government and the technology that makes it possible, I will briefly address these alternative views of the antichrist, and summarize why I think they are unbiblical.

The Antichrist a Jew?

Some interpreters suggest that the antichrist will be a Jew. They point to an early tradition that the antichrist would come from the tribe of Dan (one of the 12 tribes of Israel). Some relate this to the fact that the tribe of Dan fell into deep apostasy and idolatry, creating for themselves a graven image (Judges 18:30). The Testament of Dan (5:6) names Satan as the prince of the tribe. Irenaeus, writing in the latter part of the second century, noted that the omission of Dan in the listing of tribes in Revelation 7 was due to a tradition that the antichrist was to come from that tribe (Adv. Haer. v.30.2.).

However, Revelation 13:1 pictures the antichrist rising up out of the sea. Scripture often uses the sea as a way to refer to the Gentile nations. According to *The Bible Knowledge Commentary*, "The fact that the beast comes out from the sea indicates that he is a Gentile, for the sea of humanity is involved as his source (Revelation 17:15)."[1] Revelation 17:15 tells us that "the waters that you saw…are peoples and multitudes and nations and languages" (in other words, Gentile peoples). Moreover, Antiochus Epiphanes—himself a Gentile—seems to typify the future antichrist in Daniel 11. Therefore, it seems unlikely the antichrist will be a Jew.

The Antichrist a Muslim?

More recently, many have claimed that the antichrist will be a Muslim. However, such a view has significant problems in terms of theological consistency. For one thing, Daniel 11:36 tells us the antichrist "shall exalt himself and magnify himself above every god." We also read in 2 Thessalonians 2:4 that the antichrist ultimately "opposes and exalts himself against every so-called god or object of worship, so that he takes his seat in the temple of God, proclaiming himself to be God." To say the least, the idea of a Muslim antichrist claiming to be God—exalting himself against every so-called god, presumably including Allah— would represent an absolute and heinous trashing of the Muslim creed, which affirms that "there is one God named Allah, and Muhammad is his prophet." No true Muslim would make any claim that he was God, especially over and against Allah. Just as it is anathema to Muslims to say Jesus is God incarnate or the Son of God, so it would be anathema to Muslims for any human to claim he was God. (Keep in mind that Muslims are radical monotheists.) A Muslim antichrist would thus be viewed as an infidel among Quran-believing Muslims.

Further, Islam teaches that Allah is so radically unlike any earthly reality—so transcendent and beyond anything in the finite realm—that he cannot be described using earthly terms. How, then, could a human Muslim antichrist claim to be God—a God described in earthly terms?

Moreover, why would a Muslim antichrist make a covenant with Israel (Daniel 9:24-27), guaranteeing Israel protection? Many evangelical expositors have believed that this covenant is what allows Israel to live in peace and safety so it can rebuild the Jewish temple. It seems hard to believe that a Muslim leader would protect Israel in this regard.

Is Gog the Antichrist?

Contrary to the assumptions of some today, Gog—the leader of the northern military coalition that will one day invade Israel (Ezekiel 38:1-6)—is not just another name for the antichrist. Bible interpreters will end up in prophetic chaos if they try to make this identification. The antichrist heads up a revived Roman empire (Daniel 2; 7), while Gog heads up an invasion force made up of Russia and a number of Muslim nations. Moreover, Gog's invasion into Israel constitutes a direct challenge to the antichrist's covenant with Israel (Daniel 9:27). Further, Gog's moment in the limelight is short-lived (it is all over when God destroys the invading force—Ezekiel 39), whereas the antichrist is in power over the span of a significant part of the tribulation (see Revelation 4–18). By allowing Scripture to interpret Scripture, it is impossible to identify Gog as the antichrist. (For more on Gog, see my book *Northern Storm Rising: Russia, Iran, and the Emerging End-Times Military Coalition Against Israel* [Harvest House, 2008].)

FAST FACTS ON THE ANTICHRIST

The Scriptures reveal many facts about the antichrist—his person and his agenda. In summary, the antichrist...

- is coming (1 John 2:18)
- is now restrained, apparently by the Holy Spirit
  (2 Thessalonians 2:6)
- will rise up out of the sea of Gentile nations
  (Revelation 13:1; 17:15)
- will be a beast, ferocious and predatory
  (Revelation 13:1-10)
- will be a commercial genius, heading up a one-world economy (Daniel 11:43; Revelation 13:16-17)
- will be an intellectual genius, solving many problems of
  the world (Daniel 8:23)
- will be a military genius, conquering other earthly leaders
  (Revelation 6:2; 13:2)
- will be an oratorical genius (Daniel 11:36)
- will be a political genius, rising to global prominence
  (Revelation 17:11-13)
- will be energized by Satan (2 Thessalonians 2:9)
- will perform counterfeit signs and wonders
  (2 Thessalonians 2:9-10)
- will be a man of lawlessness and sin
  (2 Thessalonians 2:1-10)
- will be a son of perdition, full of evil (2 Thessalonians 2:3)
- will initially emerge from a reunited Roman Empire
  (Daniel 7:8; 9:26)
- will head up this revived Roman Empire
  (Daniel 2; 7; Revelation 17:8-9)
- will make a covenant with Israel (Daniel 9:27)
- will gain global dominion during the tribulation
  (Revelation 13)

- will speak arrogant, boastful words (2 Thessalonians 2:4)
- will be worshipped by the inhabitants of the earth (Revelation 13:8,11-12)
- will deceive many worldwide (Revelation 19:20)
- will persecute Christians (Revelation 13:7)
- will be defeated by Jesus at the second coming (2 Thessalonians 2:8; Revelation 19:11-16)

Clearly, the antichrist plays a central role in the unfolding of Bible prophecy in the end times. He will one day rule the world.

A GLOBAL LEADER AND FALSE GOD

When the antichrist first comes into power, he will appear to be a dynamic, charismatic leader who can solve the problems of the world. But in the middle of the tribulation period, he will deify himself. He will even set up an image of himself in the Jewish temple, thereby committing the "abomination of desolation" (Matthew 24:15).

In the book of Daniel (see 9:27; 11:31; 12:11), variations of the term *abomination of desolation* convey a sense of outrage or horror at the witnessing of a barbaric act of idolatry in God's holy temple. Such acts utterly profane and desecrate the temple.

In Daniel 11:31 we read of the antichrist, "Forces from him shall appear and profane the temple and fortress, and shall take away the regular burnt offering. And they shall set up the abomination that makes desolate." We find further clarity on this "abomination that causes desolation" in the New Testament. It will take place halfway through the future tribulation period when the antichrist—the "man of sin" (2 Thessalonians 2:4)—sets up an image of himself inside the Jewish temple (see Daniel 9:27; Matthew 24:15). This amounts to the antichrist enthroning himself in the place of deity, displaying himself as God (compare with Isaiah 14:13-14; Ezekiel 28:2-9). This blasphemous act will utterly desecrate the temple, making it abominable and therefore desolate. The antichrist—the world dictator—will then demand that the world worship and pay idolatrous homage to him. Any who refuse will be persecuted and even martyred. The false prophet, who is the antichrist's first lieutenant, will see to this.

THE MESMERIZING FALSE PROPHET

The first lieutenant of the antichrist, the false prophet, will not be walking around with a nametag that says *false prophet* on it. Only the Bible informs us of his true identity. From the perspective of those who live on earth, he will be an incredible religious leader whose words are persuasive and who effectively exalts the person of the antichrist. Bible scholar John Phillips summarizes the mesmerizing and magnetic personality of this future leader.

> The role of the false prophet will be to make the new religion appealing and palatable to men. No doubt, it will combine all the features of the religious systems of men, will appeal to man's total personality, and will take full advantage of his carnal appetite. The dynamic appeal of the false prophet will lie in his skill in combining political expediency with religious passion, self-interest with benevolent philanthropy, lofty sentiment with blatant sophistry, moral platitude with unbridled self-indulgence. His arguments will be subtle, convincing, and appealing. His oratory will be hypnotic, for he will be able to move the masses to tears or whip them into a frenzy. He will control the communication media of the world and will skillfully organize mass publicity to promote his ends. He will be the master of every promotional device and public relations gimmick. He will manage the truth with guile beyond words, bending it, twisting it, and distorting it. Public opinion will be his to command. He will mold world thought and shape human opinion like so much potter's clay. His deadly appeal will lie in the fact that what he says will sound so right, so sensible, so exactly what unregenerate men have always wanted to hear. [2]

THE REVIVED ROMAN EMPIRE:
THE BEGINNING OF WORLD DOMINION

Prophetic Scripture reveals that in the end times, the political and economic powerhouse of the world will be a revived Roman Empire—what we might call the United States of Europe. God's Word prophetically addresses this in the book of Daniel. Indeed, Daniel 7:3-8 refers to four beasts, representing four successive kingdoms in the unfolding of human history. Daniel begins in verse 3 by affirming, "Four great beasts came up out of the sea, different from one another."

The first beast, Daniel says, was "like a lion and had eagles' wings," but "its wings were plucked off" (verse 4). This imagery apparently represents Babylon, its lion-like quality indicating power and strength. Winged lions guarded the gates of ancient Babylon's royal palaces (see Jeremiah 4:7,13). The wings indicate rapid mobility, while the plucking of the wings indicate a removal of mobility—perhaps a reference to Nebuchadnezzar's insanity or to Babylon's deterioration following his death.

Daniel continued in verse 5 by referring to "another beast, a second one, like a bear. It was raised up on one side. It had three ribs in its mouth between its teeth; and it was told, 'Arise, devour much flesh.'" This kingdom is Medo-Persia, and the "ribs" are vanquished nations—perhaps Lydia, Babylon, and Egypt. Medo-Persia was well known for its strength and fierceness in battle (see Isaiah 13:17-18).

Daniel then referred to a third beast. "[It was] like a leopard, with four wings of a bird on its back. And the beast had four heads, and dominion was given to it" (Daniel 7:6). The leopard was an animal that was known for its swiftness, cunning, and agility. This imagery represents Greece under Alexander the Great. The reference to the "four heads" are the four generals who divided the kingdom following Alexander's death, ruling Macedonia, Asia Minor, Syria, and Egypt.

Finally, in verse 7, Daniel refers to the fourth beast—a mongrel beast composed of parts of a lion, bear, and leopard that was more terrifying and powerful than the three preceding beasts:

> Behold, a fourth beast, terrifying and dreadful and exceedingly strong. It had great iron teeth; it devoured and broke in pieces and stamped what was left with its feet. It was different from all the beasts that were before it, and it had ten

horns. I considered the horns, and behold, there came up among them another horn, a little one, before which three of the first horns were plucked up by the roots. And behold, in this horn were eyes like the eyes of a man, and a mouth speaking great things.

This wild imagery refers to a revived Roman Empire. Rome already existed in ancient days, but it fell apart in the fifth century AD. It will be revived, however, in the end times, apparently comprised of ten nations ruled by ten kings (ten horns). As a backdrop, animals used horns as weapons. For this reason, the horn became a symbol of power and might. As an extension of this symbol, horns in biblical times were sometimes used as emblems of dominion, representing kingdoms and kings, as is the case in the books of Daniel and Revelation (see Daniel 7–8; Revelation 13:1,11; 17:3-16). So the ten horns in Daniel 7 refer to ten kings who rule ten nations.

An eleventh horn—a little horn (the antichrist)—starts out apparently in an insignificant way but grows powerful enough to uproot three of the existing horns (kings). He eventually comes into absolute power and dominion over this revived Roman Empire (see 2 Thessalonians 2:3-10; Revelation 13:1-10).

Rome has never consisted of a ten-nation confederacy with ten corulers. If it has not happened in the past, this prophecy must deal with the future. Note that the prophecies regarding the first three world empires have been literally fulfilled, but the last—dealing with the revived Roman Empire—has not yet been fulfilled. It must be yet future. The precedent has been set. Those prophecies that have not yet been fulfilled will be fulfilled just as literally as those that have already been fulfilled. This final form of the Roman Empire will be prominent during the future tribulation period.

In Daniel 2, we read of Nebuchadnezzar's prophetic dream. In this dream, this end-times Roman Empire was pictured as a mixture of iron and clay (see verses 41-43). Daniel, the great dream-interpreter, saw this as meaning that just as iron is strong, so this latter-day Roman Empire would be strong. But just as iron and clay do not naturally mix with each other, so this latter-day Roman Empire would have some divisions. The component parts of this empire would not be completely integrated with each other.

Many modern biblical interpreters see the European Union as a primary prospect for the ultimate fulfillment of this prophecy. Thomas Ice explores this idea.

> The goal of the European Union is to unite all of Europe into one union that will also promote peace, harmony, and prosperity and prevent future world conflicts. This "European Dream," as it is often labeled, proposes a single government that will eliminate national rivalries and conflicts within Europe.

In Daniel 2, the clay mixed with iron may point to the diversity (racial, religious, and political) of the peoples in the ten nations that make up the empire. The clay and iron indicate weakness and strength at the same time, something that is true of the European Union even today. That is, even today the European Union possesses great economic and political strength, but the nations that comprise this union are diverse in culture, language, and politics, so they are not perfectly united. At present, the European Union has its own parliament, a rotating presidency, a supreme court, and a common currency used in many member nations. It allows for unrestricted travel of citizens among member nations and is working toward a unified military.[3] Perhaps the stage is now being set for the ultimate fulfillment of Daniel 2 and 7. What is taking place in Europe today would appear to be a prelude to the eventual revival of the Roman Empire according to Daniel's prophecy!

The antichrist initially emerges in this revived Roman Empire, but during the tribulation he rises into global dominion.

> The whole earth marveled as they followed the beast. And they worshiped the dragon, for he had given his authority to the beast, and they worshiped the beast, saying, "Who is like the beast, and who can fight against it?"...It was allowed to exercise authority for forty-two months...

> Authority was given it over every tribe and people and language and nation, and all who dwell on earth will worship it...[The false prophet] makes the earth and its inhabitants worship the first beast (Revelation 13:3-12).

And no one on earth can buy or sell without taking the mark of the beast (verses 16-17). Very clearly, the antichrist will rule the entire globe.

NEW TECHNOLOGIES AND THE EMERGING GLOBALISM

Prophecy enthusiasts note that even at present, we witness a movement toward globalism in economics, banking, commerce and trade, business, management, manufacturing, environmentalism, population control, education, religion, agriculture, information technologies, entertainment, publishing, science and medicine, and government. We have just seen that the book of Revelation tells us that the antichrist will ultimately lead a global union—an anti-god union. It will be a political union, an economic union, and a religious union.

When one considers the multiple cascading problems now facing humanity—including peak oil (the ultimate end of oil on the earth),* the Middle East conflict,† terrorism, overpopulation, starvation, pollution, national and international crime, cyber warfare, and economic instability‡—increasing numbers of people may come to believe that such problems can be solved only on a global level. They may think that the only hope for human survival is a strong and effective world government.

As the danger continues to mount in the world, people worldwide are yearning for a leader who can take control and fix everything. The world wants a leader who can bring stability in the midst of global chaos. The global economy is reeling, people are suffering, and there is a sense of urgency for a powerful leader who can chart a clear global

---

* See my book *The Coming Oil Storm: The Imminent End of Oil...and Its Strategic Global Role in End-Times Prophecy* (Harvest House, 2010).

† See my book *Northern Storm Rising: Russia, Iran, and the Emerging End-Times Military Coalition Against Israel* (Harvest House, 2008).

‡ See my books *The Topical Handbook of Bible Prophecy* and *The Popular Dictionary of Bible Prophecy* (Harvest House, 2010).

course toward stability. People desire a leader who can bring about a new world order. Such a leader is coming, and he may already be alive in the world. Scripture identifies him as the antichrist.

The technology that makes possible a world government—including instant global media through television and radio, cyberspace, and computers—is now in place. In other words, technology has greased the skids for the emergence of globalism in our day. Without such technology, a true globalism would be impossible.

A GLOBALIZED ECONOMY

The world is moving more and more toward a globalized economy. A number of financial advisors to the U.S. president have gone on record as affirming that a global economy is inescapable. There is every possibility, they say, that the current financial tsunami that has engulfed the entire planet may well lead to a financial new world order.

Many today believe that a global solution is needed because we have a global crisis. Some world financial leaders are even speaking about the possibility of a global economic financial regulatory commission to police the globe's financial affairs and to ensure that we never again get globally engulfed by a financial tsunami. The nation-state system—with separate economies—is not working, many believe. People are ready for a new system, a global system.

In the new age of cyberspace, national economies are more deeply interconnected and intertwined than ever before. Each nation's economy is built on global trade, global capital markets, and global communication. These national economies rise or fall together. What is good for one is good for all. What is bad for one is bad for all.

If one country suffers an economic crisis, the domino effect spans the entire world. From an economic perspective, nations do not rise or fall alone. Because of our current interconnected technologies, economic woes in one country are felt almost instantly in other countries. "An economic eruption or disturbance in New York sends financial shockwaves throughout the globe. The economic scene is highly complex, technologically integrated, and extremely unstable."[4]

Consequently, people from a variety of countries—including Germany, Russia, China, and Brazil—are calling for a new way of doing things. Voices from around the world are saying the same thing: We need some kind of global financial regulation. Some countries, such as Russia and China, are open to the creation of a globalized currency to replace America's ailing dollar. The days of nation-states protecting their own economic interests in an isolationist fashion are over; everything must be done now with a view to what is good for the global economy. That is the mind-set of many today.

Many are insisting that we need tougher global laws and regulations on big banks and financial institutions—laws and regulations that ensure global economic stability and growth instead of protecting the interests of isolationist nation-state economies. Meanwhile, various nations around the world are forming alliances to collectively stay afloat in these uncertain times. Globalism is taking shape before our very eyes.

One can easily see how closely all this relates to biblical prophecy. We have reviewed prophetic Scripture predicting that following the rapture of the church, a revived Roman Empire will emerge—an empire that will be aligned under ten leaders (Daniel 2; 7). There can be little doubt that the alliance will exist for the economic and political benefit of the group as a whole.

This will especially be a necessity after the rapture, for after millions of Christians vanish off the planet, the United States could be affected worse than any other nation because the United States is probably home to more Christians than is any other country (though admittedly, not per capita—by far). Mortgages, loans, and college tuitions will go unpaid. Millions of people will not show up for work. In their panic, the people who are left behind will stop buying. The U.S. economy—which heavily influences the global economy—will likely collapse. Politically and economically, then, it makes sense for a group of ten nations in Europe to join forces for their mutual benefit following the rapture. Things seem to be taking shape just as the ancient prophets predicted.

GREASING THE SKIDS FOR GLOBALISM

I have dealt with a lot of prophetic theology (*eschatology*) in this chapter. It is important to thoroughly understand the antichrist, the false prophet, and the one-world government that we are headed toward. Now I want to talk about the technologies that will make it all possible.

In the past, people interested in prophecy would read the books of Daniel and Revelation and wonder how it could all come about. After all, the end-times world described in these prophetic books seemed so unlike anything that existed in their day. But in our day, technology has changed everything. Indeed, as we have seen, technology has greased the skids for the emergence of globalism—a global political arena, a global economy, and a global religion. Allow me to share a few highlights with you.

Supercomputers and a Cashless Society

We know from the book of Revelation that eventually, no one will be able to buy or sell who is unwilling to receive the mark of the beast (Revelation 13:16-17). Our technology has certainly made this a possibility. Keeping global track of all people and all selling establishments is now possible through advanced computer technology. Every business and every person around the globe could have a unique account number that would enable instant tracking and processing of all financial transactions on a global basis. Today's supercomputers—such as Sequoia, which can do 20,000 trillion calculations per second—could track billions of people on the earth, millions of small businesses engaged in commerce, millions of grocery stores around the planet, millions of banks and financial institutions, and much more. These supercomputers could also support a complex biometric identification system as well as a GPS system that would keep track of the location of every person on the planet.

Biometrics and Identification

We have seen that biometrics is the technology that enables identification of people by measuring and analyzing biological data and/or behavioral traits. More specifically, it enables identification by measuring and analyzing people's bodily characteristics (including their fingerprints, facial patterns, odor/scent, hand geometry, palm print, iris recognition, retina recognition, and even DNA) as well as their behavioral traits, such as their gait or their keyboard typing pattern. Such technology will no doubt play a role in the emerging globalization of the future and the antichrist's control over all people.

How so? Through biometric identification, there will be no question that people are who they claim to be. There will be no mix-ups on identification. Those clearly identified as followers of the antichrist will be able to buy and sell. Those clearly identified as rebels against the antichrist will not be able to buy or sell.

Biometric scanning may someday include scanning the forehead or the right hand for the mark of the beast. A biometric hand scan measures the dimensions of fingers in conjunction with finger joints and the overall shape and size of the hand. That part of the scan verifies the actual identity of a person. But if the biometric process added into the mix a simultaneous scan for the mark of the beast on the right hand, the combined result of the scan would be a confirmation of the person's actual identity as well as a confirmation that the person is a follower of the antichrist. If the scan reveals no mark of the beast, then that person's bank account—which will be stored on a person's smart card, or a cell phone with a microchip, or a microchip that has been injected into the palm of the hand—could be blocked.

Biometric technology may also be used as a means of intimidating people into submission to the antichrist's leadership. For example, if facial recognition scanners were scattered throughout the major cities, the comings and goings of each person would be known to the government. Such facial scans are a nonintrusive biometric method that is suitable for both covert and overt identity checks. A typical facial biometric recognition approach measures the location and shape of such facial attributes as the eyes, eyebrows, nose, lips, and chin, and their overall spacial relationship to each other. The combined effect of these features makes for a unique biometric. With facial scanners scattered about all the major cities (and even lesser cities), authorities could be covertly watching everyone.[5] And if authorities do not like what they see, they could intervene in a nasty way. Scripture reveals that the end-times authority will be the antichrist.

Smart Cards

A smart card is just like a MasterCard or Visa card or American Express card—except that it is a tad thicker. It is called *smart* because it contains a microchip (like a computer with memory) that can store large amounts of personal information, such as banking information, medical information, information about one's personal tastes, and other kinds of information. Many today believe that smart cards will play a significant role in buying and selling in the future. One will merely need wave the smart card over a product to purchase it.

Combined with biometrics (especially a biometric approach that scans the hand and/or forehead), this could be a prime means of enforcing the no-buy/no-sell policy for those who refuse the mark of the beast. Such technology could make life difficult for believers during the tribulation.

RFID Technologies

Radio Frequency Identification (RFID) technology can easily be placed in a number of devices that people carry around with them—including smart phones.[6] In the future, products in stores will probably have RFID tags. That means that if people have smartphones that contain RFID technology, they could pay for products in an instant. The process would be fully automated. Such technology could possibly play a role in the antichrist's economic control of people in the end times. Like the smartcard/biometrics combination, the RFID/smartphone/biometrics combination could make it easy for the forces of the antichrist to enforce the no-buy/no-sell policy for those who reject the mark of the beast.

Cyberspace as a PR Tool

Even in our own day, cyberspace has become an effective PR tool. Just ask any candidate who runs for office—every candidate has his or her own website. Cyberspace has also been used as a tool to influence public perception. For example, during the second Russian–Chechen war (1997–2001), both Russia and Chechnya utilized cyberspace to control and shape public perception of the conflict.

Earlier in the chapter I noted that the false prophet will seek to mold world thought and shape human opinion like so much potter's clay—especially as related to his overall goal to exalt the antichrist. There can be little doubt that cyberspace will be one of the primary PR tools in his arsenal.

Cyber Espionage and the Enforcement of Submission

Cyber espionage involves the unauthorized probing of a target computer or network to engage in the unauthorized viewing and copying of data files. There can be little doubt that cyber espionage will play a role during the tribulation as the antichrist's cyber command center watches for any global challenges to his leadership. This cyber espionage will also likely play a role as the antichrist seeks to find and monitor individual rebels (believers who have refused the mark of the beast). Because of cyber espionage, privacy will be a thing of the past. Even today, we are witnessing privacy evaporate before our very eyes. I will address this in a bit more detail later in the book.

Smart Weaponry in Enforcing Globalism

High-tech weaponry—including laser-guided missiles, nuclear submarines, fighter jets with cyber technologies, smart bombs, GPS technology applications on the battlefield, cyber attacks, and the like—will no doubt play a role in the antichrist's enforcement of obedience to his world government. Much like shoot-'em-up video games, many attacks against opponents can be launched conveniently from a computer console—including unmanned aerial vehicles that carry a weapons payload. The antichrist will do whatever is necessary to protect his turf—the entire globe.

IS THE ANTICHRIST ALIVE TODAY?

We cannot be sure whether the antichrist is alive today. But because of what I call the *convergence factor*, there is a good chance that he is alive. By this I mean that the fulfillment of many ancient prophecies of the end times seem to be converging at a point in the not-too-distant future. Therefore, the antichrist could possibly be alive somewhere in the world today, waiting in the wings. Consider the way prophecies are being fulfilled in our time.

- Israel has been reborn as a nation (see Ezekiel 36–37).

- The nations that will participate in the Ezekiel invasion against Israel are already building alliances with each other (see Ezekiel 38).

- Steps toward globalism are evident all around us (see Revelation 13).

- Nations in Europe are uniting with each other, which could lead to a revived Roman empire (see Daniel 2; 7).

- The "signs of the times" are pointing us to the end times (Matthew 24–25).

CHRIST WILL BE VICTORIOUS

As a fitting close to this chapter, let's remember that Christ Himself will defeat the antichrist. In Revelation 19:20 we read that the beast and the false prophet—two malevolent foes who come into power during the future tribulation period—will be consigned to the lake of fire. "The beast was captured, and with it the false prophet who in its presence had done the signs by which he deceived those who had received the mark of the beast and those who worshiped its image. These two were thrown alive into the lake of fire that burns with sulfur." This takes place before Christ's millennial kingdom—that thousand-year period following the second coming of Christ in which Christ will physically rule the earth from the throne of David.

At the end of the millennial kingdom—a thousand years after the beast and the false prophet are thrown into the lake of burning sulfur—the devil himself will also be consigned to the lake of fire. "The devil who had deceived them was thrown into the lake of fire and sulfur where the beast and the false prophet were, and they will be tormented day and night forever and ever" (Revelation 20:10).

Notice that the beast and false prophet are not burned up or annihilated at the time the devil is thrown into the lake of burning sulfur. They are still burning after a thousand years. These sinister beings, along with unbelievers of all ages, will be tormented day and night forever (Revelation 20:14-15). This will mark the end of this satanic trinity.

CYBER ESPIONAGE AND END-TIMES PERSECUTIONS

Many Christians—myself included—believe the rapture of the church will take place prior to the seven-year tribulation period. This means the church will not go through the judgments prophesied in the book of Revelation (chapters 4–18).

In support of this view, Revelation 3:10 indicates that believers will be kept from the actual hour of testing that is coming on the whole world. That hour of testing is the tribulation period.

Further, no Old Testament passage on the tribulation mentions the church (Deuteronomy 4:29-30; Jeremiah 30:4-11; Daniel 8:24-27; 12:1-2). Nor does any New Testament passage on the tribulation mention the church (Matthew 13:30,39-42,47-50; 24:15-31; 2 Thessalonians 2:1-12; Revelation 4–18). The absence of the church in tribulation contexts would seem to indicate that the church is not there.

As well, a pretribulational rapture best explains the sudden apostasy that comes upon the world by the removal of the restrainer, who is apparently the Holy Spirit (2 Thessalonians 2:3-7). The Holy Spirit indwells all believers (John 14:16; 1 Corinthians 3:17), so He will essentially be removed when the church is taken in the rapture, thus making possible the fast eruption of apostasy in the tribulation.

Scripture also assures us that the church is not appointed to wrath (Romans 5:9; 1 Thessalonians 1:9-10; 5:9). This means the church cannot go through the tribulation period, which is the "great day of their wrath" (Revelation 6:17).

Finally, all throughout Scripture, God protects His people before judgment falls (see 2 Peter 2:5-9). Enoch was transferred to heaven before the judgment of the flood. Noah and his family were in the ark before the floodgates opened. Lot was taken out of Sodom before fire and brimstone fell. The firstborn among the Hebrews in Egypt were sheltered by the blood of the Paschal lamb when Egyptian's first-born were slain. The spies were safely out of Jericho and Rahab was secured before judgment fell on Jericho. So too will the church be secured safely (through the rapture) before judgment falls in the tribulation period.

However, Scripture is equally clear that many people will become believers during the tribulation period. For example, at the second coming of Christ, Christ will separate the sheep from the goats, based on how they treated Christ's brothers (see Matthew 25:31-46). The term *sheep* refers to believers, and *goats* refers to unbelievers. The sheep enter into Christ's kingdom, and the goats enter into eternal punishment. The *brothers* are apparently the 144,000 Jewish brothers of Christ who, having become believers some time after the rapture, evangelize during the tribulation period.

There are a number of ways a person might become a believer during the tribulation period. Perhaps many become convinced of the truth of Christianity after witnessing millions of Christians supernaturally vanish at the rapture. (Many Bibles and Christian books will be left behind to explain the event.) Or perhaps they become Christians as a result of the ministry of the 144,000 Jewish evangelists introduced in Revelation 7 (who also apparently come to faith in Christ after the rapture). It may also be that many become believers as a result of the miraculous ministry of the two witnesses of Revelation 11, prophets whose powers are similar to those of Moses and Elijah.

The book of Revelation certainly indicates that many people will respond to the gospel of the kingdom during the tribulation.

> After this I looked, and behold, a great multitude that
> no one could number, from every nation, from all tribes

and peoples and languages, standing before the throne and before the Lamb, clothed in white robes, with palm branches in their hands, and crying out with a loud voice, "Salvation belongs to our God who sits on the throne, and to the Lamb!" (Revelation 7:9-10).

MARTYRDOM DURING THE TRIBULATION

Though many of these believers will still be alive at the second coming, which occurs after the tribulation (see Matthew 25:31-46), many others will be martyred during the tribulation.

> When he opened the fifth seal, I saw under the altar the souls of those who had been slain for the word of God and for the witness they had borne. They cried out with a loud voice, "O Sovereign Lord, holy and true, how long before you will judge and avenge our blood on those who dwell on the earth?" Then they were each given a white robe and told to rest a little longer, until the number of their fellow servants and their brothers should be complete, who were to be killed as they themselves had been (Revelation 6:9-11).

Some of these martyred "fellow servants" are mentioned in Revelation 7:9-17. As well, the two witnesses of Revelation 11 will experience martyrdom. These two, however, will be raised from the dead after three days and then ascend into heaven (verses 8-12).

Of course, such martyrdom is nothing new. In Revelation 2 Christ speaks to the church in Pergamum about one of His faithful martyrs. "I know where you dwell, where Satan's throne is. Yet you hold fast my name, and you did not deny my faith even in the days of Antipas my faithful witness, who was killed among you, where Satan dwells" (verse 13).

When Christ spoke words of comfort to the church in Smyrna, He exhorted them to remain strong in the face of martyrdom: "Do not fear what you are about to suffer. Behold, the devil is about to throw some of you into prison, that you may be tested, and for ten days you will have tribulation. Be faithful unto death, and I will give you the crown of life" (verse 10).

WAR AGAINST THE SAINTS

Revelation 13:5-7 describes the antichrist's war against God's people during the tribulation period.

> The beast was given a mouth uttering haughty and blasphe-
> mous words, and it was allowed to exercise authority for
> forty-two months. It opened its mouth to utter blasphe-
> mies against God, blaspheming his name and his dwelling,
> that is, those who dwell in heaven. Also it was allowed to
> make war on the saints and to conquer them.

Such verses indicate that great persecution will break out against the saints during the tribulation.

We have seen that martyrs who are now in heaven are informed that still more believers will be killed (Revelation 6:11). *The Bible Knowledge Commentary* explains that these martyrs were "informed that the Tribulation is not over and that others must be martyred before God's judgment on the wicked and deliverance of the righteous occurs at the Second Coming."[1] God often affirms in Scripture that "vengeance is mine" (Deuteronomy 32:35; Romans 12:19), but only according to His sovereign timing.

Scripture is also quite clear that the nation of Israel—which gave birth to the divine Messiah, Jesus Christ—will come under heavy persecution by the antichrist. This will take place in the middle of the tribulation when the antichrist moves into Jerusalem and sets up an image of himself in the Jewish temple, proclaiming himself to be God (see Daniel 9:27). Matthew 24:16-22 describes the horrific persecution that will break out.

> Then let those who are in Judea flee to the mountains. Let
> the one who is on the housetop not go down to take what
> is in his house, and let the one who is in the field not turn
> back to take his cloak. And alas for women who are preg-
> nant and for those who are nursing infants in those days!
> Pray that your flight may not be in winter or on a Sabbath.
> For then there will be great tribulation, such as has not
> been from the beginning of the world until now, no, and

never will be. And if those days had not been cut short, no human being would be saved. But for the sake of the elect those days will be cut short.

Daniel 7:25 prophetically affirms that the antichrist "shall speak words against the Most High, and shall wear out the saints of the Most High, and shall think to change the times and the law; and they shall be given into his hand for a time, times, and half a time." The phrase "time, times, and half a time" obviously refers to the last half (three and a half years) of the seven-year period of antichrist's power.

NO RELIGIOUS ALTERNATIVES PERMITTED

It was Augustine who called the devil *Simius Dei*—"the ape of God." Satan is the great counterfeiter. He mimics God in many ways. Theologian Charles Ryrie tells us that "the principle tactic Satan uses to attack God and His program in general is to offer a counterfeit kingdom and program."[2] This is hinted at in 2 Corinthians 11:14, which refers to Satan masquerading as an angel of light. In what ways does Satan act as the ape of God?

- Satan has his own church—the "synagogue of Satan" (Revelation 2:9).

- Satan has his own ministers and apostles (2 Corinthians 11:4-5,13).

- Satan has formulated his own system of theology—called "doctrines of demons" (1 Timothy 4:1 NASB; see also Revelation 2:24).

- His ministers proclaim his false gospel—"a gospel contrary to the one we preached to you" (Galatians 1:8).

- Satan has his own throne and worshipers (Revelation 13:2-4).

- Satan inspires false, self-constituted messiahs (Matthew 24:4-5).

- Satan employs false teachers who bring in "destructive heresies" (2 Peter 2:1).

- Satan sends out false prophets (Matthew 24:11).

"Satan's plan and purposes have been, are, and always will be to seek to establish a rival rule to God's kingdom. He is promoting a system of which he is the head and which stands in opposition to God and His rule in the universe."[3]

I make this critically important point because many theologians believe—based on clear theological inferences from Scripture—that Satan will indwell the antichrist in the middle of the tribulation. This will take place after Satan is definitively thrown down to the earth after suffering defeat in battle with the archangel Michael and the holy angels (Revelation 12:7-9). That Satan indwells or at least empowers the antichrist is clear from 2 Thessalonians 2:9, which informs us, "The coming of the lawless one [the antichrist] is by the activity of Satan with all power and false signs and wonders." The antichrist will then portray himself as deity and will seek to force all who are on the earth to worship him (see verse 4). The antichrist—empowered by Satan— will allow no competing religious views. That is, he will stand against any who claim allegiance to Jesus Christ. This will be a prime motivation for his persecution against the saints during the tribulation.

SATAN: A LIAR AND MURDERER

Jesus describes the devil's character in John 8:44: "He was a murderer from the beginning, and has nothing to do with the truth, because there is no truth in him. When he lies, he speaks out of his own character, for he is a liar and the father of lies."

There are two relevant factors to note here as related to the persecution of the saints in the book of Revelation. First, Satan "was a murderer from the beginning." When he persecutes the saints, he is acting in character. Hatred is the motive that leads one to commit murder. Satan hates both God and His children, so he has a genuine motive for murder. He will murder the people of God during the tribulation by motivating the antichrist to persecute God's people.

Second, Satan is a liar. He is a deceiver. He is dishonest to the core. He is the "father of lies." The word *father* is used here metaphorically of the originator of a family or company of persons animated by a deceitful character.

The late Ray Stedman notes the twofold strategy of the devil in murder and deception. His words are wise: "Because he is a liar and a murderer, the devil's work is to deceive and to destroy. There you have the explanation for all that has been going on in human history throughout the whole course of the record of man...Whom the devil cannot deceive, he tries to destroy, and whom he cannot destroy, he attempts to deceive."[4]

I firmly believe that during the future tribulation period, Satan will motivate the antichrist to diabolically deceive people around the world to worship him as God (2 Thessalonians 2:4; Revelation 13:16-17). But I believe he will also use deceptive methods to capture and persecute the people of God (Revelation 13:7). The antichrist's deceptive tactics in capturing Christians will likely involve the use of some of the technologies I have discussed in this book, all of which he will have unrestricted access to as planetary leader.

SATAN'S TITLES ARE REVEALING

Because the antichrist will be empowered by Satan to persecute the saints, Satan's names shed light on the antichrist's character and motivations. What is true of Satan will also be reflected in the antichrist. Satan is...

- Our adversary (1 Peter 5:8). He opposes us in every way he can.

- The devil (Matthew 4:1). This name carries the idea of "adversary" as well as "slanderer." The devil was and is the adversary of Christ and all who follow Christ.

- Our enemy (Matthew 13:39). This word comes from a root meaning "hatred." It characterizes Satan's attitude—he hates both God and His children.

- A roaring lion (1 Peter 5:8-9). This graphic simile depicts Satan's strength, ferociousness, and destructiveness. He seeks to utterly and completely mutilate Christians.

Such titles indicate that Satan can cause immeasurable suffering among human beings—especially Christians, those who love and follow Christ. Satan hates Christ and all of His representatives. This same hatred will be manifest in the antichrist because Satan empowers him (2 Thessalonians 2:9).

THE ANTICHRIST AND THE USE OF TECHNOLOGY

As planetary leader, the antichrist will undoubtedly use various technologies to pursue and persecute the people of God during the tribulation, just as governments today utilize technologies to find and attack their enemies. Biblical prophecies do not explicitly state this, but we have good reason to believe it.

As we have seen, biblical prophecies are quite specific, but very often people living during the time of the prophets had no awareness of the providential circumstances that would one day emerge to bring about their fulfillment. When the Bible prophesies that the antichrist will pursue and persecute the people of God, it does not mention computers or cyberspace or the Internet or biometrics. But these very technologies are already being used today to track people and verify their identities, so we can infer that the antichrist will take advantage of these same technologies to pursue those who oppose him. As planetary leader, he will have unrestricted access to intelligence agencies and all technological advantages, including a cyber command center.

So, what are some of the cutting-edge technologies that the antichrist may use during the tribulation to persecute God's people? I will offer some admittedly speculative suggestions—but I believe they are likely to be accurate. Some of these suggestions are based on tactics that governments have already used.

CYBER ESPIONAGE

One use of cyber espionage is to view and copy data files on someone's computer or network without authorization. Governments currently engage in cyber espionage against other countries, so the antichrist's cyber command center could just as easily engage in cyber espionage to pursue God's people around the world. A specific budget may be allocated for the cyber command center to pursue religious extremists and rebels (followers of Jesus).

How might the antichrist's cyber command center accomplish this? Perhaps his own forces will set up some bogus Christian websites that automatically and secretly download malware to the computers of those who visit them. This malware could be a keyboard logger, recording all of the user's keystrokes and transmitting the recorded data back to the cyber command center.

The data transmitted back to cyber command will then likely be run through a diagnostic software program with algorithms designed to compare the data against a master list of Christian buzzwords. Those deemed to be Christians, based on the analysis, will become targets for capture and persecution.

Keep in mind something I said earlier in the chapter. Satan is the "father of lies" (John 8:44). And he will empower the antichrist, so the antichrist too will be characterized by lies and deception. So creating bogus Christian websites in order to deceive and trap Christians will be entirely consistent with his character.

PHISHING SCAMS

Previously in the book, I noted that people sometimes receive what appear to be legitimate e-mails from their banks. These e-mails copy the banks' own graphics and logos. The e-mails might request that people click on a link to go to the bank website and enter their usernames and passwords. But the e-mails and websites are bogus—all designed to deceive and plunder!

During the future tribulation period, similar phishing scams could be widespread. However, the e-mails will not appear to come from banks, but from churches, Bible study groups, or other Christian organizations. The real senders will want unsuspecting Christians to sign up with them, providing personal information. There will be plenty of graphics on the e-mails and websites—including crucifixes, churches, the Bible, the Christian fish symbol, clip art of Jesus, and the like. Once personal information is obtained from gullible Christians, it can then be utilized by the forces of the antichrist to pursue and persecute them.

FREE BIBLE SOFTWARE AND CHRISTIAN BOOK DOWNLOADS

The forces of antichrist may also post Bible software and Christian books on the Internet that can be downloaded for free. As this spiritually uplifting software is downloaded, malware also downloads to the computer in the background without the Christian computer user knowing what is happening. Again, the malware would likely be a form of spyware that utilizes a keystroke logger, which records everything typed into the keyboard of an infected machine. The spyware then transmits this information back to the cyber command forces of the antichrist.

The malware will not only identify the person downloading the software as a Christian but also, through use of the spyware, enable the antichrist's cyber command to gather e-mail addresses and even physical addresses of other Christians with whom the computer user interacts.

These newly discovered e-mail addresses will then be sent e-mails pretending to be from the Christian who originally downloaded the software (this is called spear phishing), inviting them to download the same software. Or the e-mail might say, "Hey, Chuck, I think this article about prayer will interest you..." and then provide a link to a "Christian" website. Once these Christian friends download the software or click on the link, spyware is downloaded to their computers, and even more Christians are discovered in the process.

This spyware tactic could also employ worms—computer viruses that spread to other computers even if users don't open the infected e-mails or click on bad links. This form of malware worms its way throughout cyberspace from computer to computer. If one Christian downloaded spyware, it could easily spread to other Christians' computers so a wide network of Christians could be located and targeted.

SPEAR PHISHING AND SOCIAL NETWORKS

Social networks like Facebook and MySpace are not likely to vanish in the years to come. They are more popular than ever. This makes these social networks ideal for doing cyber espionage against Christians. These social networks provide an unprecedented source of personal information about people that can be easily hacked.

Once a Christian is identified, cyber command forces could easily penetrate that person's Facebook account, gather the name of Christian family members and friends, and send them spear-phishing e-mails. These e-mail messages typically ask the recipients to click on a link or open an attachment. When they do, some form of malware is downloaded to the victims' computers. By using such methodology, it would be easy to find more and more unsuspecting Christians.

WEBCAM AND MICROPHONE SPYING

Earlier in the book, I documented that in 2009 a sophisticated computer program known as GhostNet penetrated some 1300 computers at the embassies of several countries. GhostNet remotely activated webcams and microphones on computers without alerting the users. This enabled the senders (based in China) to see and hear what was happening at these embassies. GhostNet remained active for almost two full years before being discovered.

The cyber command forces of the antichrist could do the same thing as they seek out rebels (believers in Jesus). Using this method, cyber officials could not only discover Christians but also watch them as they have Bible studies, listen in on their strategies for staying hidden from the forces of the antichrist, and much more.

FREE BIBLES AND CHRISTIAN BOOKS

There is a very real possibility that the forces of the antichrist could publish copies of the Bible as well as Christian books (perhaps such classics as *The Imitation of Christ*, *Pilgrim's Progress*, or C.S. Lewis' *Mere Christianity*) and put them in churches, Christian schools, or anywhere else where people might grab one.

These Bibles and books will be a little different from other Bibles and books. They will all have a tiny GPS chip implanted in the binding, completely hidden from view. The Global Positioning System will allow the forces of the antichrist to know where those Bibles are, anywhere in the world, any time of day. A concentration of these Bibles in one location will clearly indicate that a meeting of Christians is underway.

GPS devices could also be planted in cars of known Christians and monitored by antichrist authorities watching for meetings of Christians. At these meetings, authorities could plant GPS devices on all the Christians' cars. Entire networks of Christians could be monitored and ultimately captured.

Earlier in the book, I explained how stalkers have used GPS technology. During the future tribulation period, the antichrist may well engage in the cyber stalking of Christians in order to capture and persecute them.

BIOMETRIC FACE-RECOGNITION TECHNOLOGY

Facial recognition technology measures the location and shape of such facial attributes as the eyes, eyebrows, nose, lips, and chin as well as their spacial relationships to each other. Some people believe that facial recognition technology could be a great benefit to law enforcement. A large crowd of people could be scanned, and the images of the faces could be compared to a master database. Such technology could enable the easy capturing of wanted persons.

But the same technology could be used not only to identify and apprehend individual Christians but to also identify other Christians with whom they associate publicly.

RFID CHIPS

As we have seen, RFID (Radio Frequency Identification) chips can be programmed with personal information and placed in smart cards or cell phones or even be injected underneath the skin in the fatty area of the palm. This technology is currently being used by businesses to monitor employees' activities and productivity.

The technology could easily be adapted for use during tribulation times to monitor all people—including Christians who are not techno-savvy enough to recognize the dangers of possessing RFID technology.

RFID readers can detect people's RFID devices up to 90 feet away. This means that if RFID readers were scattered about the city, someone could monitor the comings and goings of people—including Christians and their friends. The combination of RFID chips and biometrics would practically do away with privacy in public settings. Big Brother will be watching.

WE WIN IN THE END

You get the picture. I have presented only the tip of the iceberg regarding how technology and deception might be used by the forces of the antichrist in his relentless pursuit of Christians during the tribulation period. Those will be difficult days, and there will be many martyrs.

However, let's not forget the purpose of the book of Revelation. The recipients of the book of Revelation were already undergoing severe persecution, with some of them even being killed (Revelation 2:13). Things were about to get even worse. John wrote this book to give his readers a strong hope that would help them patiently endure in the midst of suffering. At the time, evil seemed to be prevailing at every level. However, Revelation indicates that evil will one day come to an end. Indeed, Scripture reveals that Christians are destined for an eternity without sin, sorrow, or death—and with perpetual and uninterrupted fellowship with God (Revelation 21–22). Hallelujah!

CYBER INJURY AND THE END-TIMES DECLINE OF THE UNITED STATES

Have you ever wondered whether God will judge America?

Judgment plays a major role in any discussion of end-times Bible prophecy. A brief look at what Scripture teaches about the tribulation period makes this quite clear.

The Greek word translated *tribulation* (*thlipsis*) literally means "to press" (as grapes) and refers to a time of oppression, affliction, and distress. It is translated variously as tribulation, affliction, anguish, persecution, trouble, and burden. The word has been used in relation to...

- those hard-pressed by the calamities of war (Matthew 24:21)

- a woman giving birth to a child (John 16:21)

- the afflictions of Christ (Colossians 1:24)

- those pressed by poverty and lack (Philippians 4:14)

- great anxiety and burden of heart (2 Corinthians 2:4)

- a specific period in the end times that will have unparalleled tribulation (Revelation 7:14)

Of course, we all suffer *some* tribulation. However, the tribulation we all endure in the course of daily living is to be distinguished from the tribulation period of the end times.

- Scripture refers to a definite period of time at the end of the age (Matthew 24:29-35).

- It will be of such severity that no period in history—past or future—will equal it (Matthew 24:21).

- It will be shortened for the sake of the elect (Matthew 24:22); otherwise, no one could survive.

- It is called the time of Jacob's trouble, for it is a judgment on Messiah-rejecting Israel (Jeremiah 30:7; Daniel 12:1-4).

- The nations will also be judged for their sin and rejection of Christ during this time (Isaiah 26:21; Revelation 6:15-17).

- This tribulation period lasts seven years (Daniel 9:24,27).

- It will be so bad that people will want to hide and even die (Revelation 6:16).

This period of tribulation has three sets of judgments that will be poured out on the world—the seal judgments, the trumpet judgments, and the bowl judgments.

The first set of judgments to be unleashed on earth are the seal judgments, and these involve bloodshed and war, famine, death, economic upheaval, a great (and deadly) earthquake, and cosmic disturbances (Revelation 6).

The trumpet judgments include hail and fire mixed with blood, the sea turning to blood, water turning bitter, severe cosmic disturbances, affliction by demonic scorpions, and the death of a third of humankind (Revelation 8:6–9:21).

Human suffering comes to its culmination in the horrific bowl judgments, which include horribly painful sores on human beings, bodies of water turning to blood, the death of all sea creatures, people being scorched by the sun, rivers drying up, total darkness engulfing the land, a devastating earthquake, widespread destruction, and much more (Revelation 16). Such is the judgment of a holy God on a Christ-rejecting world. Woe unto those dwelling on the earth in those days.

IS JUDGMENT IN STORE FOR AMERICA?

Because judgment plays such a central role in end-times prophecy, I have always wondered about the role of the United States in the end times. This issue is worth considering, especially in view of the spiritual and moral degeneration that we have witnessed in this country.

Whether due to spiritual ignorance or national pride (even arrogance), many Americans think the United States is invulnerable and could never fall. But the Bible is clear—God is in sovereign control of all nations and has the power to bring devastating judgment on any nation that has turned its back on Him. God rules the universe, controls all things, and is Lord over all (see Ephesians 1).

Psalm 50:1 refers to God as the Mighty One, who "speaks and summons the earth from the rising of the sun to its setting." Psalm 66:7 affirms that He rules by his might forever. Psalm 93:1 assures us that the Lord reigns. God Himself asserts, "My counsel shall stand, and I will accomplish all my purpose" (Isaiah 46:10). He assures us, "As I have planned, so shall it be, and as I have purposed, so shall it stand" (Isaiah 14:24). Proverbs 16:9 tells us that "the heart of man plans his way, but the LORD establishes his steps." Proverbs 19:21 says, "Many are the plans in the mind of a man, but it is the purpose of the LORD that will stand."

In the book of Job we read, "He makes nations great, and he destroys them; he enlarges nations, and leads them away" (Job 12:23). We are told that "[God] made from one man every nation of mankind to live on all the face of the earth, having determined allotted periods and the boundaries of their dwelling place" (Acts 17:26). Daniel 2:20-21 tells us that "He changes times and seasons; he removes kings and sets up kings."

God is not only all-powerful and sovereign over all things in the universe; Scripture reveals that He is also a God of judgment. In his modern classic *Knowing God*, J.I. Packer forcefully reminds us of this sobering, oft-forgotten truth.

> The reality of divine judgment, as a fact, is set forth on page after page of Bible history. God judged Adam and Eve, expelling them from the Garden and pronouncing curses on their future earthly life (Gen. 3). God judged the corrupt world of Noah's day, sending a flood to destroy mankind (Gen. 6–8). God judged Sodom and Gomorrah, engulfing them in a volcanic catastrophe (Gen. 18–19). God judged Israel's Egyptian taskmasters, just as He foretold He would (see Gen. 15:14), unleashing against them the terrors of the ten plagues (Ex. 7–12). God judged those who worshipped the golden calf, using the Levites as His executioners (Ex. 32:26-35). God judged Nadab and Abihu for offering Him strange fire (Lev. 10:1ff.), as later He judged Korah, Dathan, and Abiram, who were swallowed up in an earth tremor. God judged Achan for sacrilegious thieving; he and his family were wiped out (Josh. 7). God judged Israel for unfaithfulness to Him after their entry into Canaan, causing them to fall under the dominion of other nations (Judg. 2:11ff., 3:5ff., 4:1ff.).[1]

I have often heard people express the idea that the God of the Old Testament is characterized by judgment, but the God of the New Testament is all about love. God *is* a God of love, but He continues to be a God of judgment in the New Testament. Indeed, there we find that judgment falls on the Jews for rejecting Jesus Christ (Matthew 21:43), on Ananias and Sapphira for lying to God (Acts 5), on Herod for his self-exalting pride (Acts 12:21-23), and on Christians in Corinth who were afflicted with serious illness and even death in response to their irreverence in connection with the Lord's Supper (1 Corinthians 11:29-32; see also 1 John 5:16). Christians will one day stand before the judgment seat of Christ (1 Corinthians 3:12-15; 2 Corinthians 5:10). Unbelievers, by contrast, will be judged before the great white throne (Revelation 20:11-15).

We must avoid confusion on this essential biblical point: God is a God of judgment. That being the case, consider this possibility:

> If God is absolutely sovereign over the nations, and God is, in fact, a God of judgment, and America continues to plummet morally and spiritually, then might God judge America for turning from Him?

I hate to say it, but I think this is a real possibility. And I am not the only one who thinks so. Prophecy scholar Mark Hitchcock, in his book *The Late Great United States*, agrees.

> One often-overlooked aspect of God's judgment is His dealing with nations. God has often judged entire nations in the past. Lengthy sections in the Old Testament are devoted to God's prophesied judgment against nations. God repeatedly pronounced judgment against Judah and Israel for their disobedience. The majority of the Old Testament prophets are devoted to this subject—Isaiah, Jeremiah, Hosea, Joel, Amos, Micah, Zephaniah, Habakkuk, Zechariah, Haggai, and Malachi. But Judah and Israel were not the sole recipients of God's just displeasure. God also announced judgment on Gentile nations for their sin...In light of the biblical record, we would be shortsighted to believe that God no longer judges nations for their sin.[2]

Those who doubt God's present role as Judge should consult what the apostle Paul says in Romans 1:18-28:

> For the wrath of God is revealed from heaven against all ungodliness and unrighteousness of men, who by their unrighteousness suppress the truth. For what can be known about God is plain to them, because God has shown it to them. For his invisible attributes, namely, his eternal power and divine nature, have been clearly perceived, ever since the creation of the world, in the things that have been made. So they are without excuse. For although they knew God, they did not honor him as God or give thanks to him,

but they became futile in their thinking, and their foolish hearts were darkened…

Therefore God gave them up in the lusts of their hearts to impurity, to the dishonoring of their bodies among themselves, because they exchanged the truth about God for a lie and worshiped and served the creature rather than the Creator, who is blessed forever!…

For this reason God gave them up to dishonorable passions. For their women exchanged natural relations for those that are contrary to nature; and the men likewise gave up natural relations with women and were consumed with passion for one another, men committing shameless acts with men and receiving in themselves the due penalty for their error.

And since they did not see fit to acknowledge God, God gave them up to a debased mind to do what ought not to be done.

If this passage tells us anything, it is that when people willfully reject God and His Word, turning their backs on His moral requirements, God eventually reveals His wrath against them. God has a long track record of wrath against ungodly nations. This passage reveals that one way God reveals His wrath is by allowing the people of that nation to experience the full brunt of the ravaging consequences of their sin. God hands them over to the consequences of sin.

With that fact in mind, it is a sobering historical reality that there have been many great nations that have risen and fallen throughout human history. In each case, the nation had no expectation of its impending demise. Indeed, those who lived within these nations probably believed their nation could never fall. As one researcher put it, "Anthropology tells us that many of the fallen civilizations in history also thought they were superior to their neighbors and forebears. Few of their citizens could have imagined their society would suddenly collapse."[3] But the harsh reality of documented history is that great nations do fall.

Studies have demonstrated that no civilization is invulnerable. One study, published in *Scientific American*, researched 60 ancient and modern civilizations in order to discover the lifespan of the average civilization. For each extinct civilization, the total number of years of its existence was calculated. For civilizations still in existence, the current age in years was calculated. The study found that the average lifespan of a civilization is 421 years. An unexpected finding of the study was that modern civilizations do not last as long as ancient ones. Indeed, among the 28 most recent civilizations, the average lifespan has been only 305 years.[4]

Two books—*Collapse*, by Jared Diamond, and *The Collapse of Complex Societies*, by Joseph Tainter—document how past civilizations have fallen because of a failure to prepare for possible future problems.[5] As well-known economist Stephen Leeb put it, "Lack of foresight and an almost childlike decision not to worry about the future seem to be human characteristics that are timeless. Ultimately, these psychological weaknesses may be more responsible for why civilizations have failed."[6]

How about a small dose of real history? Babylon lasted less than a century. Persia capitulated after about two centuries. Greece waned in less than three centuries. The mighty Roman Empire waned after holding out for nine centuries. The people in these empires surely thought they were invincible. In each of these cases, the fall was preceded by a gross moral decline, and God rendered appropriate judgment.

If what we are witnessing in America today—pornography, premarital sex, extramarital sex, widespread homosexuality, same-sex marriages, abortions, drinking, drugs, divorce, the disintegration of the family unit, and the like—were taking place in ancient Babylon, would you think that Babylon was ripe for judgment? I think so! The problem today is that many in our country have become desensitized to moral issues because immorality is so rampant. That is a dangerous state to be in, for God's patience will not last forever.

Let's briefly explore some possible scenarios relating to the United States in Bible prophecy. We'll also consider how a cyber meltdown may tie in to all of this.

POSSIBLE ALLUSIONS TO AMERICA

We begin with the recognition that no Bible verse mentions

America by name. But there are quite a number of theories regarding possible indirect references or allusions to America in Bible prophecy.

America may be just one of many unspecified nations. According to this theory, there are no direct references to the United States in Bible prophecy, but a number of general prophetic references to the nations in the tribulation at least include the United States (Isaiah 66:18-20; Haggai 2:6-7; Zechariah 12:2-3). Such unspecified passages, however, do not tell us anything specific about the role of the United States in the end times.

Others believe that perhaps the Babylon of Revelation 17–18 is the United States. Note the parallels between Babylon the Great in the book of Revelation and the United States: Both are dominant, both are immoral, both are excessively rich, and both think they are invulnerable. This scenario, however, is not given much credence by most serious Bible interpreters. It involves more *eisegesis* (reading a meaning into the text of Scripture) than *exegesis* (drawing the meaning out of the text of Scripture).

Others suggest that perhaps the United States might be the nation "whose land the rivers divide" (Isaiah 18:1-7). After all, the United States is divided by the Mississippi River. The passage also refers to the nation being feared because of its military conquests, something believed to fit the way many people around the world view the United States. The obvious problem with this view is that the nation is explicitly identified in Isaiah 18:1-2 as ancient Cush, or modern Sudan.

Still others suggest that perhaps the reference to the "merchants of Tarshish" in Ezekiel 38:13 is an allusion to the United States. According to this passage, when the great northern military coalition (Gog and his forces) invades Israel in the end times, a small group of nations will lamely protest the invasion: "Sheba and Dedan and the merchants of Tarshish and all its leaders will say to you, 'Have you come to seize spoil? Have you assembled your hosts to carry off plunder, to carry away silver and gold, to take away livestock and goods, to seize great spoil?'" It is speculated that perhaps *Tarshish* refers to all the Western nations, which would include the United States. Scholars, however, differ widely on their interpretation of this term, so being dogmatic here would be unwise.

NO MENTION IN THE BIBLE

My studied opinion is that the Bible contains no explicit or implicit references to the United States. Using proper hermeneutics and sound exegesis, I cannot see America in any of the verses so often suggested by some prophecy buffs. If I am correct in this belief, then we might ask, why isn't America mentioned in Bible prophecy? A number of explanations are possible.

Most Nations Not Mentioned

Let's begin by stating the obvious—most nations in the world are not mentioned in Bible prophecy, so it really may be no big deal if the United States is not mentioned. Still, the United States is the world's single remaining superpower and Israel's principal ally. One therefore might naturally expect at least a passing reference to this country.

No Significant Role

Perhaps America is not mentioned simply because America plays no significant role in the unfolding of God's end-time plans. Again, however, because of the United States' position and its financial support of Israel, one might naturally expect at least some reference. So again, why no reference?

Implosion Due to Degeneration

One possible reason America is not mentioned in Bible prophecy is that our country may eventually implode due to spiraling moral and spiritual degeneration. Plenty of statistics reveal this country's moral and spiritual troubles. At present, four out of five adults—some 83 percent—say they are concerned about the moral condition of the United States. If the moral fiber of this country continues to erode, the demise of this country is only a matter of time.

Nuclear Attack

Perhaps the United States is not mentioned in Bible prophecy because it will be destroyed or at least greatly weakened by nuclear weapons and will play no significant role in the end times. The United States stands a good chance of being attacked with nuclear weapons at some point in the future. Some government advisors are presently saying that a nuclear attack on U.S. soil within the next ten years is more likely than not. Of course, it may be a stretch to say that the entire United States could be destroyed, but the destruction of one major city—such as New York—would have a devastating effect on the U.S. economy.

Electro-Magnetic Pulse Attack

Perhaps the United States is not mentioned in Bible prophecy because it will become incapacitated by an electro-magnetic pulse (EMP) attack. This possibility is documented in a report issued in 2004 by a blue-ribbon Congressional commission called Commission to Assess the Threat to the United States from Electromagnetic Pulse Attack. Based on this report, government officials lamented that the technology is now here to bring America's way of life to an end.

The commission found that a single nuclear weapon, delivered by a missile to an altitude of a few hundred miles over the United States, would yield catastrophic damage to the nation. Such a missile could easily be launched from a freighter off the coast of the United States. The commission explained that the higher the altitude of the weapon's detonation, the larger the affected geographic area would be. At a height of 300 miles, the entire continental United States would be exposed, along with parts of Canada and Mexico.

The commission warned that the electromagnetic pulse produced by such a weapon would have a high likelihood of severely damaging the electrical power systems, electronics, and information systems that Americans depend on. At high risk would be electronic control, the infrastructures for handling electric power, sensors and protective systems of all kinds, computers, cell phones, telecommunications, cars, boats, airplanes, trains, fuel and energy, banking and finance, emergency services, and even food and water. Anything that uses electricity is at risk.

The consequences of an EMP attack would be especially harmful to American society today because the infrastructure of our society—civilian and military—virtually runs on electricity and electronic components. The commission estimated that "months to years" could be required to fully recover from such an attack.

Starvation and disease could result in some parts of the country following an EMP attack. Expert testimony presented before the U.S. Congress indicated that an EMP attack could reduce the United States to pre–Industrial Age levels of transportation and access to food and water. Instead of cars, buses, and trains, people would be reduced to using bikes, horses, and buggies.

Oil Crisis

In my book *The Coming Oil Storm* (Harvest House, 2010), I discuss the real possibility that our country could suffer substantial economic weakening due to its gross overdependence on oil. As I document in the book, the world is undeniably running out of oil. Top experts in this field are now telling us that a progressive lessening in the oil supply will progressively weaken the economy of our oil-driven society. (Our infrastructure runs totally on oil—including our transportation, farming equipment, manufacturing equipment, and much more.) When the oil supply begins to dwindle, the shortages will cause global recession, conflict, and more.

Stephen Leeb, Wall Street analyst and author of *The Coming Economic Collapse*, warns that just because a nation has been around for two or three hundred years does not mean it will last forever. He suggests that our next major crisis will likely be a shortfall in energy production, which could severely injure the country. He raises the possibility that as nations start to run out of oil, this could escalate to war—even nuclear war.

> Energy is essential to wealth. Just as the United States will feel compelled to defend its access to oil, other nations, who feel they have an equal right to enjoy a share of the world's wealth, may fight to secure some of the remaining oil deposits. With nuclear weapons becoming more widespread, the possibility of nuclear war grows greater, and with it the most dramatic, large-scale collapse of civilization the world has ever witnessed.[7]

The Rapture

Another possible reason the United States is not mentioned in Bible prophecy is that the United States will be affected catastrophically by the rapture. It seems fair to say that the United States will be negatively affected by the rapture more so than most other nations. That is because more Christians may live in the United States than in any other country. Following the moment of the rapture, many executives and their employees will not show up for work, many bills and mortgages will go unpaid, many college tuition bills and loans will go unpaid, many law enforcement personnel will no longer be here to keep the peace, and the stock market will likely crash because of the panic that ensues when millions of people suddenly vanish. This and much more will result following the rapture.

Cyber Attack

One final possibility that could lead to the demise of the United States is a lethal cyber attack. Presently, advisors to our government are affirming that our country could suffer catastrophic damage through cyberspace in just 15 minutes. In that short time, we could experience an electronic equivalent to Pearl Harbor.

During such an attack, computer networks affiliated with the Department of Defense would likely fail and grind to a halt, as would Pentagon computers. The major Internet providers would melt down. Major financial centers in New York and elsewhere would likely be slammed with a potent computer virus that erases terabytes of stored data. Computer systems affiliated with air traffic control would go down, resulting in countless midair collisions. Refinery fires and explosions would likely take place, chemical plants would begin emitting clouds of poisonous chemicals into the air, major pipelines would explode, trains would crash in subways, electrical grids would go down, traffic lights would go (resulting in countless automobile accidents), and all communication devices would go silent—and all this in 15 minutes.[8]

You may recall my earlier discussion of Cyber ShockWave, an exercise in 2010 that simulated our government's reaction to a real cyber attack. After the exercise was complete, Michael Chertoff, former secretary of homeland security, warned that cyberterrorism "ought to be treated as a threat of sufficient seriousness that we give it the priority attention we've given weapons of mass destruction."[9] Director Stephen Friedman of the National Economic Council agreed that immediate action is necessary. "There is no question in my mind that this is a predictable surprise and we need to get our act together."[10]

Such comments reflect the sobering reality that a lethal cyber attack could yield the same number of casualties in the United States as a weapon of mass destruction. When we consider the midair collisions, auto accidents, poisonous fumes, and the like, we can reasonably expect significant injury to the civilian population. The enemy would not even need to set foot on American soil to make all this happen. It would be accomplished entirely through cyberspace.

Other countries are not the only potential sources of such an attack—terrorists are now getting in on the act. A small group of hackers could develop a cyber attack that could be lethal to the United States.[11] Major terrorist groups now have the financial backing of some oil-rich Muslim countries, so they could afford a substantial hacker budget. As Wayne Simmons, former CIA operative, put it, "The major funding of terror is definitely oil."[12] For example, according to author Rachel Ehrenfeld, al-Qaeda funding comes from the oil-rich Saudi royal family, Saudi charitable organizations, Saudi banks and financial networks, Saudi businesses, and Saudi criminal activities.[13] Hamas funding comes from Iran, Saudi Arabia, the Gulf States, the United Arab Emirates, Syria, and Iraq. Hezbollah receives its funding from oil-rich Tehran. Palestinian Islamic Jihad receives its funding from Iran and Syria.

The United States is sending a tidal wave of wealth to Middle Eastern nations as we purchase their oil. Much of that oil money is then used to fund terrorist acts against the United States. Our government's leaders are concerned that a lot of that oil money may be used to finance a large team of highly trained and religiously motivated cyber hackers that are assigned a single task: to bring down the United States. At the very least, their goal would be to inflict terror on Americans. Recall this definition of cyberterrorism: "A computer based attack or threat of attack intended to intimidate or coerce governments or societies in pursuit of goals that are political, religious, or ideological. The attack should be sufficiently destructive or disruptive to generate fear comparable to that from physical acts of terrorism."[14] To bring about such terror, these cyber attacks would be purposefully engineered to cause injury, death, power outages, jets crashing, and major economic losses. Some Islamic hackers speak about such cyber attacks in religious terms, affirming that their attacks are tantamount to fighting jihad against Islam's enemies.[15] And their number one target is the United States—the "Great Satan."

Meanwhile, U.S. military technology has been so compromised through cyber espionage that our physical defenses may be far from what they need to be. Recall that in 2009, the People's Republic of China successfully penetrated the cyber security of the Pentagon's multi-billion-dollar Joint Strike Fighter F-35 project.[16] Between ten and twenty terabytes of data were stolen from the U.S. Army Information Systems Engineering Command, the Naval Ocean Systems Center, the Missile Defense Agency, and Sandia National Laboratories. Security breaches such as this enable our military adversaries to discover vulnerabilities in our new technologies. If a physical conflict develops between us, they will already know how to defend against such technologies.

A massive cyber attack could also be launched as a prelude to—or in conjunction with—a kinetic (physical) attack. For example, consider the possibility of a nuclear weapon being shipped into the United States. Of the 50,000 cargo containers that are shipped into the United States each day, only 5 percent are screened.[17] That leaves 95 percent that are unscreened. A bomb could easily make its way into the country in one of the unscreened containers.

As a prelude to detonating this bomb in New York City, a massive distributed denial of service (DDoS) attack could be launched against the Department of Defense computer networks, the Pentagon computer networks, other military networks, and all our country's primary Internet providers. As we have seen, in a DDoS attack, a preprogrammed flood of Internet traffic shuts down or at least jams targeted websites or computer networks. It is "distributed" because thousands of computers—in some cases, more than a million computers—distributed over a wide geographical area receive electronic instructions from a remote user to flood the targeted website or network with messages.

Because the U.S. military depends so heavily on the Internet, a DDoS attack launched just prior to a nuclear detonation in New York City would completely disrupt communications and significantly hinder command and control efforts from responding to the attack. We might have no idea who launched the cyber attack and who nuked us.

CONCLUSION

A genuine cyber threat exists for the people of the United States today. We face a "real and present danger." In fact, one or more catastrophic cyber events may play a role in the eventual demise of the United States in the end times. We now understand why the U.S. government has allocated such a significant portion of its annual budget to beefing up the country's cyber defenses. Will it be enough?

CYBER STRATEGIES IN END-TIME WARS

Biblical prophecy reveals that battles and wars—even between allies—will take place during the future tribulation period. The bloodshed and loss of life will be staggering, on a scale never before seen.

In the pages that follow, I will briefly summarize two of these—the Ezekiel invasion and Armageddon—and then provide my take on how cyber warfare may well relate to them. I noted previously in the book that man initially fought all his battles on land. As the technology increased, he added another domain—the sea. Eventually he developed the technology to engage in battle beneath the sea. Still later, after a quantum leap forward in technological advancements, another physical domain for battle was added—the air. And still later, after further technological gains, man attained the capability of going into outer space, where man placed satellites for military use (such as reconnaissance, communication, and navigation). With each new technology, human beings have discovered new ways to do battle against each other.[1] In our present day, yet another domain for doing battle has emerged—only this time, it is not a physical domain. I am talking, of course, about cyberspace.[2] The turf of end-time battles will undoubtedly include all of these domains.

THE EZEKIEL INVASION

About 2600 years ago, the prophet Ezekiel predicted that the Jews would be regathered from many nations to the land of Israel in the end times (Ezekiel 36–37). He then prophesied that sometime later, there would be an all-out invasion into Israel by a massive northern assault force, with Russia heading up a coalition of Muslim nations, including modern Iran, Sudan, Turkey, and Libya. Their goal will be to utterly obliterate the Jews. With the sheer size of this assault force, Israel will have virtually no chance of defending itself. Ezekiel specifies the invading force in Ezekiel 38:1-6 (NASB).

> The word of the LORD came to me saying, "Son of man, set your face toward Gog of the land of Magog, the prince of Rosh, Meshech and Tubal, and prophesy against him and say, 'Thus says the Lord GOD, "Behold, I am against you, O Gog, prince of Rosh, Meshech and Tubal. I will turn you about and put hooks into your jaws, and I will bring you out, and all your army, horses and horsemen, all of them splendidly attired, a great company with buckler and shield, all of them wielding swords; Persia, Ethiopia and Put with them, all of them with shield and helmet; Gomer with all its troops; Beth-togarmah from the remote parts of the north with all its troops—many peoples with you."'"

A look at a few ancient history books, Hebrew lexicons, and archaeological discoveries clarifies the territory intended by these strange-sounding names.

- *Rosh*, to the uttermost north of Israel, refers to Russia.

- *Magog* refers to the southern portion of the former Soviet Union—probably including the former southern Soviet republics of Kazakhstan, Kyrgyzstan, Uzbekistan, Turkmenistan, Tajikistan, and possibly even northern parts of modern Afghanistan.

- *Meshech* and *Tubal* refer to the territory south of the Black and Caspian seas, which is modern Turkey.

- *Persia* refers to modern Iran. Persia became Iran in 1935 and the Islamic Republic of Iran in 1979.

- *Ethiopia* refers to the territory south of Egypt on the Nile River—what is today known as Sudan.

- *Put* refers to a land to the west of Egypt—modern-day Libya. The term may also include the modern-day countries of Algeria and Tunisia.

- *Gomer* apparently refers to part of modern Turkey.

- *Beth-togarmah* also apparently refers to modern-day Turkey, though it may also include Azerbaijan and Armenia.

More than a few students of the Bible have recognized that the very nations prophesied to join this alliance in the end times are already coming together. Significantly, this alliance is emerging after Israel became a nation again in 1948—with Jews continuing to stream into their homeland ever since, so that today there are more Jews in Israel than anywhere else on earth. The stage is apparently being set for this prophesied future invasion into Israel.

Note that an invasion into Israel on the scale of what is described in Ezekiel 38–39 has never occurred. Nor have the specific nations mentioned in the passage ever invaded Israel. The fulfillment of this prophecy must therefore yet be future. Ezekiel himself affirmed that the things of which he spoke would be fulfilled "in the latter years" (Ezekiel 38:8) and "in the latter days" (38:16) from the standpoint of his day. Such phrases point to the end times.

Ezekiel also affirmed that the invasion will occur after Israel is regathered from all around the earth to a land that had been a wasteland (Ezekiel 38:8,12). Certainly there were occasions in Israel's history in which the Jews were held in bondage. For example, they were slaves in Egypt. They went into captivity in Assyria and in Babylon. But in each of these cases, they were freed from a single nation, not many nations around the world. The only regathering of Jews from "many nations" around the world in Israel's history is that which is occurring in modern days. And since chapters 36–37 of Ezekiel are apparently being literally fulfilled (a regathering from "many nations"), we can reasonably and consistently assume that chapters 38–39 will likewise be literally fulfilled.

Notice also that the alliance between many of the nations mentioned in Ezekiel 38–39 may not necessarily have made good sense in Ezekiel's day because these nations are not located right next to each other. It makes great sense today, however, because the nations that make up the coalition are predominantly Muslim. Of course, Islam did not even exist in Ezekiel's day. This religion emerged in the seventh century AD.

Today, many Islamic nations appear to hate Israel. Jerusalem is at the heart of the conflict. It is the holiest of cities for the Jews and the third-holiest city for Muslims, behind Mecca and Medina. Jews believe Jerusalem belongs to them alone by divine right. And of course, Muslims believe Jerusalem belongs to *them* alone by divine right.

Anwar Sadat once proclaimed the Arab or Muslim view: "Jerusalem is the property of the Muslim nation…Nobody can ever decide the fate of Jerusalem. We shall retake it with the help of Allah."[3] Likewise, Yasser Arafat once promised that "whoever does not accept the fact that Jerusalem will be the capital of a Palestinian state, and only that state, can go drink from the Dead Sea."

On the Jewish side, Binyamin Netanyahu—with equal vigor—made this promise: "I will never allow Jerusalem to be divided again. Never! Never! We will keep Jerusalem united and…we will never surrender those ramparts."

Muslim political leaders today say they want to "wipe Israel off the map" and "push Israel into the sea." Iranian president Mahmoud Ahmadinejad has been particularly vitriolic in his hatred of Israel. Muslim nations clearly have a strong motive to unite and attack Israel. In fact, there have been hostilities in the Middle East for some 60 years, and things today seem more heated than ever.[4]

Russia also has a track record of aggression against Israel. For example, during the 1967 Six-Day War, Russia was poised to attack Israel and had been preparing to do so for a substantial time. Soviet warships, submarines, bombers, and fighter jets were mobilized and ready for action. However, President Johnson ordered the U.S. Sixth Fleet to steam toward Israel as a show of solidarity with Israel, and the Russians backed down.

Russia showed military aggression toward Israel again in 1973. Egypt, Syria, and some other Arab/Islamic countries launched an attack against Israel, and the Russians provided the military muscle behind the attack—including weaponry, ammunition, intelligence, and military training to help this Arabic coalition destroy Israel. While Russia provided help to the Arabs, the United States provided help to Israel. Russian general secretary Leonid Brezhnev fired off a threatening communiqué, couched in diplomatic language, to President Richard Nixon. Both Soviet and U.S. forces were put on high alert. Nixon promptly returned the favor and sent a communiqué to Brezhnev, warning him that his actions could lead to "incalculable consequences." This strongly worded communiqué, combined with the presence of U.S. military forces in the region, again served to stare down the Russian bear.

As well, I noted earlier in the book that in 1982, then-Israeli prime minister Menachem Begin revealed that a secret but massive cache of Russian weaponry had been discovered in deep underground cellars in Lebanon, apparently prepositioned for later use in a future invasion by Russia into Israel and perhaps other Middle East nations. Investigators found massive quantities of ammunition, armored vehicles, tanks, small arms, heavy weapons, communications devices, and other paraphernalia useful to military forces. Much of what was discovered was highly sophisticated—equipment that crack military units would use. So much was found that hundreds of trucks were required to remove it all. Israel's leaders admitted they had no idea that such extensive plans had been made for a future ground assault into Israel.

In view of such facts, a military alliance between Russia and the Muslim nations is not surprising.

A POWER VACUUM, AND THE RISE OF ANTICHRIST

Ezekiel 39 informs us that even though Israel will be vastly outnumbered, God Himself will come to the rescue of His people and annihilate the invading force. When God destroys the northern coalition either prior to the tribulation or in the early part of it, the resulting power vacuum will allow for the quick ascendancy of the antichrist. With no more Russia and no more Muslims, the antichrist will have a much easier time attaining world domination (see Revelation 13). As John F. Walvoord put it, "When the invading armies are defeated, the ruler of the ten nations will elevate himself and proclaim himself ruler of the entire world."[5] Thomas Ice elaborates:

> I have always thought that one of the strengths of this view is the way in which it could set the stage for the biblical scenario of the tribulation. If the tribulation is closely preceded by a failed regional invasion of Israel (by Russia and her Muslim allies), then this would remove much of the Russian and Muslim influence currently in the world today and allow a Euro-centric orientation to arise.[6]

A United States of Europe—that is, a revived Roman Empire—will become the seat of power for the antichrist.

If the Muslim invaders are destroyed before the tribulation begins, the antichrist might more easily sign a peace pact with Israel (Daniel 9:27), guaranteeing that Israel will be protected. (In other words, Israel will be easier to protect if the Muslim forces are already out of the picture.)

This would also give Israel time to rebuild its temple by the middle of the tribulation period, as Matthew 24 requires. If the Muslims were still in power in the early part of the tribulation period, they would prohibit Israel from building its temple on the temple mount in Jerusalem. But if all the Muslim armies are destroyed by God, this major obstacle to Israel's rebuilding of the temple is removed.

The destruction of Muslim forces in the first half of the tribulation will also allow for the emergence of a one-world religion. Christians will have already been removed in the rapture, and the Muslim forces will have been destroyed in the Ezekiel conflict. The emergence of a one-world religion will be much easier in this religious vacuum.

ARMAGEDDON

Aside from the Ezekiel invasion, which will result in countless casualties, Scripture reveals that human suffering will steadily escalate during the seven-year tribulation period. First are the seal judgments, involving bloodshed, famine, death, economic upheaval, a great earthquake, and cosmic disturbances (Revelation 6). Then come the trumpet judgments, involving hail and fire mixed with blood, the sea turning to blood, water turning bitter, further cosmic disturbances, affliction by demonic scorpions, and the death of a third of humankind (Revelation 8:6–9:21). Then come the bowl judgments, involving horribly painful sores on human beings, more bodies of water turning to blood, the death of all sea creatures, people being scorched by the sun, total darkness engulfing the land, a devastating earthquake, and much more (Revelation 16). Worse comes to worst, however, when these already traumatized human beings find themselves engaged in a catastrophic series of battles called Armageddon (see Daniel 11:40-45; Joel 3:9-17; Zechariah 14:1-3; Revelation 16:14-16). This takes place at the end of the tribulation period. Millions of people will perish in the worst escalation of conflict in the history of the planet.

The word *Armageddon* literally means "Mount of Megiddo" and refers to a location about 60 miles north of Jerusalem. This is the location of Barak's battle with the Canaanites (Judges 4) and Gideon's battle with the Midianites (Judges 7). This will be the site for the final horrific battles of humankind just prior to the second coming (Revelation 16:16).

Napoleon is reported to have once commented that this site is perhaps the greatest battlefield he had ever witnessed. Of course, the battles Napoleon fought will dim in comparison to Armageddon. So horrible will Armageddon be that no one would survive if it were not for Christ coming again (Matthew 24:22). The campaign of Armageddon includes several stages:

- the assembling of the antichrist's allies (Psalm 2:1-6; Joel 3:9-11; Revelation 16:12-16)
- Babylon's destruction (Isaiah 13–14; Jeremiah 50–51; Zechariah 5:5-11; Revelation 17–18)
- Jerusalem's fall (Micah 4:11–5:1; Zechariah 12–14)

- the antichrist's armies at Bozrah (Jeremiah 49:13-14)

- Israel's national regeneration (Psalm 79:1-13; Isaiah 64:1-12; Hosea 6:1-13; Joel 2:28-32; Zechariah 12:10; Romans 11:25-27)

- the second coming (Isaiah 34:1-7; Micah 2:12-13; Habakkuk 3:3)

- the horrific battle from Bozrah to the Valley of Jehoshaphat (Jeremiah 49:20-22; Joel 3:12-13; Zechariah 14:12-15)

- the ascent on the Mount of Olives (Joel 3:14-17; Zechariah 14:3-5; Matthew 24:29-31; Revelation 16:17-21; 19:11-21)

In view of all that occurs at Armageddon, the "battle" of Armageddon is not a single event. Armageddon will involve an extended, escalating conflict, and it will be catastrophic.

CYBER COMPONENTS OF END-TIMES WARFARE

The escalation of battles during the tribulation period will no doubt involve the use of some of the same cyber technologies that are available and already in use in modern warfare. To avoid speculating on specific, highly detailed cyber scenarios for these end-time battles and campaigns, I will describe in general terms the kinds of cyber technologies that will likely be employed in these conflicts, based on what we know about current military cyber strategies.

Preliminary Cyber Espionage

Before hostilities break out early in the tribulation period, various countries around the globe will undoubtedly spy on each other's military networks to gather as much information as possible about emerging military technologies. (Keep in mind that in the tribulation, nations will war against each other before the one-world government develops [see Matthew 24:7; Revelation 13].) Cyber espionage will likely be the primary means each country will utilize in spying on the others.

The effectiveness of this type of espionage was illustrated when China penetrated U.S. Department of Defense and Pentagon networks to download many terabytes of highly sensitive data about the new F-35 fighter jet. Hackers have also penetrated and compromised the networks of civilian companies doing contract work for the military—and we can expect this type of activity to continue during the tribulation.

In addition to directly hacking into a network, cyber espionage employs keyboard loggers. As we have seen, this type of malware might find its way onto a private network in any number of ways, including someone using an infected thumb drive. Once loaded into the network, the keyboard logger records all keystrokes and then transmits them to a remote location. Are Israeli keyboard loggers already transmitting data from Muslim keyboards in, say, Syria or Turkey or other Muslim countries? I suspect that keyboard loggers will be in extensive use during the tribulation.

As related specifically to the future Ezekiel invasion, there can be little doubt that even today, Israel's hackers—among the most talented in the world—are gathering all the intelligence data they can from the military networks of the Russians as well as Muslim nations such as Iran, Syria, and Turkey. Likewise, Russian and Muslim hackers are surely doing all they can to spy on Israel's networks. Every country is spying on every other country.

What is the goal of such spying? Among other things, each country spies on other countries to gain reliable information on new weapons technologies, military strategies, deployments, and vulnerabilities. Armed with such information, countries are more likely to be able to defeat their enemies. This is one of the reasons that Sun Tzu, in his book *The Art of War*, said it is a good policy to stay close to your friends but to stay even closer to your enemies. This tactic is faster, easier, and safer than ever before because of cyberspace.

Social Networks and Spear Phishing

Assuming that social networks will continue to exist during the tribulation (and we have no reason to expect their demise), intelligence gathering will likely continue on Facebook, MySpace, Twitter, and other such services. Many soldiers around the world make continual postings on such sites—including information about family members and friends. By gathering this data, an enemy hacker could launch a spear-phishing attack against a particular soldier.

We have seen that spear-phishing attacks involve e-mails that appear to be legitimate messages from someone you actually know (using real names) and include a link to something of interest. When the soldier-victim clicks on the link (thinking the e-mail was from someone he trusts), he may well be taken to a website that has an interesting article—but also, in the background, a virus downloads a keyboard logger, which records all his keystrokes and transmits them to a remote location. The more soldiers who are fooled in this way, the better it is for the enemy! Such deceptive techniques work well now; they will continue to work well in the end times.

Spying on Foreign Embassies

As documented earlier in the book, GhostNet software penetrated some 1300 computers at foreign embassies in several countries in 2009. This software remotely activated webcams and microphones without alerting the computer users that this was happening. This enabled the sources in China to engage in cyber eavesdropping for almost two years before being discovered.

I have no doubt that such spying will continue now as well as during the future tribulation. Intelligence gathering is a key to all successful warfare. This type of cyber espionage will certainly play a role in the Ezekiel invasion, for all the countries involved in that invasion—Russia, various Muslim nations, and Israel—are already engaged in cyber espionage against each other. The forces of the antichrist will likely engage in this type of cyber spying, always on the watch for those who may resist his globalized government.

Prepositioned Military Cyber Advantage Through Foreign Trade

In some cases, countries can gain prepositioned military cyber advantages over other countries through foreign trade. For example, the United States was victimized by China in recent years. China manufactured and distributed a network router and sold it at greatly reduced prices. Unbeknownst to anyone else, this router was specially designed to allow the Chinese government to bring down the networks of foreign countries. Buyers of these bogus routers included the U.S. Pentagon, the Marine Corps, the Air Force, and many defense contractors. Just imagine how easily the U.S. military could have been victimized if U.S. military hackers had not caught on!

One can only wonder if such bogus hardware has been manufactured and distributed by a number of countries around the world—hardware that may one day be instructed to crash during a future tribulation military engagement. Will the forces of the antichrist manufacture and distribute such equipment during the tribulation? He will be energized by Satan, the father of lies (John 8:44) and master of deception, so I don't doubt that as a possibility.

Disruption of the Power Supply

Civilian populations and the military depend on a reliable power supply, so in any military conflict, each side tries to knock out the power grids of enemy combatants. The military usually has alternative power sources, but knocking out the main power source of a country will definitely hinder its military from completing its objectives.

This is accomplished in cyberspace utilizing logic bombs, which I discussed earlier in the book. Such logic bombs can be used to inflict damage on physical hardware. For example, a hacker could infect a computer network that runs an electrical power grid with a logic bomb that initiates instructions to cause a power surge sufficient to fry the circuits of the transformers. When that happens, the electricity goes out. And if all the transformers are blown all over the country, electricity will be out for a very long time.

Chinese and Russian government hackers have already penetrated United States electrical power grids and laced the power infrastructure with logic bombs. Once those logic bombs are activated by foreign hackers—*boom*, there goes our power! Of course, U.S. hackers have probably also laced foreign power grids with logic bombs.

When Armageddon breaks out at the end of the tribulation period, I can envision logic bombs going off all over the globe. Everything will go haywire. Power outages will be the norm. The resulting confusion will be staggering.

More than 140 countries currently wield cyber warfare capabilities. These countries can plant a variety of electronic viruses and bugs into key utility, military, and financial network systems that can wreak all kinds of havoc. When Armageddon emerges, you can bet that all of these countries will be busy launching their cyber attacks.

Disabling or Disrupting Hardware

Earlier in the book, I noted that the Stuxnet worm is the most lethal computer virus ever launched into cyberspace. It has been called "a cyber shot heard around the world," a "first-of-its-kind guided cyber missile," a "cyber superweapon," the "first direct example of weaponized software," and "a working and fearsome prototype of a cyber-weapon that will lead to a new arms race in the world…a cyber arms race." A cyber analyst commented that Stuxnet "could produce the kind of damage only seen in Hollywood disaster films."

This type of worm targets certain computer systems—"programmable logic controllers" (or PLCs)—that monitor and manage such things as oil pipelines, factories, power plants, nuclear reactors, and other industrial facilities. It is a virus that can control the computers that control machinery. Prior to the launching of Stuxnet, no other malware program has ever managed to move from cyberspace to the real world. This is what makes Stuxnet so revolutionary. It is not a tool of industrial espionage. It is a weapon of war.

In future end-time military conflicts, including both the Ezekiel invasion and Armageddon, we can expect predesigned worms to be launched against enemy combatants and disable or disrupt military hardware systems. This type of disabling or disruption will not allow for a quick fix (as has been more than amply demonstrated with Stuxnet). When a piece of hardware has been disabled, it may become a useless piece of junk so far as military use is concerned.

What kinds of hardware might be targeted? Missile guidance

systems, unmanned aerial vehicle guidance systems, smart bombs with laser targeting, communications systems, nuclear facilities (as was the case with Iran's reactors that were crippled by Stuxnet), and much more. For such a worm to hit just prior to an enemy launching a kinetic (physical) attack may well spell defeat.

Disruption of Critical Military Networks

The computer networks at the U.S. Department of Defense and the Pentagon have already been hacked, and the computer networks of foreign militaries are also vulnerable. It can be assumed that in any kinetic (physical) attack, cyber attacks will be launched to disrupt the functioning of military networks. Military strategists say that significant military advantage can be gained by launching a cyber attack just prior to a kinetic attack. This ensures that the enemy will be reeling from the cyber attack when the physical attack is launched.

North Korea has successfully brought down the servers of the Department of Homeland Security, the U.S. Treasury, several other government departments, and regular Internet providers by flooding them with requests for data. This was a DDoS (distributed denial of service) attack. A Pentagon server used by the military for logistical communications in armed conflict was also impeded by such a cyber attack.

North Korea accomplished this with a botnet. Recall from my earlier discussion that a botnet is a network of robot computers that have been infected with a virus that forces them to operate according to the commands of unauthorized remote users—in this case, North Koreans. This usually takes place without any knowledge of the computer's owner or user. Such a network of robot computers are typically used to launch an attack against a target website, often by flooding the target website with messages. This causes the website to become jammed or to shut down altogether. By using this strategy, North Korea shut down some U.S. computer servers that have military applications.

We can count on this type of thing happening in the future tribulation battles and wars. The more computers are jammed up during wartime, the more sluggish military response is. During the Ezekiel invasion, the computer networks of Russia, Israel, and Muslim nations will almost certainly become targeted for DDoS attacks. Of course, the country that launches the *preemptive* attack might be able to so damage the enemy's computer networks that cyber retaliation is thwarted. So Russia, for example, might launch a preemptive lethal cyber attack against Israel, thereby completely disrupting Israel's cyber abilities. If Israel is attacked by a massive assault force of Russian and Muslim invaders when their Internet service and communication systems are down, it would seem to stand no chance of survival. However, Ezekiel 39 reveals that God Himself will come to the rescue of Israel and utterly annihilate all the invaders. God is always watchful—"He who keeps Israel will neither slumber nor sleep" (Psalm 121:4)—and He will be Israel's defender, thus guaranteeing the defeat of the coalition.

Hacking Enemy Radar

Earlier in the book, we saw that Israel successfully hacked Syrian air radar so that it remained blank while Israel's jets invaded Syria. It is still being debated as to just how Israel pulled this off. Suffice it to say that Israel has some very talented hackers.

In the future Ezekiel invasion, as well as at Armageddon, it is entirely possible that some of the nations involved will follow Israel's lead by using this same kind of cyber hacking to disrupt enemy radars. The major governments of the world all have cyber command centers with thousands of hackers on the payroll and are even now perfecting such cyber capabilities.

□ □ □

So effective will man's military attacks be in the end times—both cyber and kinetic—that if the Lord did not return at the height of it, not a single human being would survive: "If those days had not been cut short, no human being would be saved" (Matthew 24:22).

LIVING AS AN END-TIMES CHRISTIAN

et's summarize a few of the fundamental facts we have considered in our brief journey together.

- Cyber attacks and cyber warfare are increasingly the norm in our troubled day.

- Vulnerabilities exist at virtually every level of our infrastructure—including our banking institutions, our power grids, and our Internet service providers.

- Our personal computers are vulnerable—including all the information stored on our personal computers as well as our online financial transactions.

- Our military is vulnerable on many different levels, including networks at the Pentagon and the Department of Defense.

- Cyber espionage is at epidemic levels. Massive amounts of private and sensitive data is stolen daily.

- Cyber technologies and cyber events seem closely connected to the fulfillment of end-times Bible prophecies.

Understandably, many Bible prophecy students believe the stage is currently being set for what the ancient prophets predicted. Thomas Ice and Timothy Demy, for example, make this observation: "Today, the world is similar to a stage being set for a great drama. The major actors are standing in the wings waiting for their moment in history. The main stage props have been put in place. The curtain is about to rise for a prophetic play."[1]

PROPHETIC INTEREST ON THE RISE

With all that is happening in our world today, Americans' interest in biblical prophecy is steadily increasing.

- In 1999, 40 percent of all Americans said they believed the world would end just as the Bible predicts.[2]

- A 2006 poll revealed that 42 percent of Americans said they agreed that Israel's rebirth as a nation, the instability of the Middle East, and other such events are indications that we are living in what the Bible calls the last days.

- The same poll reveals that 52 percent of Americans (that is, more than 150 million people) agree that the rebirth of Israel as a nation in 1948 and the return of millions of Jews to the Holy Land is a direct fulfillment of biblical prophecy.[3]

We are living in exciting times. A studied examination of biblical prophecies and a thorough and rational survey of the world scene today indicate we may indeed be living in the last days. Prophecy experts agree. "Never before in the history of the world has there been a confluence of major evidences of preparation for the end."[4] "Today, for the first time in two thousand years, we are seeing all of these signs come true, and the rebirth of Israel is the most dramatic sign of them all. We can, therefore, have confidence that Jesus' return is closer than ever."[5]

This postscript is not the place for me to go into a detailed chronological examination of the various biblical prophecies related to the second coming. Instead, I will mention two resources I have written that will help you do this on your own: *The Popular Dictionary of Bible*

Prophecy and *The Topical Handbook of Bible Prophecy* (both from Harvest House, 2010). These are available for quick and easy purchase at my website (www.ronrhodes.org) or at your local Christian bookstore.

As we bring this book to a close, let's consider how we ought to live as Christians in the end times.

LIVING AS END-TIME CHRISTIANS

As the stage is being set for the direct fulfillment of end-time Bible prophecies, we ought to think about the way we Christians should live our lives. Should we make any changes? Should we be worried about the future? Should we be discouraged about world events? What should be our attitude as we live in the end times?

Many extremists have taken unhealthy paths as a result of their understanding of prophecy. I want to avoid such extremism. I advise people to live their lives as if the rapture could happen today but also to plan their lives as if they will live a long life on the earth. That way they are prepared for time and eternity.

Yet I feel it necessary to go beyond this because Scripture gives us many helpful exhortations that clarify what our attitude should be as we live in the end times. We will see that Scripture never endorses extreme changes or policies. Rather, Scripture takes a reasoned and sound approach in guiding Christians in this regard. I urge you to meditate on these scriptural truths so that when things seem to be going haywire in our world, you will have an anchor to keep your soul on track.

DISCERN THE SIGNS OF THE TIMES

Some people today utterly ignore biblical prophecy. Other people have been misled by some Christians (*preterists*) who teach that most biblical prophecies have already been fulfilled in the first century and that we should therefore not look for future fulfillments of Bible prophecies relating to the tribulation or the rapture. This viewpoint is as unfortunate as it is unbiblical. Scripture indicates that just as biblical prophecies about the first coming of Christ were fulfilled literally (such as Isaiah 7:14; Micah 5:2; Zechariah 12:10), so the prophecies that relate to the second coming (for example, a one-world government—Revelation 13) will also be literally fulfilled. In view of this, we should all make an effort to stay aware of what Scripture teaches about the end times and then accurately observe the times. Consider these words from the gospel of Matthew:

> The Pharisees and Sadducees came up, and testing Jesus, they asked Him to show them a sign from heaven. But He replied to them, "When it is evening, you say, 'It will be fair weather, for the sky is red.' And in the morning, 'There will be a storm today, for the sky is red and threatening.' Do you know how to discern the appearance of the sky, but cannot discern the signs of the times?" (Matthew 16:1-3 NASB).

What a rebuke! These Pharisees and Sadducees—the religious elite of the time—were supposed to know the teachings of Scripture, and yet they were completely unable to properly discern the times. They had been inundated by prophetic signs that revealed that Jesus was the divine Messiah, yet they had missed them all. They were blind to the reality that the Messiah was in their midst. The miracles Jesus wrought were clear signs to His divine identity, just as dark clouds in the sky are signs of impending rain. These miracles—sight for the blind, hearing for the deaf, and the like—had been prophesied of the Messiah in the Old Testament (Isaiah 35:5-6), and the Pharisees and Sadducees (experts in the Old Testament) should have seen that Jesus fulfilled these messianic verses. But in their blindness, they could not "discern the signs of the times." Let's not follow their example.

Jesus also urged, "Now learn the parable from the fig tree: when its branch has already become tender and puts forth its leaves, you know that summer is near; so, you too, when you see all these things, recognize that He is near, right at the door" (Matthew 24:32-33 NASB). Jesus indicates in this verse that God has revealed certain things through prophecy that ought to cause people who know the Bible to understand that a fulfillment of prophecy is taking place (or that the stage is being set for a prophecy to eventually be fulfilled). Jesus is thus exhorting His followers to be accurate observers of the times so that when biblical prophecies are fulfilled, they will recognize it (see also Luke 21:25-28).

LIVE IN PURITY

God is not showing off when He tells us about the future. God does not give us prophecy to teach us mere intellectual facts about eschatology. Many verses in the Bible that deal with prophecy lead to exhortations to personal purity in the way we live our lives. This means that studying Bible prophecy ought to change the way we live. It ought to have an effect on our behavior. Consider these biblical examples.

> Do this, knowing the time, that it is already the hour for you to awaken from sleep; for now salvation is nearer to us than when we believed. The night is almost gone, and the day is near. Therefore let us lay aside the deeds of darkness and put on the armor of light. Let us behave properly as in the day, not in carousing and drunkenness, not in sexual promiscuity and sensuality, not in strife and jealousy. But put on the Lord Jesus Christ, and make no provision for the flesh in regard to its lusts (Romans 13:11-14 NASB).

> The day of the Lord will come like a thief, in which the heavens will pass away with a roar and the elements will be destroyed with intense heat, and the earth and its works will be burned up.
>
> Since all these things are to be destroyed in this way, what sort of people ought you to be in holy conduct and godliness, looking for and hastening the coming of the day of God, because of which the heavens will be destroyed by burning, and the elements will melt with intense heat! But according to His promise we are looking for new heavens and a new earth, in which righteousness dwells.
>
> Therefore, beloved, since you look for these things, be diligent to be found by Him in peace, spotless and blameless (2 Peter 3:10-14 NASB).

> Beloved, now we are children of God, and it has not appeared as yet what we will be. We know that when He appears, we will be like Him, because we will see Him just as He is. And everyone who has this hope fixed on Him purifies himself, just as He is pure (1 John 3:2-3 NASB).

This last passage is referring to the future rapture. And what a glorious day that will be. One scholar put it this way: "The hope of the rapture, when we will meet the Savior, should be a sanctifying force in our lives. We will be made completely like Him then; so we should endeavor with His help to serve Him faithfully now and to lead lives of purity."[6]

A helpful analogy is found in ancient Jewish marriages. In biblical times, a betrothed woman eagerly awaited the coming of her groom to take her away to his father's house in marriage celebration. During this time of anticipation, the bride's loyalty to her groom was tested. Likewise, as the bride of Christ (the church) awaits the coming of the messianic Groom, the church is motivated to live in purity and godliness until He arrives at the rapture.

USE SOUND JUDGMENT

First Peter 4:7-10 is jam-packed with wisdom for how we ought to live in view of biblical prophecy.

> The end of all things is near; therefore, be of sound judgment and sober spirit for the purpose of prayer. Above all, keep fervent in your love for one another, because love covers a multitude of sins. Be hospitable to one another without complaint. As each one has received a special gift, employ it in serving one another as good stewards of the manifold grace of God (NASB).

Many people tend to become sensationalistic and alarmist about end-time prophecies. But God tells us to be sober-minded. God instructs us to maintain sound judgment. The best way to be sober-minded and maintain sound judgment is to regularly feed our minds with the Word of God. Keeping our minds stayed on the Scriptures will keep us on track in our thinking and in our life choices in the light of biblical prophecy.

NEVER PREDICT THE DATES OF THE FULFILLMENT OF BIBLE PROPHECIES

The timing of end-time events is in God's hands, and we have not been given the details. In Acts 1:7 we read Jesus' words to the disciples before He ascended into heaven: "It is not for you to know times or epochs which the Father has fixed by His own authority." This means that we can be accurate observers of the times, as Jesus instructed (Matthew 24:32-33; Luke 21:25-28), and we can be excited about the fulfillment of Bible prophecy, but we do not have details on the precise timing of end-time events. We must simply resolve to trust God with these matters.

Christians who get caught up in predicting dates (for the rapture, for example) can do damage to the cause of Christ. For example, non-Christians enjoy scorning Christians who have put stock in end-time predictions—especially when specific dates have been attached to specific events. Why discredit the Christian message? We can be excited about events that appear to be setting the stage for the eventual fulfillment of prophecy without engaging in such sensationalism. Remember, Christ calls His followers to live soberly and alertly as they await His coming (Mark 13:32-37).

DO NOT LET YOUR HEART BE TROUBLED

> Do not let your heart be troubled; believe in God, believe also in Me. In My Father's house are many dwelling places; if it were not so, I would have told you; for I go to prepare a place for you. If I go and prepare a place for you, I will come again and receive you to Myself, that where I am, there you may be also (John 14:1-3 NASB).

My former Bible prophecy mentor, John F. Walvoord, has a great insight on this passage:

> These verses are the Bible's first revelation of the rapture, in which Christ will come back to take His own to heaven. He exhorted the disciples not to be troubled. Since they trusted the Father, they also should trust Christ, whose power was demonstrated in His many miracles. Having referred to Himself as the Source of peace, Jesus spoke of His coming to take them to heaven. They need not be anxious about His leaving because later He would return for them.[7]

So regardless of what happens in this world, we need not be troubled. Why not? Because we know the Prince of Peace, Jesus Christ. He is the source of peace, and the peace He gives does not depend on circumstances (John 14:27). We need not worry or fear. As Jesus said, He is now preparing our eternal homes. That future reality is enough to strengthen us through any present difficulties.

RECALL GOD'S GREATNESS

We should ever keep in mind that Bible prophecy constantly and relentlessly points to the awesome greatness of God.

> Behold, the former things have come to pass, now I declare new things; before they spring forth I proclaim them to you (Isaiah 42:9 NASB).

> Thus says the LORD, the King of Israel and his Redeemer, the LORD of hosts:

> "I am the first and I am the last, and there is no God besides Me. Who is like Me? Let him proclaim and declare it; yes, let him recount it to Me in order, from the time that I established the ancient nation. And let them declare to them the things that are coming and the events that are going to take place. Do not tremble and do not be afraid; have I not long since announced it to you and declared it? And you are My witnesses. Is there any God besides Me, or is there any other Rock? I know of none" (Isaiah 44:6-8 NASB).

> Remember this, and be assured; recall it to mind, you transgressors. Remember the former things long past, for I am God, and there is no other; I am God, and there is no one like Me, declaring the end from the beginning, and from ancient times things which have not been done, saying, "My purpose will be established, and I will accomplish all My good pleasure" (Isaiah 46:8-10 NASB).

Let the name of God be blessed forever and ever, for wisdom and power belong to Him. It is He who changes the times and the epochs; He removes kings and establishes kings; He gives wisdom to wise men and knowledge to men of understanding. It is He who reveals the profound and hidden things; He knows what is in the darkness, and the light dwells with Him (Daniel 2:20-22 NASB).

As Rich Mullins wrote in his popular contemporary Christian song, our God is an awesome God! Amen!

KEEP AN ETERNAL PERSPECTIVE IN THE MIDST OF TEMPORAL TURMOIL

Regardless of what takes place on earth, we each have a splendorous destiny ahead. I never tire of saying that a daily pondering of the incredible glory of the afterlife is one of the surest ways to stay motivated to live faithfully during our relatively short time on earth. We are but pilgrims on our way to another land—to the final frontier of heaven, where God Himself dwells.

J.I. Packer, one of my favorite Christian authors, once said that the "lack of long, strong thinking about our promised hope of glory is a major cause of our plodding, lackluster lifestyle."[8] Packer points to the Puritans as a much-needed example for us, for they believed that "it is the heavenly Christian that is the lively Christian." The Puritans understood that we "run so slowly, and strive so lazily, because we so little mind the prize…So let Christians animate themselves daily to run the race set before them by practicing heavenly meditation."[9]

A daily habit of Puritan Richard Baxter was to "dwell on the glory of the heavenly life to which one was going."[10] He daily practiced "holding heaven at the forefront of his thoughts and desires."[11] The hope of heaven brought him joy, and joy brought him strength. Baxter once said, "A heavenly mind is a joyful mind; this is the nearest and truest way to live a life of comfort…A heart in heaven will be a most excellent preservative against temptations, a powerful means to kill thy corruptions."[12]

REMEMBER THAT THE RAPTURE IS IMMINENT

The term *imminent* literally means "ready to take place" or "impending." The New Testament teaches that the rapture is imminent—that is, nothing else must happen before the rapture occurs (see 1 Corinthians 1:7; 16:22; Philippians 3:20; 4:5; 1 Thessalonians 1:10; Titus 2:13; Hebrews 9:28; 1 Peter 1:13; Jude 21). The rapture could occur at any moment—no signs will precede it. This is in contrast to the second coming of Christ, which is preceded by many events during the seven-year tribulation period (see Revelation 4–18).

The imminence of the rapture is certainly implied in the apostle Paul's words in Romans 13:11-12: "You know the time, that the hour has come for you to wake from sleep. For salvation is nearer to us now than when we first believed. The night is far gone; the day is at hand. So then let us cast off the works of darkness and put on the armor of light." Salvation in this context must be eschatological, referring to the rapture, for Paul refers to this salvation as a specific future event. At the end of each day, the Christian is that much closer to the rapture.

The imminence of the rapture is also implied in James 5:7-9:

> Be patient, therefore, brothers, until the coming of the Lord. See how the farmer waits for the precious fruit of the earth, being patient about it, until it receives the early and the late rains. You also, be patient. Establish your hearts, for the coming of the Lord is at hand. Do not grumble against one another, brothers, so that you may not be judged; behold, the Judge is standing at the door.

The fact that no signs will precede the rapture, that it could occur at any moment, ought to spur the Christian to faithful living (see Titus 2:13-14). How blessed it will be for the Christian to be living in righteousness at that moment. How embarrassing it will be for the Christian to be engaged in sin at that moment.

DWELL ON COMFORTING TRUTHS FROM THE WORD OF GOD

Here are some verses to get you started.

Maintain Faith in God

Blessed are those who trust (Jeremiah 17:7).

Cling tightly to faith (1 Timothy 1:19).

Do not throw away trust (Hebrews 10:35).

Faith brings answered prayer (Matthew 15:28; 21:22).

Faith grows from hearing God's Word (Romans 10:17).

Faith is assurance and conviction of what we do not see (Hebrews 11:1).

Faith without works is dead (James 2:17-18).

Trusting God brings joy (Psalm 40:4).

Live by faith, not by sight (2 Corinthians 5:7).

Faith opens the door to miracles (Matthew 21:21).

The righteous live by faith (Romans 1:17; Hebrews 10:38).

Small faith yields big results (Luke 17:5-6).

Trials are tests of faith (1 Peter 1:7).

Trust in the Lord with your whole heart (Proverbs 3:5).

Trust in the Lord, not man (Psalm 118:8).

Faith pleases God (Hebrews 11:6).

Keep Your Hope Firm

Jesus gives us eternal comfort and good hope (2 Thessalonians 2:16).

God's plans for His people give hope (Jeremiah 29:11).

Hope empowers us to endure (1 Thessalonians 1:3).

Hope in God (Psalm 39:7; 42:5; Lamentations 3:24).

We can hope in God's unfailing love (Psalm 33:18,20,22).

We can hope in God's Word (Psalm 119:74,81; 130:5; Romans 15:4).

Hope in the Lord will not be disappointed (Isaiah 49:23 NIV).

Hopes of godly people result in joy (Proverbs 10:28).

We can have eager expectation and hope (Philippians 1:20).

Hope is laid up for us in heaven (Colossians 1:5).

Those who hope in the Lord renew their strength (Isaiah 40:31 NIV).

Three things endure: faith, hope, love (1 Corinthians 13:13).

We have a living hope (1 Peter 1:3).

Remain Optimistic Regardless of What Happens

Have good courage (2 Corinthians 5:6).

Always rejoice (1 Thessalonians 5:16).

Be strong and take courage (Psalm 31:24).

A joyful heart is good medicine (Proverbs 17:22).

God has plans for His people (Jeremiah 29:11).

Rejoice and be glad (Psalm 118:24).

Our help comes from the Lord (Psalm 121:1).

The righteous need not be afraid of bad news (Psalm 112:7-8).

There is a future for people of peace (Psalm 37:37).

Do Not Worry

Pray and give thanks instead of worrying (Philippians 4:6-7).

Anxious hearts weigh us down (Proverbs 12:25).

Banish anxiety from your heart (Ecclesiastes 11:10).

Cast your anxiety on God (1 Peter 5:7).

Circumstances need not cause us to worry (Luke 8:22-25).

God's consolation cheers us (Psalm 94:19).

Seek the kingdom instead of worrying about your needs (Matthew 6:25-34).

Life's worries will choke the word if you let them (Mark 4:19).

The Lord is always at hand (Acts 2:25-28).

Be Faithful to God Regardless of What Happens

Always be faithful (Proverbs 3:3).

Be a faithful servant (Matthew 25:23).

Be faithful in prayer (Romans 12:12 NIV).

Choose whom you will serve (Joshua 24:15).

Be faithful in small matters (Luke 16:10).

The fruit of the Spirit includes faithfulness (Galatians 5:22).

God preserves the faithful (Psalm 31:23).

Hold tightly to hope (Hebrews 10:23).

Keep a grip on the traditions you have learned (2 Thessalonians 2:15).

Hold fast your confession (Hebrews 4:14).

Pay attention to what you have heard (Hebrews 2:1).

The Lord will not forsake you (Psalm 37:28).

The Lord preserves the lives of His saints (Psalm 97:10).

Remain faithful even in face of death (Revelation 2:10).

Stand firm in the faith (1 Corinthians 16:13).

Let your life be worthy of the gospel (Philippians 1:27).

Continue in what you have learned (2 Timothy 3:14).

As we close our prophetic journey in this book, let's resolve to live as this kind of end-time Christian. Let's resolve not to fall into the snare of being satisfied with mere intellectual facts about prophecy. Instead, let's live expectantly that we may be face-to-face with our Lord this very day.

MARANATHA

The Aramaic term *maranatha* is found at the end of the apostle Paul's first letter to the Corinthians (1 Corinthians 16:22). The term literally means, "Our Lord, come." May all Christians who joyfully await the soon coming of the Lord affirm in unison, *Maranatha*!

APPENDIXES

THE HARD FACTS

*(These statistics are gleaned from the text of this book.
Endnote citations occur at their first occurrence.)*

Seventy-three percent of people in the world have experienced some form of cyber crime, 55 percent have been victims of computer viruses, and only 13 percent feel "very safe" while online.

Cyber experts warn that an electronic equivalent of Pearl Harbor could be inflicted on the U.S. in a mere 15 minutes.

When analysts at Google examined several million Web pages for the presence of malicious software in 2010, they determined that 4.5 million of the pages they examined were suspicious. Further tests revealed that more than a million automatically downloaded malicious software to users.

Stuxnet, a highly virulent computer virus introduced in 2009 (and still active as of December 2010), has been called "a cyber shot heard around the world," a "first-of-its-kind guided cyber missile," a "cyber superweapon," the "first direct example of weaponized software," and "a working and fearsome prototype of a cyber-weapon that will lead to a new arms race in the world...a cyber arms race."

One cyber attack from North Korea knocked out the websites of the U.S. Treasury, Secret Service, Federal Trade Commission, and Department of Transportation. Also hit were the websites of NASDAQ, New York Mercantile, the New York Stock Exchange, and the *Washington Post*.

Logic bombs—packets of malicious software code—have infected the computers and networks that control U.S. power grids. They have been positioned there by Russian and Chinese governments for future use. These logic bombs are waiting for a signal from one of these countries, and once they are activated, electricity will be knocked out in the U.S. for a significant time.

The number of U.S. Senate "security events" per month is now about 1.8 billion (yes, *billion*).

Each day, 13.9 million computer attacks are launched against the Senate Security Operations Center.

Thousands of terabytes of data has been stolen from U.S. networks through cyber espionage—ten times the amount of information stored in the U.S. Library of Congress.

For 18 minutes in April of 2010, China's state-controlled telecommunications company hijacked 15 percent of the entire world's Internet traffic, including data from the U.S. military and civilian organizations in America and allied countries.

Chinese hackers stole multiple terabytes of data on the new F-35 jet fighter from the computer networks of the U.S. Army Information Systems Engineering Command, the Naval Ocean Systems Center, the Missile Defense Agency, and Sandia National Laboratories.

Chinese hackers penetrated 1300 computers at several embassies and were able to remotely activate computer webcams and microphones without embassy users' knowledge. This Peeping Tom and eavesdropping cyber espionage continued for two years before being discovered.

Israel utilized a sophisticated cyber attack to render Syria's radar system completely blind to incoming fighter jets.

More than 140 countries possess cyber warfare capabilities.

Malicious computer hackers often tweak their viruses until they are no longer recognized by today's popular antivirus software programs.

Online services provide cyber attacks against targeted websites or networks. Economy attack packages start at $20 a month; deluxe attack capabilities go for about $100 a month.

CYBER GLOSSARY

antivirus software

Antivirus software identifies malware and prevents users from installing it or, if it has already been installed, removes it from the computer. Such software performs on-access scanning, which means that every time a software program runs or a file is accessed, it is examined to see if any viruses are present. The software also performs on-demand scanning, in which the program is activated specifically to look for viruses on the computer.

botnet

A botnet is a network of zombie or robot computers (*bot* is short for "robot," and *net* is short for "network") infected by a computer virus that allows them to be controlled by an unauthorized remote user—so remote that he or she could be in another country. This usually takes place without any knowledge of the computer's owner or user, though the computer may seem to run a bit slower. Such a network of robot computers is typically used to launch an attack against a target website, often by flooding the target website with messages. This causes the website to become jammed or to shut down altogether.

carder

A carder is someone who makes illegal credit card transactions. Carders abound in cyberspace.

cyber attack

A cyber attack is an action or an assault that damages other computer systems or networks, scans their data, or gains control of them. These systems are then used to perform actions contrary to their programming, thereby providing the hacker with some strategic benefit or advantage.

cyber criminal

A cyber criminal engages in illegal activities in cyberspace—such as using malware to steal credit card information from other computer users or gain control of their systems.

cyber espionage

Cyber espionage is unauthorized probing of a target computer's configuration to evaluate its system defenses or to view and copy data files. Cyber espionage typically results in information theft.

cyber strategy

Cyber strategy is the development and employment of strategic capabilities to operate in cyberspace, integrated and coordinated with other operational domains (air, land, sea, and outer space), to achieve objectives of vital interest.

cyber warfare

Cyber warfare includes hostile attempts to penetrate a nation's computers or networks to gain strategic or military advantage or to cause damage or disruption in the system. Cyber warfare may be used in concert with kinetic attacks (such as ground, air, or naval attacks).

cyberpower

Cyberpower is a measurement of a group's ability to use cyberspace to create advantages and influence events in all the other operational environments (land, sea, air, and outer space).

cyberspace

Cyberspace is a vast electronic global domain within the information environment. It includes the Internet, where one "surfs the Web" and retrieves e-mail, but it also includes other networks and associated infrastructures where information is stored, modified, and retrieved. Cyberspace includes all of the computer networks in the world and everything they connect and control.

cyberterrorism

Cyberterrorism is the use of Internet-based attacks in terrorist activities, including acts of deliberate, large-scale disruption of computers and computer networks. Goals include jamming or shutting down Internet service providers, disrupting information systems, damaging infrastructure (for example, an electrical grid), and rendering economic damage by penetrating banking and financial networks.

DDoS

Distributed Denial of Service attack.

distributed denial of service attack

Also known as a DDoS, this attack sends a preprogrammed flood of Internet traffic to a website or computer network in order to shut it down. It is *distributed* because thousands of computers—in some cases, hundreds of thousands of computers—distributed over a wide geographical area are given electronic instructions by a remote user to flood the targeted website or network with messages.

The computers participating in this attack are collectively called a *botnet*—a robotic network of zombie computers that have been infected by malware that brings them under remote control.

logic bomb

A logic bomb is malware or computer code that contains instructions that cause a computer system or network of computers to perform destructive operations, such as shutting down or erasing all data on a network. Once a logic bomb activates on a computer or network, the hardware often becomes useless. Logic bombs can also be used to inflict damage on other physical hardware controlled by computers. For example, a hacker or cyber criminal (or a hostile foreign country) could infect a computer network that runs an electrical power grid with a logic bomb that initiates instructions to cause a power surge sufficient to fry the circuits of the transformers, causing a power outage.

malware

Malware is malicious software code that causes computers to engage in actions contrary to the computer's programming or contrary to the desires of the computer's users. The various kinds of malware include viruses, worms, logic bombs, and spyware. Such malware can be destructive, invasive, and deceptive (operating by stealth).

phishing

Phishing involves sending an e-mail that is apparently (but not really) from a trusted sender. It may use the stolen name, logo, and graphics of a bank or credit card company. The e-mail recipients are asked to click on a link to go to the bank or credit card website and sign on with their usernames and passwords so their data can be updated. But the website is bogus, designed by a hacker who illegally obtains and uses the usernames and passwords to steal money from the victims' accounts. (See also *spear phishing*.)

root kits

Talented hackers can penetrate and gain access to private networks. Once they do so, they often leave behind *trapdoors*—malicious software code that permits easier and faster access to that same private network in the future. These trapdoors provide hackers with a *root*. Hackers trade or sell *root kits* to each other in a black market. Buyers of these root kits gain *root access* to private networks. After these buyers access the private network, they can erase any evidence that they were ever there.

spear phishing

Spear-phishing attacks use e-mail messages that appear to be from people you actually know. The names of friends, family members, or acquaintances may have been gathered from social networks such as Facebook and then used in the spear-phishing attack. The e-mail message typically asks the recipient to click on a link or open an attachment. Once the user clicks on the link, malware is downloaded to his computer.

spyware

Spyware is installed on a user's computer by stealth (without the user's consent or knowledge). The installation may occur when the user opens an attachment or clicks on a link in an e-mail.

Spyware is specifically designed to gather information from a user's computer, including usernames and passwords for signing onto the user's bank or credit card company website. This form of spyware utilizes a *keystroke logger*, which records everything typed on the keyboard of an infected machine. Spyware can also be used in corporate settings to steal sensitive or proprietary documentation. Corporate executives and employees must be especially cautious, for at some business conventions and conferences, free flash drives are handed out as gifts, and *some* of these flash drives—once plugged into a computer—*may* load keystroke loggers.

trapdoor

Hackers can gain access to private networks and leave behind a *trapdoor*. This is malicious software code that hides in the background and provides the hacker with easier and faster access to that private network in the future.

Trojan horse

A Trojan horse is malware that purports to perform a desirable function for the computer user but actually allows unauthorized remote access of the user's computer system.

virus

A virus is a malicious software program that passes from computer to computer over the Internet or a network. Viruses can also be transmitted by storage devices, such as thumb drives. There are a variety of computer viruses, including spyware, Trojan horses, keyboard loggers, and worms.

worm

Worms are computer viruses that do not require computer users to do anything to spread the virus from one computer to another. Rather, computer worms can copy themselves from one computer to another by taking advantage of known vulnerabilities in other software programs (such as Microsoft Internet Explorer). This form of malware "worms" itself throughout cyberspace from computer to computer to computer. Such worms can infect hundreds of thousands of computers and can go global in a very short time period.

THE DANGER OF PREDICTING THE DATES OF END-TIME EVENTS

I have presented plenty of evidence showing that the stage is being set for the fulfillment of end-times Bible prophecies, and I've shown how cyber technology may play a part. The natural temptation of some might be to speculate that the Lord will definitely return within the next decade or so. I certainly hope that happens, but I must emphasize that the coming of the Lord could still be a long way off. For that reason, we should avoid predicting dates for the fulfillment of end-time events. Here's why.

- During the past 2000 years, those who predicted the time of the rapture or second coming were wrong 100 percent of the time. Certainly the rapture will occur one day, and the Lord will come again one day, and we should be excited about that. But in our excitement, let's not succumb to predicting the date.

- Those who make these predictions may then make harmful decisions for their lives—such as delaying their college education or not saving money for their retirement. Do not make that mistake!

- Christians who succumb to predicting dates may damage

their faith in the Bible when their expectations fail. That would be tragic.

- If people lose confidence in the prophetic portions of Scripture, biblical prophecy may cease to be a motivation to holiness in their daily lives (see Titus 2:12-14).

- Christians who succumb to predicting dates may damage the faith of new or immature believers when the predictions are proved false.

- People who predict the dates of end-time events tend to be sensationalistic, and sensationalism is unbefitting to a Christian. Christ calls His followers to live soberly and alertly as they await His second coming (Mark 13:32-37).

- Skeptics have often scorned Christians who attached dates to end-time events.

- The precise timing of end-time events is in God's hands, and we have not been given the details (Acts 1:7).

A wise person once said that we ought to plan our lives as if we will be here for our full lifetime expectancy, but we should live our lives as if the Lord is coming today. That way we are prepared for both time and eternity.

So by all means, let's be excited about Bible prophecy. Let's be thrilled that the rapture of the church could happen this very day. But let's also be wise and make prudent plans for the future, trusting in the Lord's sovereign timing for all end-time events.

IF YOU ARE
NOT A CHRISTIAN...

The decision to enter into a personal relationship with Jesus is the most important one you could ever make. A relationship with Him is unlike any other. If you leave this life without this relationship, you will spend eternity apart from Him.

If you will allow me, I would like to explain how you can begin a personal relationship with Jesus. The first step is to recognize that He is ready and willing.

God Desires a Personal Relationship with You

God created you (Genesis 1:27)—not to exist all alone and apart from Him, but to share a personal relationship with Him. Just as God fellowshipped with people in Bible times (Genesis 3:8-19), so He desires to fellowship with you (1 John 1:5-7). God loves you (John 3:16). Never forget that fact. But unfortunately, there is one problem.

Our Sin Blocks a Relationship with God

When Adam and Eve chose to sin against God in the Garden of Eden, they catapulted the entire human race—to which they gave birth—into sin. Since that time, every human being has been born into the world with a propensity to sin—to do things that are wrong, to engage in actions that are hurtful or inappropriate, to do things that are immoral.

Sin then brought about death. The apostle Paul affirmed that "just as sin came into the world through one man, and death through sin… so death spread to all men because all sinned…By the one man's disobedience the many were made sinners" (Romans 5:12,19). Ultimately this means that "in Adam all die" (1 Corinthians 15:22).

Jesus often used metaphors that illustrate the havoc sin can wreak in one's life. He described sin as blindness (Matthew 23:16-26), sickness (Matthew 9:12), slavery (John 8:34), and darkness (John 8:12; 12:35-46). He also taught that this is a universal condition and that all people are guilty before God (Luke 7:37-48).

Jesus also taught that both inner thoughts and external acts render a person guilty (Matthew 5:28). He taught that from within the human heart come evil thoughts, sexual immorality, theft, murder, adultery, coveting, wickedness, deceit, sensuality, envy, slander, pride, and foolishness (Mark 7:21-23). Moreover, the Gospel record shows that Jesus is fully aware of every person's sins, both external acts and inner thoughts; nothing escapes His notice (Matthew 22:18; Luke 6:8; John 4:17-19).

Of course, some people are more morally upright than others. However, we all fall short of God's infinite standards (Romans 3:23). In a contest to see who can throw a rock to the moon, I am sure a muscular athlete would be able to throw the rock much farther than I could. But everyone ultimately falls short. Similarly, all of us fall short of measuring up to God's perfect holy standards.

Though the sin problem is a serious one, God has graciously provided a solution.

Jesus Died for Our Sins and Made Salvation Possible

God's absolute holiness demands that sin be punished. The good news of the gospel, however, is that Jesus has taken this punishment on Himself. God loves us so much that He sent Jesus to bear the penalty for our sins!

Jesus affirmed that He came into the world for the very purpose of dying (John 12:27). He perceived His death as a sacrificial offering for the sins of humanity (Matthew 26:26-28). He took His sacrificial mission with utmost seriousness, for He knew that without Him, humanity would certainly perish (Matthew 16:25; John 3:16) and spend eternity apart from God in a place of great suffering (Matthew 10:28; 11:23; 23:33; 25:41; Luke 16:22-28).

Jesus therefore described His mission this way: "The Son of Man came not to be served but to serve, and to give his life as a ransom for many" (Matthew 20:28). "The Son of Man came to seek and to save the lost" (Luke 19:10). "God did not send his Son into the world to condemn the world, but in order that the world might be saved through him" (John 3:17).

This is great news indeed! But the benefits of Christ's death on the cross are not automatically applied to your life. To receive the gift of salvation, you must believe.

Believe in Jesus Christ, the Savior

By His sacrificial death on the cross, Jesus took the sins of the entire world on Himself and made salvation available for everyone (1 John 2:2). But this salvation is not automatic. Only those who personally choose to believe in Christ are saved. This is Jesus' consistent testimony.

- "For God so loved the world, that he gave his only Son, that whoever believes in him should not perish but have eternal life" (John 3:16).

- "For this is the will of my Father, that everyone who looks on the Son and believes in him should have eternal life, and I will raise him up on the last day" (John 6:40).

- "I am the resurrection and the life. Whoever believes in me, though he die, yet shall he live" (John 11:25).

Choosing *not* to believe in Jesus, by contrast, leads to eternal condemnation: "Whoever believes in him is not condemned, but whoever does not believe is condemned already, because he has not believed in the name of the only Son of God" (John 3:18).

Free at Last—Forgiven of All Sins

When you believe in Christ the Savior, a wonderful thing happens. God forgives you of all your sins. *All of them!* He puts them completely out of His sight. Ponder for a few minutes the following verses, which speak of the forgiveness of those who have believed in Christ.

- "In him we have redemption through his blood, the forgiveness of our trespasses, according to the riches of his grace" (Ephesians 1:7).

- "I will remember their sins and their lawless deeds no more" (Hebrews 10:17).

- "Blessed is the one whose transgression is forgiven, whose sin is covered. Blessed is the man against whom the LORD counts no iniquity, and in whose spirit there is no deceit" (Psalm 32:1-2).

- "For as high as the heavens are above the earth, so great is his steadfast love toward those who fear him; as far as the east is from the west, so far does he remove our transgressions from us" (Psalm 103:11-12).

Such forgiveness is wonderful indeed, for none of us can possibly work our way into heaven or be good enough to warrant God's good favor. Because of what Jesus has done for us, we can freely receive the gift of salvation. It is a gift provided solely through the grace of God (Ephesians 2:8-9). It becomes ours when we place our faith in Jesus.

Don't Put It Off

To put off turning to Christ for salvation is highly dangerous, for you do not know the day of your death. What if it happens this evening? "Death is the destiny of everyone; the living should take this to heart" (Ecclesiastes 7:2 NIV).

If God is speaking to your heart now, then now is your door of opportunity to believe. "Seek the LORD while he may be found; call on him while he is near" (Isaiah 55:6).

Follow Me in Prayer

Would you like to place your faith in Jesus for the forgiveness of sins, thereby guaranteeing your eternal place in heaven along His side? If so, pray the following prayer with me. Keep in mind that the prayer itself doesn't save you. The faith in your heart saves you. So let the following prayer be a simple expression of the faith that is in your heart.

> *Dear Jesus,*
> *I want to have a relationship with You.*
> *I know I cannot save myself, because I am a sinner.*
> *Thank You for dying on the cross in my place.*
> *I believe You died for me, and I accept Your free gift of salvation.*
> *Thank You, Jesus.*
> *Amen.*

Welcome to God's Forever Family

On the authority of the Word of God, I can now assure you that you are a part of God's forever family. If you prayed the prayer above with a heart of faith, you will spend all eternity by Jesus' side in heaven. Welcome to God's family!

What to Do Next

1. Purchase a Bible and read from it daily. If you have never read a Bible before, you might start with one of the easier-to-read translations, such as The New Living Translation or the New International Version. Other good translations include the English Standard Version, the Holman Christian Standard Version, and the New American Standard Version. Read at least one chapter a day, followed by a time of prayer. I recommend starting with the Gospel of Luke. It has many interesting stories that illustrate important spiritual truths.

2. Send me an e-mail at ronrhodes@earthlink.net. I will send you a free e-book that will explain everything you need to know about Christianity and walking daily with Jesus.

3. Join a Bible-believing church immediately. Get involved in it. Join a Bible study group at the church so you will have regular fellowship with other Christians.

4. Please visit my website, where you will find many materials that will help you: www.ronrhodes.org.

BIBLIOGRAPHY

Ankerberg, John, and Dillon Burroughs. *Middle East Meltdown*. Eugene, OR: Harvest House, 2007.

Ansari, Ali. *Confronting Iran: The Failure of American Foreign Policy and the Next Great Conflict in the Middle East*. New York: Basic Books, 2006.

Berman, Ilan. *Tehran Rising: Iran's Challenge to the United States*. New York: Rowman & Littlefield, 2005.

Block, Daniel. *The Book of Ezekiel: Chapters 25–48*. Grand Rapids: Eerdmans, 1998.

Carr, Jeffrey. *Inside Cyber Warfare: Mapping the Cyber Underworld*. Cambridge: O'Reilly, 2010.

Clarke, Richard. *Cyber War: The Next Threat to National Security and What to Do About It*. New York: HarperCollins, 2010.

Corsi, Jerome. *Atomic Iran: How the Terrorist Regime Bought the Bomb and American Politicians*. Nashville: WND Books, 2005.

Ehrenfeld, Rachel. *Funding Evil: How Terrorism Is Financed—and How to Stop It*. Chicago: Bonus Books, 2005.

Feinberg, Charles. *The Prophecy of Ezekiel*. Eugene, OR: Wipf and Stock, 2003.

Fruchtenbaum, Arnold. *The Footsteps of the Messiah*. San Antonio: Ariel Publishers, 2004.

Gabriel, Mark. *Islam and the Jews: The Unfinished Battle*. Lake Mary, FL: Charisma House, 2003.

———. *Journey into the Mind of an Islamic Terrorist*. Lake Mary, FL: Front Line, 2006.

Gaffney, Frank. *War Footing: Ten Steps America Must Take to Prevail in the War for the Free World*. Annapolis: Naval Institute Press, 2006.

Geisler, Norman. *Systematic Theology*. Vol. 4, *Church/Last Things*. St. Paul: Bethany House, 2005.

Gold, Dore. *The Fight for Jerusalem: Radical Islam, the West, and the Future of the Holy City*. Washington, DC: Regnery, 2007.

Guisnel, Jean. *Cyberwars: Espionage on the Internet*. New York: Basic Books, 1999.

Halpin, Edward F., Philippa Trevorrow, David Webb, and Steve Wright, eds. *Cyberwar, Netwar and the Revolution in Military Affairs*. New York: Palgrave Macmillan, 2006.

Hays, J. Daniel, J. Scott Duvall, and C. Marvin Pate. *Dictionary of Biblical Prophecy and End Times*. Grand Rapids: Zondervan, 2007.

Hitchcock, Mark. *Bible Prophecy*. Wheaton: Tyndale House, 1999.

———. *Cashless: Bible Prophecy, Economic Chaos, & The Future Financial Order*. Eugene, OR: Harvest House, 2009.

———. *The Coming Islamic Invasion of Israel*. Sisters, OR: Multnomah, 2002.

———. *Iran: The Coming Crisis*. Sisters, OR: Multnomah, 2006.

———. *Is America in Bible Prophecy?* Sisters, OR: Multnomah, 2002.

———. *The Second Coming of Babylon*. Sisters, OR: Multnomah, 2003.

Hoyt, Herman. *The End Times*. Chicago: Moody Press, 1969.

Ice, Thomas, and Randall Price. *Ready to Rebuild: The Imminent Plan to Rebuild the Last Days Temple*. Eugene, OR: Harvest House, 1992.

Ice, Thomas, and Timothy Demy. *The Coming Cashless Society*. Eugene, OR: Harvest House, 1996.

———. *Prophecy Watch*. Eugene, OR: Harvest House, 1998.

———. *When the Trumpet Sounds*. Eugene, OR: Harvest House, 1995.

Jeremiah, David. *The Coming Economic Armageddon: What Bible Prophecy Warns About the New Global Economy*. Nashville: FaithWords, 2010.

Klein, Aaron. *The Late Great State of Israel: How Enemies Within and Without Threaten the Jewish Nation's Survival*. New York: WND Books, 2009.

Kramer, Franklin D., Stuart H. Starr, and Larry K. Wentz, eds. *Cyberpower and National Security*. Washington, DC: Potomac Books, 2010.

LaHaye, Tim, and Ed Hindson, eds. *The Popular Bible Prophecy Commentary*. Eugene, OR: Harvest House, 2006.

———, eds. *The Popular Encyclopedia of Bible Prophecy*. Eugene, OR: Harvest House, 2004.

LaHaye, Tim, and Jerry Jenkins. *Are We Living in the End Times?* Wheaton: Tyndale, 1999.

LaHaye, Tim, and Thomas Ice. *Charting the End Times*. Eugene, OR: Harvest House, 2001.

———. *The Beginning of the End*. Wheaton: Tyndale, 1991.

———. *The Coming Peace in the Middle East*. Grand Rapids: Zondervan, 1984.

———, ed. *Prophecy Study Bible*. Chattanooga: AMG Publishers, 2001.

Leeb, Stephen. *The Coming Economic Collapse*. New York: Warner Business Books, 2006.

Libicki, Martin C. *Cyberdeterrence and Cyberwar*. Santa Monica: RAND Corporation, 2009.

Mehan, Julie E. *CyberWar, CyberTerror, CyberCrime*. United Kingdom: IT Governance Publishing, 2008.

Pentecost, J. Dwight. *Things to Come*. Grand Rapids: Zondervan, 1964.

Pollack, Kenneth. *The Persian Puzzle: The Conflict Between Iran and America*. New York: Random House, 2005.

Phares, Walid. *Future Jihad: Terrorist Strategies Against the West*. New York: Palgrave Mac-Millan, 2005.

Price, Randall. *Fast Facts on the Middle East Conflict*. Eugene, OR: Harvest House, 2003.

———. *Unholy War*. Eugene, OR: Harvest House, 2001.

Reid, T.R. *The United States of Europe: The New Superpower and the End of American Supremacy*. New York: Penguin Books, 2004.

Rhodes, Ron. *Christianity According to the Bible*. Eugene, OR: Harvest House, 2006.

———. *The Coming Oil Storm: The Imminent End of Oil...and Its Strategic Global Role in End-Times Prophecy*. Eugene, OR: Harvest House, 2010.

———. *Middle East Conflict: What You Need to Know*. Eugene, OR: Harvest House, 2009.

———. *Northern Storm Rising: Russia, Iran, and the Emerging End-Times Military Coalition Against Israel*. Eugene, OR: Harvest House, 2008.

———. *The Popular Dictionary of Bible Prophecy*. Eugene, OR: Harvest House, 2010.

———. *The Topical Guide to Bible Prophecy*. Eugene, OR: Harvest House, 2010.

Rosenberg, Joel. *Epicenter: Why Current Rumblings in the Middle East Will Change Your Future*. Wheaton: Tyndale House, 2006.

Ruthven, Jon Mark. *The Prophecy that Is Shaping History: New Research on Ezekiel's Vision of the End*. Fairfax: Xulon Press, 2003.

Ryrie, Charles. *Basic Theology*. Wheaton: Victor, 1986.

———. *Dispensationalism Today*. Chicago: Moody, 1965.

Stiennon, Richard. *Surviving Cyberwar*. Lanham, MD: Government Institutes, 2010.

Timmerman, Kenneth. *Countdown to Crisis: The Coming Nuclear Showdown with Iran*. New York: Three Rivers Press, 2006.

Venter, Al. *Iran's Nuclear Option: Tehran's Quest for the Atomic Bomb*. Philadelphia: Casemate, 2005.

Viega, John. *The Myths of Security: What the Computer Security Industry Doesn't Want You to Know*. Cambridge: O'Reilly, 2009.

Walvoord, John F. and John E. Walvoord. *Armageddon, Oil, and the Middle East Crisis*. Grand Rapids: Zondervan, 1975.

Walvoord, John F. *End Times*. Nashville: Word, 1998.

———. *The Millennial Kingdom*. Grand Rapids: Zondervan, 1975.

———. *The Prophecy Knowledge Handbook*. Wheaton: Victor Books, 1990.

———. *The Return of the Lord*. Grand Rapids: Zondervan, 1979.

Yamauchi, Edwin. *Foes from the Northern Frontier: Invading Hordes from the Russian Steppes*. Eugene, OR: Wipf and Stock, 1982.

NOTES

Except where noted, articles without page numbers and website address were accessed through online membership search engines, including HighBeam Research and Questia.

INTRODUCTION: TECHNOLOGIES THAT AMAZE

1. Thomas Ice and Timothy Demy, *The Coming Cashless Society* (Eugene, OR: Harvest House, 1996), p. 19.

2. Ice and Demy, *The Coming Cashless Society*, pp. 58-59.

3. Franklin Kramer, Stuart Starr, and Larry Wentz, eds., *Cyberpower and National Security* (Washington, DC: Potomac Books, 2009), p. xvi; see also p. 4.

4. Richard Clarke, *Cyber War: The Next Threat to National Security and What to Do About It* (New York: HarperCollins, 2010), pp. 70-71.

5. Maggie Shiels, "U.S. Cyber-Security 'Embarrassing,'" *BBC News*, April 29, 2009. news.bbc .co.uk/2/hi/technology/8023793.stm.

6. Larry Seltzer, "Congress: 1.8 Billion Cyber 'Security Events' Per Month," *PC Magazine*, March 10, 2010. www.pcmag.com/article2/0,2817,2361188,00.asp.

7. Seltzer, "Congress: 1.8 Billion Cyber 'Security Events' Per Month."

8. Samir Salama, "Cyber war poses threat to national security," *Gulf News*, May 20, 2010. gulf news.com/news/gulf/uae/general/cyber-war-poses-threat-to-national-security-expert-1.629138. Accessed via HighBeam Research.

9. "EU agencies ally to fight cyberterrorists," *UPI*, September 30, 2010. www.upi.com/Top_News/ US/2010/09/30/EU-agencies-ally-to-fight-cyberterrorists/UPI-12211285866029/.

10. "EU agencies ally to fight cyberterrorists."

CHAPTER 1: PROBING U.S. VULNERABILITIES

1. Clarke, *Cyber War*, pp. 66-68.

2. Clarke, *Cyber War*, p. 68.

3. See Alex Spillius, "Cyber attack 'could fell U.S. within 15 minutes,'" *Daily Telegraph*, May 7, 2010. www.telegraph.co.uk/news/worldnews/northamerica/usa/7691500/Cyber-attack-could-fell-US-within-15-minutes.html.

4. Eileen McMenamin, "Cyber ShockWave Hits Washington," *Bipartisan Policy Center*, February 10, 2010. www.bipartisanpolicy.org/news/press-releases/2010/02/cyber-shockwave-hits-wash ington-updated-participants.

5. Eileen McMenamin, "Cyber ShockWave Shows U.S. Unprepared for Cyber Threats," *Bipartisan Policy Center*, February 17, 2010. www.bipartisanpolicy.org/news/press-releases/2010/02/cyber-shockwave-shows-us-unprepared-cyber-threats.

6. McMenamin, "Cyber ShockWave Shows U.S. Unprepared for Cyber Threats."

7. McMenamin, "Cyber ShockWave Shows U.S. Unprepared for Cyber Threats." See also "USA failed in Cyber War Test," *Cyber Security*, February 18, 2010. security-informatica.blogspot .com/2010/02/usa-failed-in-cyberwar-test.html.

8. McMenamin, "Cyber ShockWave Shows U.S. Unprepared for Cyber Threats." See also "Cyber ShockWave exercise finds that the U.S. has many lessons to learn when it comes to cyber-attack response," *Continuity Central*, February 22, 2010. www.continuitycentral.com/news05004.html.

9. McMenamin, "Cyber ShockWave Shows U.S. Unprepared for Cyber Threats."

10. McMenamin, "Cyber ShockWave Shows U.S. Unprepared for Cyber Threats."

11. Cited in Leslie Horn, "U.S. Launches Three-Day 'Cyber Storm' Response Test," *PC Magazine*, September 28, 2010. www.pcmag.com/article2/0,2817,2369860,00.asp. See also Brian Prince, "Cyber-security Report Highlights Progress, Future," *eWeek*, July 15, 2010. www.eweek.com/c/a/Security/Cyber-Security-Report-Highlights-Progress-Future-607320/.

12. Shaun Waterman, "Cyber Storm III aims to protect against real thing," *The Washington Times*, September 28, 2010. www.washingtontimes.com/news/2010/sep/28/cyber-storm-iii-aims-pro tect-against-real-thing/.

13. Horn, "U.S. Launches Three-Day 'Cyber Storm' Response Test."

14. Grant Gross, "Cyber Storm III simulates large-scale attack," *Network World*, September 29, 2010. www.networkworld.com/news/2010/092910-cyber-storm-iii-simulates-large-scale.html.

15. Gross, "Cyber Storm III simulates large-scale attack."

16. Cited in Ice and Demy, *The Coming Cashless Society*, p. 146.

17. I document this financial backing in my recent book *The Coming Oil Storm* (Eugene, OR: Harvest House, 2010).

18. Kramer, Starr, and Wentz, eds., *Cyberpower and National Security*, p. 438.

19. See Gerald Posner, "China's Secret Cyberterrorism," Combined Arms Center Blog, January 13, 2010. usacac.army.mil/blog/blogs/fight/archive/2010/08/09/china-s-secret-cyberterrism-by-ger ald-posner.aspx.

20. Jamal Elias, *Islam* (Upper Saddle River, NJ: Prentice Hall, 1999), p. 73.

21. Ergun Mehmet Caner and Emir Fethi Caner, *Unveiling Islam: An Insider's Look at Muslim Life and Beliefs* (Grand Rapids: Kregel, 2002), p. 49.

22. David Goldmann, *Islam and the Bible: Why Two Faiths Collide* (Chicago: Moody, 2004), p. 22.

23. John Ankerberg and John Weldon, *Fast Facts on Islam* (Eugene, OR: Harvest House, 2001), p. 19.

24. Quoted in Caner and Caner, *Unveiling Islam*, pp. 183-84.

25. Jeffrey Carr, *Inside Cyber Warfare* (Cambridge: O'Reilly, 2010), p. 22.

CHAPTER 2: CYBER WARFARE

1. Cited in Tony Bradley, "Critical Infrastructure Under Siege from Cyber Attacks," *PC World*, January 28, 2010. www.pcworld.com/businesscenter/article/188095/critical_infrastructure_under_ siege_from_cyber_attacks.html.

2. Phil Elmore, "Why We Need Cyber-Warriors Now," *WorldNetDaily*, July 2, 2009. www.wnd
.com/index.php?fa=PAGE.printable&pageId=102736.

3. Kim Sengupta, "Terrorists 'Gaining Upper Hand in Cyber War,'" *The Independent*, February 6, 2010. www.independent.co.uk/news/uk/home-news/terrorists-gaining-upper-hand-in-cyber-war-1890913.html.

4. Cited in Carr, *Inside Cyber Warfare*, p. 179.

5. Cited in Clarke, *Cyber War*, p. 64.

6. Spillius, "Cyber attack 'could fell U.S. within 15 minutes.'"

7. "The Cyber-Security Menace Grows," *Compliance Week*, July 1, 2010. Accessed online through HighBeam Research.

8. Charles Billo, "Cyber Warfare: An Analysis of the Means and Motivations of Selected Nation States," Institute for Security Technology Studies at Dartmouth College, November, 2004. www.ists.dartmouth.edu/projects/archives/cyber-warfare.html.

9. Kramer, Starr, and Wentz, eds., *Cyberpower and National Security*, p. 475.

10. Stew Magnuson, "U.S. Plans to Destroy Enemy Computer Networks in Cyber-Attacks Questioned," *National Defense*, July 2009, www.nationaldefensemagazine.org/archive/2009/June/Pages/USPlanstoDestroyEnemyComputerNetworksQuestioned.aspx.

11. Jeremy Kirk, "Estonia recovers from massive DDoS attack," *ComputerWorld*, May 17, 2007, www.computerworld.com/s/article/9019725/Estonia_recovers_from_massive_DDoS_attack.

12. Carr, *Inside Cyber Warfare*, p. xiv; see also Steven Erlanger, "Tactical Cyber Warfare Capabilities," *New York Times*, November 2, 2010; Stephen W. Korns and Joshua E. Kastenberg, "Georgia's Cyber Left Hook," *Parameters*, vol. 38, no. 4, 2008, p. 60-61.

13. See John Markoff, "Before the Gunfire, Cyberattacks," *New York Times*, August 12, 2008. www.nytimes.com/2008/08/13/technology/13cyber.html.

14. See Dean Takahashi, "After the Five-day Russia-Georgia War: A Chronicle of the Cyber Battle Unfolds," *VentureBeat*, August 12, 2008. venturebeat.com/2008/08/12/after-a-five-day-war-a-chronicle-of-the-cyber-battle-unfolds/.

15. Clarke, *Cyber War*, p. 21; see also Binoy Kampmark, "Cyber Warfare between Estonia and Russia," *Contemporary Review*, vol. 289, no. 1686, 2007, p. 288.

16. "Governments Hit by Cyber Attack," *BBC*, July 8, 2009. news.bbc.co.uk/2/hi/technology/8139821.stm.

17. Clarke, *Cyber War*, p. 28.

18. James Kraska, "How the United States Lost the Naval War of 2015," *Orbis*, Winter 2010. www.fpri.org/orbis/5401/kraska.navalwar2015.pdf.

19. "FBI: China Using Bootleg CISCO Router to Infiltrate DOD," *The Security Dialogue*, May 20, 2008, Internet edition.

20. Tom Kington and Wendell Minnick, "China, GhostNet and the Tip of the Iceberg," *Defense-News*, July 6, 2009. www.defensenews.com/story.php?i=4172668.

21. Clarke, *Cyber War*, pp. 58-60; see also Byron Acohido, "china-google quarrel highlights world of cyber espionage," *TechnologyLive*, January 15, 2010. content.usatoday.com/communities/technologylive/post/2010/01/chinese-cyberspies-arent-the-only-ones-on-the-prowl/1.

22. Lewis Page, "Israeli Sky-Hack Switched Off Syrian Radars Countrywide," *The Register* (UK), November 22, 2007. www.theregister.co.uk/2007/11/22/israel_air_raid_syria_hack_network_vuln_intrusion/

23. Carr, *Inside Cyber Warfare*, pp. 25-26.

24. Carr, *Inside Cyber Warfare*, p. 21.

25. See Noah Shachtman, "Wage Cyberwar Against Hamas, Surrender Your PC," *Wired*, January 8, 2009. www.wired.com/dangerroom/2009/01/israel-dns-hack/.

26. Kramer, Starr, and Wentz, eds., *Cyberpower and National Security*, p. 313.

CHAPTER 3: WE ARE BEING WATCHED

1. Kramer, Starr, and Wentz, eds., *Cyberpower and National Security*, p. 423.

2. Matt Egan, "Cyber Spies Pose Looming Threat," *Fox Business*, November 19, 2010. www.fox business.com/markets/2010/11/19/businesses-risk-cyber-espionage/.

3. Larry Seltzer, "When Does Hacking Become Cyber Warfare?" *PC Magazine*, February 8, 2010. www.pcmag.com/article2/0,2817,2358924,00.asp.

4. Carr, *Inside Cyber Warfare*, p. 89.

5. Cited in Andrea King, "A Hacker Knows Where Your Children Are, Do You?" *WorldNetDaily*, May 17, 2010. www.wnd.com/index.php?fa=PAGE.printable&pageId=154905.

6. Egan, "Cyber Spies Pose Looming Threat."

7. See Kramer, Starr, and Wentz, eds., *Cyberpower and National Security*, p. 177; see also Ben Rothke, "Secrets of Computer Espionage: Tactics and Countermeasures," *Security Management*, vol. 49, no. 6, June 2005, p. 145; Michelle Drumheller, "Hackers Intensify Fears of Industrial Espionage," *National Defense*, vol. 84, no.549, July/August 1999, pp. 48-49.

8. Seltzer, "When Does Hacking Become Cyber Warfare?"

9. Samir Salama, "Cyber War Poses Threat to National Security."

10. Clarke, *Cyber War*, pp. 233-34.

11. John Viega, *The Myths of Security: What the Computer Industry Doesn't Want You to Know* (Cambridge: O'Reilly, 2009), p. 130.

12. Kramer, Starr, and Wentz, eds., *Cyberpower and National Security*, p. 177.

13. Carr, *Inside Cyber Warfare*, p. 4.

14. Alperovitch also notes, however, that Chinese cyber capabilities lag behind those of the United States, Russia, Israel, and France. See Jim Wolf, "The Pentagon's new cyber warriors," *Reuters*, October 5, 2010, www.reuters.com/article/idUSTRE69433120101005.

15. Stew Magnuson, "Cyber Experts Have Proof that China Has Hacked U.S.-Based Internet Traffic," *National Defense*, November 12, 2010. www.nationaldefensemagazine.org/blog/Lists/Posts/Post.aspx?ID=249.

16. Clarke, *Cyber War*, p. 58.

17. Cited in Magnuson, "Cyber Experts Have Proof that China Has Hacked U.S.-Based Internet Traffic."

18. Clarke, *Cyber War*, p. 58.

19. See Kramer, Starr, and Wentz, eds., *Cyberpower and National Security*, p. 423.

CHAPTER 4: WEAPONIZED SOFTWARE

1. See Thorsten Holz and Frederic Raynal, "Malicious Malware: attacking the attackers, part 2," *Symantec*, February 1, 2006. www.symantec.com/connect/articles/malicious-malware-attacking-attackers-part-2.

2. Mary Alice Davidson, "The Many Faces of Malware," *Security Management*, vol. 51, no. 8, September 2007, pp. 120-23.

3. See Viega, *The Myths of Security*, pp. 9-10.

4. Anne Layne-Farrar, "The Law and Economics of Software Security," *Harvard Journal of Law & Public Policy*, vol. 30, no. 1, 2006, pp. 283-87.

5. Kramer, Starr, and Wentz, eds., *Cyberpower and National Security*, p. 422.

6. Carr, *Inside Cyber Warfare*, p. 151.

7. See Clarke, *Cyber War*, pp. 91-92.

8. Clarke, *Cyber War*, p. 198; see also Richard Clarke, "War from Cyberspace," *The National Interest*, November-December 2009, pp. 31-32; Kathleen Tierney, "Why We Are Vulnerable," *The American Prospect*, July-August 2007, pp. 56-57.

9. See Viega, *The Myths of Security*, pp. 35-36.

CHAPTER 5: STUXNET

1. Ameen Izzadeen, "Cyber war is on: Apocalypse.com," *DailyMirror*, October 1, 2010.

2. Wolf, "The Pentagon's New Cyber Warriors."

3. Wolf, "The Pentagon's New Cyber Warriors."

4. "World's First 'Cyber Superweapon' Attacks China," *Physorg.com*, October 1, 2010. www.physorg .com/news205050403.html

5. Neil J. Rubenking, "Stuxnet: Cyber Attack on Iranian Nuclear Reactors?" *PC Magazine*, September 23, 2010. www.pcmag.com/article2/0,2817,2369598,00.asp.

6. Rhodri Marsden, "Has the West Declared Cyber War on Iran?," *The Independent*, September 28, 2010. www.independent.co.uk/news/science/has-the-west-declared-cyber-war-on-iran-2091320.html.

7. Wolf, "The Pentagon's New Cyber Warriors."

8. Gordon Thomas, "Links Between Spy's Death, Computer Virus Reviewed," *G2 Bulletin*, September 30, 2010, Internet edition.

9. Chris Bronk, "Stuxnet Virus Exposes Computer Risks," *Houston Chronicle*, October 30, 2010. www.chron.com/disp/story.mpl/editorial/outlook/7271330.html.

10. "World's First 'Cyber Superweapon' Attacks China."

11. "World's First 'Cyber Superweapon' Attacks China."

12. Ryan Naraine, "Inside Stuxnet: Researcher drops new clues about origin of worm," *ZDNet*, September 30, 2010. www.zdnet.com/blog/security/inside-stuxnet-researcher-drops-new-clues-about-origin-of-worm/7409.

13. Mark Clayton, "Stuxnet malware is 'weapon' out to destroy…Iran's Bushehr nuclear plant?" *Christian Science Monitor*, September 21, 2010. www.csmonitor.com/USA/2010/0921/Stuxnet-malware-is-weapon-out-to-destroy-Iran-s-Bushehr-nuclear-plant.

14. Gregg Keizer, "Secrets of the Stuxnet Worm's Travels," *PCWorld*, October 3, 2010. www.pcworld .com/article/206822/secrets_of_the_stuxnet_worms_travels.html?tk=hp_new.

15. Clayton, "Stuxnet malware is 'weapon' out to destroy…Iran's Bushehr nuclear plant?"

16. Keizer, "Secrets of the Stuxnet Worm's Travels."

17. Rubenking, "Stuxnet: Cyber Attack on Iranian Nuclear Reactors?"

18. "Stuxnet Specifically Targeted Iranian Nuclear Program," *Jerusalem Post*, November 20, 2010. www.jpost.com/IranianThreat/News/Article.aspx?id=196051.

19. Thomas, "Links Between Spy's Death, Computer Virus Reviewed."

20. Keizer, "Secrets of the Stuxnet Worm's Travels."

21. Richard Bejtlich, "On the Other Side of an Advanced Persistent Threat," *National Cyber Security*, September 30, 2010. nationalcybersecurity.com/?p=31213.

22. Bejtlich, "On the Other Side of an Advanced Persistent Threat."

23. Bejtlich, "On the Other Side of an Advanced Persistent Threat."

24. Thomas, "Links Between Spy's Death, Computer Virus Reviewed."

25. "Iran Is Bent on Avenging Cyber Attack, Raising Military Tensions," *DEBKAfile*, October 2, 2010. warsclerotic.wordpress.com/2010/10/01/iran-is-bent-on-avenging-cyber-attack-raising-military-tensions/.

26. "World's First 'Cyber Superweapon' Attacks China."

27. "World's First 'Cyber Superweapon' Attacks China."

28. Arthur Bright, "Clues Emerge About Genesis of Stuxnet Worm," *Christian Science Monitor*, October 1, 2010. www.csmonitor.com/World/terrorism-security/2010/1001/Clues-emerge-about-genesis-of-Stuxnet-worm.

29. Dana Chivvis, "Stuxnet Intrigue Deepens with Hidden Clues in Code," *AOL News*, September 30, 2010. www.aolnews.com/surge-desk/article/stuxnet-intrigue-deepens-with-hidden-clues-in-code/19656309.

30. Chivvis, "Stuxnet Intrigue Deepens with Hidden Clues in Code."

31. Aharon Etengoff, "Stuxnet Mystery Deepens," *TG Daily*, September 30, 2010. www.tgdaily.com/security-features/51811-stuxnet-mystery-deepens.

32. Thomas, "Links Between Spy's Death, Computer Virus Reviewed."

33. Bright, "Clues Emerge About Genesis of Stuxnet Worm."

34. Chivvis, "Stuxnet Intrigue Deepens with Hidden Clues in Code."

35. Clayton, "Stuxnet Malware is 'weapon' out to destroy…Iran's Bushehr nuclear plant?"

36. Rubenking, "Stuxnet: Cyber Attack on Iranian Nuclear Reactors?"

37. Marsden, "Has the West Declared Cyber War on Iran?"

38. "Stuxnet Specifically Targeted Iranian Nuclear Program."

39. "Many Hands Cooperated to Build Stuxnet Worm," *InfoSecurity*, November 5, 2010. www.infosecurity-us.com/view/13773/many-hands-cooperated-to-build-stuxnet-worm/.

40. Keizer, "Secrets of the Stuxnet Worm's Travels."

41. Clayton, "Stuxnet malware is 'weapon' out to destroy…Iran's Bushehr nuclear plant?"

42. Gregg Keizer, "Why Did Stuxnet Worm Spread?," *ComputerWorld*, October 1, 2010. www.computerworld.com/s/article/9189140/Why_did_Stuxnet_worm_spread_.

43. Keizer, "Secrets of the Stuxnet Worm's Travels."

44. Clayton, "Stuxnet Malware is 'weapon' out to destroy…Iran's Bushehr nuclear plant?"

45. Clayton, "Stuxnet Malware is 'weapon' out to destroy…Iran's Bushehr nuclear plant?"

46. Caroline Glick, "The lessons of Stuxnet," *CarolynGlick.com*, October 1, 2010. www.carolineglick.com/e/2010/10/the-lessons-of-stuxnet.php.

47. "World's First 'Cyber Superweapon' Attacks China."

48. Thomas, "Links Between Spy's Death, Computer Virus Reviewed."

49. Thomas, "Links Between Spy's Death, Computer Virus Reviewed."

50. Clayton, "Stuxnet Malware is 'weapon' out to destroy…Iran's Bushehr nuclear plant?"

51. Ellen Nakashima, "Stuxnet malware is blueprint for computer attacks on U.S." *Washington Post*, October 2, 2010. www.washingtonpost.com/wp-dyn/content/article/2010/10/01/AR2010100106981.html.

52. Shaun Waterman, "Computer worm creates an opening for copycats," *Washington Times*, October 11, 2010. www.washingtontimes.com/news/2010/oct/10/computer-worm-creates-an-opening-for-copycats/.

53. Clayton, "Stuxnet Malware is 'weapon' out to destroy...Iran's Bushehr nuclear plant?"

54. Peter Beaumont, "Stuxnet worm heralds a new era of global cyberwarfare," *Guardian.co.uk*, September 30, 2010. www.guardian.co.uk/technology/2010/sep/30/stuxnet-worm-new-era-global-cyberwar.

55. Glick, "The Lessons of Stuxnet."

56. Matt Harley, "New era of online terrorism is here, security firm says," *National Post*, November 22, 2010. www.nationalpost.com/news/features/online+terrorism+here/3869756/story.html.

CHAPTER 6: THE CYBER THREAT AGAINST THE U.S. INFRASTRUCTURE

1. Anna Mulrine, "Pentagon: The global cyberwar is just beginning," *Christian Science Monitor*, October 5, 2010. www.csmonitor.com/USA/Military/2010/1005/Pentagon-The-global-cyberwar-is-just-beginning.

2. See Carr, *Inside Cyber Warfare*, p. 8.

3. See Kramer, Starr, and Wentz, eds., *Cyberpower and National Security*, p. 113.

4. Richard Clarke, "War from Cyberspace."

5. Stewart Baker, Shaun Waterman, and George Ivanov, "In the Crossfire: Critical Infrastructure in the Age of Cyber War," McAfee, 2010. resources.mcafee.com/content/NACIPReport.

6. Baker, Waterman, and Ivanov, "In the Crossfire."

7. Kramer, Starr, and Wentz, eds., *Cyberpower and National Security*, p. 127.

8. Clarke, "War from Cyberspace."

9. Cited in Grant Gross, "U.S. Cyber War Policy Needs New Focus, Experts Say," *PCWorld*, October 29, 2009. www.pcworld.com/article/174711/us_cyber_war_policy_needs_new_focus_experts_say.html.

10. Clarke, "War from Cyberspace."

11. Cited in Gross, "U.S. Cyber War Policy Needs New Focus, Experts Say."

12. Cited in Wolf, "The Pentagon's New Cyber Warriors."

13. Wolf, "The Pentagon's New Cyber Warriors."

14. Clarke, *Cyber War*, p. 199.

15. Brian Krebs, "Cyber Incident Blamed for Nuclear Power Plant Shutdown," *The Washington Post*, June 5, 2008. www.washingtonpost.com/wp-dyn/content/article/2008/06/05/AR2008060501958.html.

16. Jerry Liao, "Critical infrastructure under constant cyberattack," *Manila Bulletin*, February 8, 2010. www.mb.com.ph/articles/242526/critical-infrastructure-under-constant-cyberattack.

17. Clarke, "War from Cyberspace."

18. Cited in Wolf, "The Pentagon's New Cyber Warriors."

19. Wolf, "The Pentagon's New Cyber Warriors."

20. Wolf, "The Pentagon's New Cyber Warriors."

21. Wolf, "The Pentagon's New Cyber Warriors."

22. Mulrine, "Pentagon: The global cyberwar is just beginning."

CHAPTER 7: CYBER THUGS AND THEIR CYBER CRIMES

1. Samara Lynn, "65 Percent of Adults Victimized by Cyber Crime," *PC Magazine*, September 8, 2010. www.pcmag.com/article2/0,2817,2368865,00.asp.

2. See Viega, *The Myths of Security*, p. 22.

3. Carr, *Inside Cyber Warfare*, p. 6. To obtain helpful information on a variety of cyber crimes, visit www.cybercrime.gov/.

4. Brian Krebs, "European Cyber-Gangs Target Small U.S. Firms, Group Says," *Washington Post*, August 25, 2009, www.washingtonpost.com/wp-dyn/content/article/2009/08/24/AR2009082402272.html. See also Brian Krebs, "Cyber Gangs Hit Healthcare Providers," *Washington Post*, September 28, 2009. voices.washingtonpost.com/securityfix/2009/09/online_bank_robbers_target_hea.html.

5. Krebs, "European Cyber-Gangs Target Small U.S. Firms, Group Says."

6. Viega, *The Myths of Security*, pp. 15-17.

7. Kramer, Starr, and Wentz, eds., *Cyberpower and National Security*, pp. 422-23.

8. Carr, *Inside Cyber Warfare*, p. 13. See also Claudine Beaumont, "Microsoft Offers $250,000 Bounty for Conficker Creators," *The Telegraph*, December 2, 2010. www.telegraph.co.uk/technology/microsoft/4611944/Microsoft-offers-250000-bounty-for-Conficker-creators.html.

9. Kramer, Starr, and Wentz, eds., *Cyberpower and National Security*, pp. 422-23. See also Davey Winder, "Stolen Australian Credit Cards Going Cheap," *iTWire*, October 11, 2008. www.itwire.com/your-it-news/home-it/21099-stolen-australian-credit-cards-going-cheap.

10. Viega, *The Myths of Security*, p. 37. See also www.clickforensics.com/.

11. See Clarke, *Cyber War*, p. 73.

12. Clarke, *Cyber War*, p. 71.

13. Viega, *The Myths of Security*, pp. 79-80. However, see Mathew J. Schwartz, "Phishing Attacks Rise Sharply but Spam Emails Decline," *InformationWeek*, October 15, 2010. www.informationweek.com/news/security/attacks/showArticle.jhtml?articleID=227900052.

CHAPTER 8: THE MILITARIZATION OF CYBERSPACE

1. See Kramer, Starr, and Wentz, eds., *Cyberpower and National Security*, p. 25.

2. See, for example, Paul D. Berg, "Dominant Air, Space and Cyberspace Operations," *Air & Space Power Journal*, vol. 21, no. 1, 2007.

3. Charles L. Jackson, "The Origins of the Internet—A research effort in the department of defense's advanced projects research agency led to many of the innovations that power today's Internet," *World and I*, October 2001, pp. 36-40.

4. Clarke, *Cyber War*, p. 34.

5. Carr, *Inside Cyber Warfare*, pp. 1-2.

6. Carr, *Inside Cyber Warfare*, pp. 1-2; see also Arnaud de Borchgrave, "Silent Cyberwar," *The Washington Times*, February 19, 2009, p. A18.

7. Kramer, Starr, and Wentz, eds., *Cyberpower and National Security*, p. 14.

8. Clarke, *Cyber War*, pp. 70-71; see also Huba Wass de Czcge, "Warfare by Internet: The Logic of Strategic Deterrence, Defense, and Attack," *Military Review*, vol. 90, no. 4, 2010, pp. 85-87.

9. Matt Kelly, "The Cyber-Security Menace Grows," *Compliance Week*, July 1, 2010.

10. Clarke, *Cyber War*, p. 45; see also Deborah A. Liptak, "Information Warfare," *Searcher*, vol. 17, no. 9, 2009, pp. 21-23.

11. Kramer, Starr, and Wentz, eds., *Cyberpower and National Security*, p. xvi.

12. Cited in Carr, *Inside Cyber Warfare*, p. 161.

13. Kelly, "The Cyber-Security Menace Grows."

14. David Jeremiah, *The Coming Economic Armageddon: What Bible Prophecy Warns About the New Global Economy* (New York: Faith Words, 2010), p. 5.

15. Jim Wolf, "The Pentagon's New Cyber Warriors," *Reuters*, October 5, 2010. www.reuters.com/article/idUSTRE69433120101005.

16. Kramer, Starr, and Wentz, eds., *Cyberpower and National Security*, p. 300.

17. These and the following personnel figures are derived from Wolf, "The Pentagon's New Cyber Warriors."

18. Wolf, "The Pentagon's New Cyber Warriors."

19. Carr, *Inside Cyber Warfare*, pp. 93-94; see also Gabriel Weimann, "Terror on Facebook, Twitter, and YouTube," *The Brown Journal of World Affairs*, vol. 16, no. 2, 2010, pp. 45-46.

20. See Carr, *Inside Cyber Warfare*, pp. 188-89.

CHAPTER 9: IS THERE NO DEFENSE?

1. Gordon Thomas, "Hackers Fight Cyberterrorism," *G2 Bulletin*, June 30, 2009.

2. Viega, *The Myths of Security*, p. xiv.

3. Seltzer, "When Does Hacking Become Cyber Warfare?"

4. Viega, *The Myths of Security*, p. 143; see also James C. Johnson, "Windows Vista: Seven Good Reasons for Upgrading to Microsoft's New Operating System," *Black Enterprise*, March 2007, pp. 60-61.

5. Cited in Maggie Shiels, "U.S. Cyber-Security 'Embarrassing,'" *BBC News*, April 29, 2009. news.bbc.co.uk/2/hi/technology/8023793.stm.

6. Al Venter, *Iran's Nuclear Option* (Philadelphia: Casemate, 2005), pp. xvii-xviii.

7. Walid Phares, *Future Jihad* (New York: Palgrave MacMillan, 2005), p. 243.

8. Phares, *Future Jihad*, p. 244.

9. Gross, "U.S. Cyber War Policy Needs New Focus, Experts Say."

10. Gross, "U.S. Cyber War Policy Needs New Focus, Experts Say"; see also Kelly A. Gable, "Cyber-Apocalypse Now: Securing the Internet Against Cyberterrorism and Using Universal Jurisdiction as a Deterrent," *Vanderbilt Journal of Transnational Law*, vol. 43, no. 1, 2010, pp. 57-61.

11. Gross, "U.S. Cyber War Policy Needs New Focus, Experts Say."

12. Kramer, Starr, and Wentz, eds., *Cyberpower and National Security*, p. 15.

13. Kramer, Starr, and Wentz, eds., *Cyberpower and National Security*, p. 7; Wass de Czege, "Warfare by Internet," pp. 85-87.

14. Clarke, *Cyber War*, p. 161.

15. Clarke, *Cyber War*, p. 175.

16. Viega, *The Myths of Security*, p. 46; Marshall Breeding, "A Prescription for Computer Health," *Information Today*, vol. 18, no. 2, 2001.

17. "The Era of Cyber Warfare," *PRWeb*, November 26, 2010. www.prweb.com/releases/2010/11/prweb4833004.htm

18. Viega, *The Myths of Security*, p. 50.

19. Clay Dillow, "An Order of Seven Global Cyber-Guardians Now Hold Keys to the Internet," *Popsci*, July 27, 2010. www.popsci.com/technology/article/2010-07/order-seven-cyber-guardians-around-world-now-hold-keys-internet.

CHAPTER 10: BIOMETRICS

1. "Now, Ears Too Can Be Used for Airport Security ID Checks," *Asian News International*, October 11, 2010.

2. "New Software Brings Facial-Recognition Technology to Mobile Phones," *ScienceDaily*, October 26, 2010. www.sciencedaily.com/releases/2010/10/101026111725.htm.

3. Derek Scheips, "Voice Recognition—Benefits and Challenges of this Biometric Application for Access Control," *SourceSecurity*, September 2010. www.sourcesecurity.com/news/articles/co-3108-ga.4100.html.

4. See Mark Hitchcock, *Cashless: Bible Prophecy, Economic Chaos, & the Future Financial Order* (Eugene, OR: Harvest House, 2010), p. 74.

5. Stew Magnuson, "Defense Department Under Pressure to Share Biometric Data," *National Defense Magazine*, January 2009. www.nationaldefensemagazine.org/archive/2009/January/Pages/DefenseDepartmentUnderPressuretoShareBiometricData.aspx.

6. Magnuson, "Defense Department Under Pressure to Share Biometric Data."

7. Hitchcock, *Cashless*, pp. 59-60.

8. Stewart Watkins, "RFID Is Set to Have a Huge Impact," *The Journal*, November 19, 2009. www.nebusiness.co.uk/business-news/science-and-technology/2009/11/19/rfid-is-set-to-have-a-huge-impact-51140-25200022/.

9. Ice and Demy, *The Coming Cashless Society*, p. 66.

10. Watkins, "RFID Is Set to Have a Huge Impact."

11. Ian Carey, "Biometric ID that 'gives Big Brother a passport to your privacy,'" *The Daily Mail*, November 5, 2009.

12. Jaya Narain, "Big Brother Cameras Scan Faces at Car Park," *The Daily Mail*, August 7, 2010.

CHAPTER 11: GPS TECHNOLOGY

1. Ice and Demy, *The Coming Cashless Society*, p. 61.

2. See Michael K. Stone, "Global Positioning Systems," *Whole Earth*, Fall 2000.

3. "What Is GPS?" *Garmin*. www8.garmin.com/aboutGPS/.

4. Michael Rosenwald, "Every Step You Take…Every Move You Make…My GPS Unit Will Be Watching You," *Popular Science*, November 11, 2004. www.popsci.com/scitech/article/2004-11/every-step-you-take-every-move-you-make-my-gps-unit-will-be-watching-you?page=1.

5. Rosenwald, "Every Step You Take…"

6. Rosenwald, "Every Step You Take…"

7. See Mark Tunick, "Privacy in Public Places: Do GPS and Video Surveillance Provide Plain Views?" *Social Theory and Practice*, vol. 35, no. 4, 2009; Arthur G. Sharp, "Taking a Position on GPS Tracking Devices," *Law & Order*, vol. 53, no. 8, 2005; Devlin M. Gualtieri, "Technology's Assault on Privacy," *Phi Kappa Phi Forum*, vol. 84, no. 4, Fall 2004.

CHAPTER 12: CYBER ECONOMICS AND OUR COMING CASHLESS SOCIETY

1. Ice and Demy, *The Coming Cashless Society*, pp. 125-26, 80.

2. Arnold Fruchtenbaum, *Footsteps of the Messiah* (Ariel Ministries, 2003), pp. 250-51.

3. Hitchcock, *Cashless*, pp. 163-64.

4. Cited in Thomas Ice and Timothy Demy, *Fast Facts on Bible Prophecy from A to Z* (Eugene, OR: Harvest House, 2004), p. 129.

5. John MacArthur, *The MacArthur Study Bible* (Nashville: Thomas Nelson, 2003). See note on Revelation 13:16.

6. David Jeremiah, *The Coming Economic Armageddon: What Bible Prophecy Warns About the New Global Economy* (New York: Faith Words, 2010), p. 146.

7. John F. Walvoord, *Prophecy: 14 Essential Keys to Understanding the Final Drama* (Nashville: Thomas Nelson, 1993), p. 125.

8. Ice and Demy, *The Coming Cashless Society*, p. 132.

9. John Walvoord, "The Beginning of the Great Day of God's Wrath," *Bible.org.* bible.org/seriespage/6-beginning-great-day-god%E2%80%99s-wrath.

10. Stanley Toussaint, *Behold the King: A Study of Matthew* (Grand Rapids: Kregel, 2005), p. 291.

11. Merrill F. Unger, *Beyond the Crystal Ball* (Chicago: Moody, 1978), pp. 134-35.

12. J. Dwight Pentecost, *The Words and Works of Jesus Christ* (Grand Rapids: Zondervan, 1978), p. 410. See also J. Dwight Pentecost, *Things to Come* (Grand Rapids: Zondervan, 1978), p. 418.

13. Herman Hoyt, *The End Times* (Chicago: Moody, 1980), p. 220.

14. John Walvoord and Roy Zuck, eds., *Bible Knowledge Commentary*, vol. 2, *New Testament* (Wheaton: Victor Books, 1981), p. 81.

15. See John 14:1-3; Romans 8:19; 1 Corinthians 1:7-8; 15:51-53; Philippians 3:20-21; Colossians 3:4; 1 Thessalonians 1:10; 2:19; 4:13-18; 5:9,23; 2 Thessalonians 2:1,3; 1 Timothy 6:14; 2 Timothy 4:1,8; Titus 2:13; Hebrews 9:28; James 5:7-9; 1 Peter 1:7,13; 5:4; 1 John 2:28–3:2; Jude 21; Revelation 2:25; 3:10.

16. Joel Kurtzman, *The Death of Money* (New York: Simon & Schuster, 1993), p. 11.

17. Hitchcock, *Cashless*, p. 43.

18. Cited in Jeremiah, *The Coming Economic Armageddon*, pp. 162-64.

19. Cited in Jeremiah, *The Coming Economic Armageddon*, pp. 162-64.

20. Ice and Demy, *The Coming Cashless Society*, pp. 85-86.

21. Jeremiah, *The Coming Economic Armageddon*, pp. 162-64.

22. "Microchip Implants Closer to Reality," *The Futurist*, vol. 33, no. 8, 1999.

23. Grant Jeffrey, *Shadow Government: How the Secret Global Elite Is Using Surveillance Against You* (Colorado Springs: Waterbrook Press, 2009), p. 18.

24. Hitchcock, *Cashless*, pp. 75-76.

25. Cited in Jeremiah, *The Coming Economic Armageddon*, pp. 162-64.

26. Cited in Ice and Demy, *The Coming Cashless Society*, p. 54.

27. Tim LaHaye and Jerry Jenkins, *Are We Living in the Last Days?* (Wheaton, IL: Tyndale House, 1999), pp. 198-99.

CHAPTER 13: CYBER CONTROL AND THE EMERGENCE OF A GLOBAL GOVERNMENT

1. John Walvoord and Roy Zuck, eds., *Bible Knowledge Commentary*, vol. 2, *New Testament* (Wheaton, IL: Victor, 1980). See entry for Revelation 13.

2. John Phillips, *Exploring Revelation* (Neptune, NJ: Loizeaux Brothers, 1991), p. 171.

3. John F. Walvoord and Mark Hitchcock, *Armageddon, Oil, and Terror* (Carol Stream, IL: Tyndale House, 2007), pp. 82-84.

4. Ice and Demy, *The Coming Cashless Society*, p. 50; see also Jeremiah, *The Coming Economic Armageddon*, p. 65.

5. See Ian Carey, "Biometric ID that 'Gives Big Brother a Passport to Your Privacy,'" *The Daily Mail*, November 5, 2009; see also Jaya Narain, "Big Brother Cameras Scan Faces at Car Park," *The Daily Mail*, August 7, 2010.

6. Stewart Watkins, "RFID Is Set to Have a Huge Impact," *The Journal*, November 19, 2009.

CHAPTER 14: CYBER ESPIONAGE AND END-TIMES PERSECUTIONS

1. John Walvoord and Roy Zuck, eds., *Bible Knowledge Commentary*, vol. 2, *New Testament* (Wheaton, IL: Victor Books, 1983).

2. Charles C. Ryrie, *Basic Theology* (Wheaton, IL: Victor Books, 1986), p. 147.

3. Charles C. Ryrie, *Balancing the Christian Life* (Chicago: Moody Press, 1978), p. 124.

4. Ray C. Stedman, *Spiritual Warfare* (Waco: Word Books, 1976), p. 22.

CHAPTER 15: CYBER INJURY AND THE END-TIMES DECLINE OF THE UNITED STATES

1. J. I. Packer, *Knowing God* (Downers Grove, IL: InterVarsity Press, 1983), p. 126.

2. Mark Hitchcock, *The Late Great United States* (Colorado Springs: Multnomah, 2009), pp. 85-86.

3. Stephen Leeb, *The Coming Economic Collapse* (New York: Warner Business Books, 2006), p. 30.

4. Michael Shermer, "Why ET Hasn't Called," *Scientific American*, August 2002. www.michael shermer.com/2002/08/why-et-hasnt-called/.

5. Jared Diamond, *Collapse: How Societies Choose to Fail or Succeed* (New York: Penguin 2005); Joseph Tainter, *The Collapse of Complex Societies* (Cambridge: Cambridge University Press, 1990).

6. Leeb, *The Coming Economic Collapse*, p. 36.

7. Leeb, *The Coming Economic Collapse*, pp. 127-28.

8. See Clarke, *Cyber War*, pp. 66-68.

9. McMenamin, "Cyber ShockWave Shows U.S. Unprepared for Cyber Threats."

10. McMenamin, "Cyber ShockWave Shows U.S. Unprepared for Cyber Threats."

11. Jim Setde, cited in Ice and Demy, *The Coming Cashless Society*, p. 146.

12. Cited in *The Third Jihad: Radical Islam's Vision for America*, Publicscope Films, 2008.

13. Rachel Ehrenfeld, *Funding Evil: How Terrorism Is Financed—and How to Stop It* (Chicago: Bonus Books, 2005), p. 35.

14. Kramer, Starr, and Wentz, eds., *Cyberpower and National Security*, p. 438.

15. Carr, *Inside Cyber Warfare*, p. 22.

16. Carr, *Inside Cyber Warfare*, pp. 37-38.

17. Joel Rosenberg, "Nuclear Terrorism: How Real Is the Threat?" April 30, 2007. lit4ever.org/revival forum/index.php?topic=5842.0;wap2.

CHAPTER 16: CYBER STRATEGIES IN END-TIME WARS

1. Kramer, Starr, and Wentz, eds., *Cyberpower and National Security*, p. 25.

2. Paul D. Berg, "Dominant Air, Space and Cyberspace Operations," *Air & Space Power Journal*, vol. 21, no. 1, 2007.

3. The quotations in this and the next paragraph are from Randall Price, *Unholy War: The Truth Behind the Headlines* (Eugene, OR: Harvest House, 2001), p. 344.

4. Wars in the region include Israel's War of Independence (1947–1948), the Suez War/Sinai Campaign (1956), the Six-Day War (1967), the War of Attrition (1968–1970), the Yom Kippur/October War (1973), the Lebanese Civil War (1975–1976), the Iran–Iraq War (1980–1988), the Lebanon War (1982–1985), the Persian Gulf War (1991), the War with Iraq (1991–2003), and the War on Terror (2001 to the present).

5. John Walvoord, *End Times* (Nashville: Word, 1998), p. 124.

6. Thomas Ice, "Ezekiel 38 and 39," Part 1, posted at the PreTrib Center website.

POSTSCRIPT: LIVING AS AN END-TIMES CHRISTIAN

1. Ice and Demy, *The Coming Cashless Society*, p. 20.

2. See Jon Mark Ruthven, *The Prophecy that Is Shaping History: New Research on Ezekiel's Vision of the End* (Fairfax: Xulon Press, 2003), pp. 1-2.

3. Joel Rosenberg, *Epicenter* (Carol Stream: Tyndale House, 2006), p. 50.

4. John Walvoord, cited in Mark Hitchcock, *Iran: The Coming Crisis* (Sisters, OR: Multnomah, 2006), p. 189.

5. Rosenberg, *Epicenter*, pp. 252-53.

6. Walvoord, *End Times*, p. 219.

7. Walvoord, *End Times*, p. 218.

8. J.I. Packer, ed., *Alive to God* (Downers Grove: InterVarsity, 1992), p. 162.

9. Packer, *Alive to God*, p. 171.

10. Packer, *Alive to God*, p. 165.

11. Packer, *Alive to God*, p. 165.

12. Cited in Packer, *Alive to God*, p. 167.

INDEX

THE 10 MOST IMPORTANT THINGS SERIES

The 10 Most Important Things
You Can Say to a Catholic

The 10 Most Important Things You
Can Say to a Jehovah's Witness

The 10 Most Important Things
You Can Say to a Mason

The 10 Most Important Things
You Can Say to a Mormon

The 10 Things You Need
to Know About Islam

The 10 Things You Need
to Know About the
Creation vs. Evolution Debate

THE REASONING FROM THE SCRIPTURES SERIES

Reasoning from the
Scriptures with Catholics

Reasoning from the Scriptures
with the Jehovah's Witnesses

Reasoning from the
Scriptures with Masons

Reasoning from the
Scriptures with the Mormons

Reasoning from the
Scriptures with Muslims

QUICK REFERENCE GUIDES

Archaeology and the Bible:
What You Need to Know

Christian Views of War:
What You Need to Know

Five Views on the Rapture:
What You Need to Know

Halloween: What You
Need to Know

Homosexuality: What
You Need to Know

Is America in Bible Prophecy?:
What You Need to Know

Islam: What You Need to Know

Jehovah's Witnesses: What
You Need to Know

The Middle East Conflict: What
You Need to Know